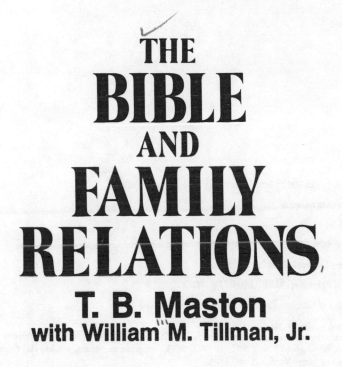

THE
BIBLE
AND
FAMILY
RELATIONS

T. B. Maston
with William M. Tillman, Jr.

BROADMAN PRESS
Nashville, Tennessee

To
Dora Etta Bridgford
faithful and efficient
secretary
for
a quarter of a century

Preface

The family in the contemporary period is in serious trouble. The traditional Christian home is threatened. Many Christians are aware of the danger and are searching for help. A considerable number of churches and church leaders also are searching for ways to strengthen and stabilize the family. One thing that will help is an understanding of biblical teachings concerning the family. What the Bible says on any subject is important, and rightly interpreted, it becomes authoritative for the church and the child of God.

This book attempts to survey the most relevant biblical material concerning the family and family relationships. Its main purpose is to serve as a reference book for busy pastors, teachers, counselors, and church and community workers in the varied areas of family ministry. We hope that teachers of courses on the family will find it acceptable as a text or required reading. Church and school librarians may decide that it should be placed in their libraries.

One of the major problems in preparing the manuscript has been the abundance of material on some of the areas discussed. Entire volumes have been written on the subjects for most of the chapters. In a case or two, such as homosexuality, many volumes have been written on a subtopic of one of the chapters. This means, among other things, that no claim is made that the present volume is exhaustive. We hope that the general picture presented will be true to the biblical material.

There is a secondary emphasis on the interpretation of Scriptures closely related to some of the major problems in the area of contemporary family living. This emphasis will be evident, to some degree, throughout the book but will be most prominent in the section on "Family Relationships." Also, limited attention is given to the application of biblical teachings and insights to some contemporary family problems. This emphasis will vary from chapter to chapter.

Where an effort is made to interpret specific Scriptures, some of the best recognized commentaries have been utilized. Also, there is considerable use of some of the better-known translations. The various translations are instruments of interpretation. Every translation of the Bible is, at least to some degree, an interpretation. That is one reason for the many translations.

The chapters of this book differ in structure. An effort has been made to let the biblical material determine the structure used. In a couple of chapters, the most logical division seemed to be threefold: Old Testament, Jesus, Paul. Other chapters have a topical structure with some more detailed than others.

A book that surveys the biblical material on any major subject, such as the family, cannot avoid some repetition. There are sections in almost every chapter that would have been incomplete without some reference to material discussed in one or more other chapters. An outstanding example is the subject of women, to which chapter 3 is devoted. However, women, in some way and to some degree, are involved, directly or indirectly, in every succeeding chapter (4-10). We have sought to keep the repetition to a minimum.

A book of this nature is the product of many people. Credit has been given in footnotes to authors who have been particularly helpful. In addition, there are other individuals to whom appreciation should be expressed. This is particularly true of William M. Tillman, Jr., a younger colleague. He helped in many ways in the preparation of the manuscript: wrote the first draft of one chapter; read the first draft of all the other chapters, making many suggestions that have contributed to a more readable volume; and prepared the indexes.

Two other professors at Southwestern Baptist Theological Seminary who again have been very helpful are J. W. MacGorman and Ralph L. Smith. They took time from busy schedules of teaching, writing, and speaking to read carefully the entire manuscript and to make numerous suggestions that resulted in improvements at many points. Mrs. Roy (Jean) Fish checked the Scripture references—a big task—and made helpful suggestions concerning structure and form. The administration of the seminary has made available for a number of years a convenient place to work and the library staff has again been uniformly courteous and helpful.

A special word of appreciation is due Mrs. Melvin (Dora Etta) Bridgford, my secretary for many years. She originally transcribed most of the material from my poorly handwritten pages. She then prepared the final typescript, as she has most of the things I have ever written. I have taken the liberty, without asking her permission, to dedicate this book to her.

My wife (Mommie), who has shared with me life's joys and sorrows for many years, has helped in innumerable ways, particularly with her added work load at home and the patience that is required when one is working on a manuscript of this type.

I was in correspondence with Broadman Press about the possibilities of this book when I had a severe heart attack and was in the hospital for four weeks. Although it may sound unusual, I want to express my appreciation to our Heavenly Father who has given me the health and strength to complete the manuscript.

T. B. Maston

Abbreviations

Commentaries that follow a verse-by-verse format are referred to, in abbreviated form, in the body of the material.

An.B.	*Anchor Bible*
LBBC	*Layman's Bible Book Commentary*
Cam.B.	*Cambridge Bible*
Ell.	*Ellicott's Commentary on the Whole Bible*
Exp.Gr.	*Expositor's Greek Testament*
ICC	*The International Critical Commentary*
Int.B.	*The Interpreter's Bible*
W.P.	*Word Pictures in the New Testament*
OTL	*Old Testament Library*

Contents

Part I: Introduction 15
  1. THE BIBLE 17
    Its Nature
    Its Message
    Its Relevance
    Its Interpretation
  2. THE FAMILY 35
    Its Source
    Its Purposes
    Its Nature
    Its Form
    Its Customs
    Its Symbolic Use
    Conclusions
Part II: Family Members 59
  3. WOMEN 61
    Old Testament
    Jesus
    Paul
    Summary and Conclusions
  4. CHILDREN 86
    Desire for Them
    Source of Them
    Concern for Them
    Customs Related to Them
    Dedication of Them
    The Childhood of Jesus
    Jesus and Children

5. SINGLE ADULTS 109
  Widows in the Bible
  Treatment of Widows
  Divorced
  Never Married
  Conclusions
6. OLDER ADULTS 130
  Age and Aging
  "Elders"
  Their Qualities
  Attitudes Toward Them
  An Example
  Their Crises
Part III: Family Relationships 157
7. HUSBANDS AND WIVES 159
  Choice of Companion
  Contrasting Perspectives
  Nature and Roles
  Equality and Submission
  Covenant and Commitment
8. SEX AND SEXUAL RELATIONS 181
  Basic Concepts
    Sex, a Good Gift of God
    Man and Woman—Created in the Image of God
    One Flesh
    Body Belongs to the Lord
    Celibacy and Virginity
  Sex Within Marriage
  Sex Outside of Marriage
    Prostitution
    Adultery
    Homosexuality
    Paul's List of Vices
    The Lustful Look
    General Exhortations
    Conclusion: Jesus and the Sinner

9. DIVORCE AND REMARRIAGE 203
   Introductory Statements
   Old Testament
   Jesus
   Paul
   The Divorced
10. PARENTS AND CHILDREN 225
   Parents to Children
      Love Them
      Discipline Them
      Teach and Train Them
      Dedicate Them
   Children to Parents
      Honor Them
      Obey Them
      Provide for Them
   Conclusion
Supplementary Resources 248
Indexes 250

PART I
INTRODUCTION

Two introductory chapters will seek to provide a background for this study of the Bible and family relations. Before we discuss the biblical perspective and teachings concerning the members of the family and their relations to one another, we will consider the general nature and the proper interpretation of the Scriptures. We also considered it wise to have a general chapter on the family or home. Much of that chapter will be based on the general impact of the Scriptures rather than specific teachings. More attention will be given to the specific teachings in later chapters, particularly in part 3: Husbands and Wives, Sex and Sex Relations, Divorce and Remarriage, Parents and Children.

1

The Bible

The Bible is the most important possession of the Christian church. This is particularly true for Protestants who consider the Bible the final authority for their faith and practice. This means that anything the Bible says concerning the family and family relations should be considered seriously and studied carefully.

Its Nature[1]

The Bible, in a very real sense, is *a divine-human book*. It is divine in its origin or initiation, human in its mediation. It was written by men but by men inspired and led by the Spirit of God. There would be no Bible without the response of men to that revelation. In other words, revelation is a transitive event. A transitive verb has a subject and an object. God, the Initiator, is the subject of the revelation; man is the object or recipient. The divine-human nature of the writing of the Scriptures is rather clearly stated in various places in the New Testament. For example, Peter said, "No prophecy ever came by the impulse of man, but men moved by the Holy Spirit spoke from God" (2 Pet. 1:21). Men did the speaking, but they spoke "from God" and, we might add, primarily "for" and "concerning" God.

There are a number of places in the New Testament where a statement or quotation is directly attributed to a specific Old Testament speaker or writer. This is true of Moses. For example, Jesus said, "For Moses said, 'Honor your father and your mother'" (Mark 7:10). Paul said, "Moses writes" (Rom. 10:5). References to Isaiah are particularly prominent in the Gospels. A few examples: "This was to fulfil what was spoken by the prophet Isaiah" (Matt.

17

12:17); "You hypocrites! Well did Isaiah prophesy of you, when he said" (Matt. 15:7); "As it is written in Isaiah the prophet" (Mark 1:2); "As it is written in the book of the words of Isaiah the prophet" (Luke 3:4); John the Baptist said, "I am the voice of one crying in the wilderness, 'Make straight the way of the Lord,' as the prophet Isaiah said" (John 1:23). For other references in the Gospels see Matthew 13:14-15; Mark 7:6-7; John 12:38-41. Paul, in Romans, also referred to something Isaiah had said (9:27-29).

There are also two or three specific references to a couple of minor prophets. Immediately preceding the above reference to Isaiah, Paul said, "As indeed he [God] says in Hosea" (Rom. 9:25-26). Peter, on the day of Pentecost, quoted at some length from the prophet Joel (Acts 2:14-21) and also from David (Acts 2:25-26).

There are several additional references in the New Testament to David as God's spokesman. For example, Jesus said, "David . . . inspired by the Holy Spirit, declared" (Mark 12:36). This statement beautifully underscores the divine-human nature of the Bible. David did the speaking or declaring. He was inspired by the Holy Spirit (see Acts 1:16; 4:25).

In addition to these references that emphasize in a particular way the divine-human nature of the Bible, there are many places where the reference is not to a particular human source but simply says, "It is written." A few examples will have to suffice. In response to each of the temptations by Satan, Jesus quoted from Deuteronomy, without identifying the source. He simply said, "It is written" (Matt. 4:4,6,10). For a few other references in Matthew to "It is written," see 11:10; 21:13; 26:24; 26:31. Several of these passages are found also in Mark and in Luke. There are additional references to "It is written" in John's Gospel and the Pauline Epistles that can be located in any good concordance.

The Bible is not only a divine-human Book in its writing but also in its content. It is a record of the revelation of God's nature and character and of his attitude toward and will for humanity. But the Scriptures also portray the life struggles, the faults and failures, as well as the successes of real men and women.

Another evident characteristic of the Bible is its *unity in* the midst of its *diversity*. The diversity of the Bible in content, emphases, general approach, and style is rather obvious. One reason for the diversity is the fact that the people, particularly in Old Testament days, were not prepared to understand and accept the full revelation of God and his will. That was the explanation by Jesus for something in the Mosaic law that was not in harmony with God's original purpose for marriage. His word was, "For your hardness of heart Moses allowed ["permitted," NASB] you to divorce your wives, but from the beginning it was not so. And I say to you" (Matt. 19:8-9). The same could be said for many other things in the Old Testament.

The diversity in the Bible means that the unity we find there, which is clearly evident, is a dynamic rather than a static unity. It is a unity of growth or movement. That movement has been compared to a musical production. The Old Testament may be and is a part of the sonata but the New Testament is the climax.

The dynamic unity, so clearly evident in the Old Testament and the New Testament, stems basically from the Divine Person revealed in and through the Scriptures. In turn, that Divine Person is supremely revealed in and through the central divine event: the birth, life, teachings, death, and resurrection of Christ. It is this divine event that the Old Testament looks forward to and the New Testament records, interprets, and reflects upon.

The climax of the revelation of God is in Christ, his Son, a divine-human Person. In him we discover the fullest revelation of the nature and character of God, the Father. Jesus himself said, "He who has seen me has seen the Father" (John 14:9; see 17:22). He also said, "I and the Father are one" (John 10:30). Paul said, "For in him all the fulness of God was pleased to dwell," or "For in him the complete being of God, by God's own choice, came to dwell" (Col. 1:19, NEB). Paul also said, "For in Christ all the fullness of the Deity lives in bodily form" (Col. 2:9, NIV). The writer of Hebrews said that the Son "reflects the glory of God and bears the very stamp ["the exact representation," NASB] of his nature" (Heb. 1:3).

Christ was also the climax of God's revelation of his attitude toward and will for humanity. This revelation was embodied not only in what he taught but also in the kind or quality of life he lived. This has tremendous implications for family relationships, as well as for human relations in general.

The fact that Christ was the final and full revelation of the Father makes Christianity primarily a religion of a Person rather than a religion of a book. The Book is reverenced largely because of the Person whose life, ministry, death, and resurrection are recorded there. He is the Way, the Truth, the Resurrection, the Bread of life, and the Light of the world. He is God's final and full word to humanity. It is a word that not only reveals God to people but also reveals people to themselves. We see in Christ, the God-man, what God is like and what people, by the grace of God, should become.

The preceding means that the New Testament, and particularly the *life and teachings of Jesus*, is *normative* for the children of God in every aspect and relationship of their lives. The Old Testament has many contributions to make, but it should be read and particularly evaluated in the light of the full revelation of the New Testament. One who attributes equal authority to the Old Testament tends to become what might be termed "an Old Testament Christian." He may defend attitudes that he has and things he does that are definitely contrary to the teachings and spirit of the New Testament. On the same basis, he will tend to defend or advocate some practices and conditions in the social order that clearly fall short of the spirit of Jesus.

Its Message

Broadly speaking, the Bible contains *a twofold message*: (1) how people can be saved and (2) how saved people should live. The latter involves more than one dimension. Those dimensions, in the main, can be compressed into two: (1) the vertical or right relations to God, and (2) the horizontal or right relations to other persons and to the society of which they are a part.

While the Bible clearly reveals that right relations to God and persons belong together, it reveals just as clearly that right relations to God are most basic. When stated together, right relations to God are stated first, followed by right relations to other people. The latter is, in a sense, a derivative of the former, but it is such an inevitable derivative that if one is not right with other people that is a valid reason to conclude that he is not right with God.

The fact that right relations to God are basic and that right relations to other people naturally and inevitably follow is illustrated over and over again in the Scriptures. For example, the first of the Ten Commandments, which incidentally summarizes the fundamental moral law, sets forth the requirements regarding one's relation to God. The second portion of the Commandments deals with one's duties or responsibility to his neighbor. Several of these are directly related to the family: honor father and mother; do not commit adultery; do not covet a neighbor's wife.

The prophets struggled with a people who evidently thought they could be right with God and wrong with other people. They, particularly the great eighth-century prophets, over and over again stressed that this could not be true. Just a few examples will suffice. For instance, Isaiah (1:10-20), speaking for God, said that the latter rejected their offerings; they were vain, "worthless" (NASB), "useless" (NEB), "detestable" (NIV). He also said, "I cannot endure iniquity and solemn assembly" (Isa. 1:13) (what a combination— "iniquity and solemn assembly"). Their prayers would not be heard. Then he told the people what God expects:

> Wash yourselves; make yourselves clean,
>> remove the evil of your doings
>> from before my eyes;
> cease to do evil,
>> learn to do good;
> seek justice,
>> correct oppression [Reprove the ruthless, NASB];
> defend the fatherless,
>> plead for the widow (Isa. 1:16-17).

Amos represented God as saying to his people:

> I hate, I despise your feasts,
>> and I take no delight in your solemn assemblies.
> Even though you offer me your burnt offerings and
>> cereal offerings,

> I will not accept them,
> and the peace offering of your fatted beasts
> I will not look upon.
> Take away from me the noise of your songs;
> to the melody of your harps I will not listen.

Then he tells them what he wants:

> But let justice roll down like waters,
> and righteousness like an everflowing stream
> (Amos 5:21-24; see 2:6-8; 5:10-12).

The preceding passages illustrate a continuing emphasis of the prophets. One of the greatest summaries of the basic requirements of our biblical faith is in Micah, another one of the eighth-century prophets. It is as follows:

> He has showed you, O man, what is good;
> and what does the Lord require of you
> but to do justice, and to love kindness,
> and to walk humbly with your God?
> (Mic. 6:8).

Surely these words from the prophets underscore the necessity of being right with our neighbors if we are to be right with or acceptable to our Heavenly Father. Again, let us suggest that this includes right relations of husbands and wives, parents and children, and other family relationships.

We could cite many illustrations of the two-dimensional nature of the requirements of our biblical faith, but we will restrict ourselves to a few additional examples from the New Testament. One of the most pointed illustrations is the answer of *Jesus* when he was asked to identify "the great commandment in the law." The reply of Jesus, quoting from Deuteronomy 6:5, was: "You shall love the Lord your God with all your heart, and with all your soul, and with all your mind. This is the great and first commandment" (Matt. 22:37-38). And then, possibly after a pause for emphasis, quoting Leviticus 19:18, he added: "And a second is like it, you shall love your neighbor as yourself" (Matt. 22:39; see Rom. 13:8-10; Gal. 5:14).

Why did Jesus add the second when he was only asked for *the* great commandment? It is possible that he thought the first was incomplete without the second. Also, Jesus may have thought the second was particularly needed by his questioner. But what did he mean by "a second is like it"? Possibly like it because it was a commandment of love. But also possibly because it was like it in importance. The first was really incomplete without the second. At least without the second, it could not have been said, by Jesus or someone else, "On these two commandments depend ["hangs," NEB] all the law and the prophets" (v. 40).

On another occasion Jesus gave the disciples a Model Prayer. There is a petition in that prayer and some comments concerning that petition that emphasize the two-dimensional nature of our Christian faith. Among other things in the prayer are the words

> And forgive us our debts,
> As we also have forgiven our debtors.
>
> (Matt. 6:12)

The petition was the only one commented on following the prayer. "For if you forgive men their trespasses, your heavenly Father also will forgive you; but if you do not forgive men their trespasses, neither will your Father forgive your trespasses" (Matt. 6:14-15). In other words, the forgiving are the forgiven—and we might add the forgiven should be the forgiving.

Many other references could be given that stress the two-dimensional emphasis in the Scriptures. Among these are the relation of faith and works (Eph. 2:8-10; Jas. 2:14-26), the "therefore" perspective, which is prevalent in some of the prophets (Jer. 20—21; Amos 3:11; 5:10-13), in Paul's Epistles (Rom. 1:1; Eph. 4:1), and in 1 Peter (4:7-10).

This should be enough to underscore the fact that we cannot be right with God and that our worship will not be acceptable to him unless we are right with others, including members of our families—husbands and wives, parents and children, grandparents, aunts, uncles, and others. Right relations with others also include neighbors and friends, fellow church members, those with whom we work and play, casual acquaintances, and even strangers we may meet at shops or on the streets. The horizontal dimension also includes our relations to those of different races and cultures, to society in general, and to the institutions and agencies of society: the family as such, the church, the school, the community, the state, the nation, and the world.

The *cross* is *an appropriate symbol* of the two-dimensional nature of our biblical faith and of the Christian life in general. The upright or vertical bar represents people reaching up to God and God reaching down to people. The transverse beam symbolizes people reaching out to other people and to the society of people. In other words, the cross is the unifying symbol of the Christian life.[2]

Its Relevance

Does a book, such as the Bible, written so long ago have any relevant or authoritative word for us today? Many contemporary trends and issues, including some in the area of family relations, were largely if not entirely unknown in biblical days. It is possible, however, if we study the Bible carefully and interpret it properly, we may discover that basically the Bible is ahead rather than behind us and our times.

Let us first suggest two or three ideas concerning the *relevance of the Bible in general.* The Bible's abiding relevance stems primarily from *the Person revealed* in it. He is the eternal "I Am," the same yesterday, today, and forever. When Moses, at the burning bush, asked God what he was to reply when the people of Israel asked, "What is his name?" the word of God to Moses was, "I AM WHO I AM. . . . Say this to the people of Israel, 'I AM has sent me to you'" (Ex. 3:14-15). The word to John on Patmos was: "'I am the Alpha and the Omega,' says the Lord God, who is and who was and who is to come, the Almighty" (Rev. 1:8). The self-disclosure or self-revelation of the eternally I AM One gave birth to the Bible. That self-revelation is abidingly relevant for people because they were created for fellowship with him.

Also, *the redemptive message* of the Bible is continuously relevant. People of our age and every age need that message. The testimony of the Scriptures and of our own hearts is that

> All we like sheep have gone astray;
> we have turned every one to his own way (Isa. 53:6).

Or, as Paul, citing Psalm 14:1-3, wrote, "None is righteous, no, not one" (Rom. 3:10). Paul also concluded that "all have sinned and fall short of the glory of God" (Rom. 3:23).

Furthermore, *the great promises* of the Scriptures are abidingly relevant. This is true of promises, such as "underneath are the everlasting arms" (Deut. 33:27); "When I sit in darkness, the Lord will be a light to me" (Mic. 7:8); that great promise of Jesus, "Come to me, all who labor and are heavy laden, and I will give you rest" (Matt. 11:28); the statement by Paul so hard to comprehend and yet so comforting when life caves in—"We know that in everything God works for good with those who love him, who are called according to his purpose" (Rom. 8:28)—things do not work together for good automatically. God works them together "with those who love him," requiring their cooperation. In addition to these great promises, there is the statement of God to Paul, "My grace is sufficient for you" (2 Cor. 12:9). These and other promises of God can be just as meaningful to us today as to and for those of past generations.

What about our *day-to-day decisions, problems, and relationships*? Does the Bible have a relevant message for us? What about where we work and worship? Does it or can it speak to the needs of the contemporary home? Can we find any help, direct or indirect, in the Scriptures concerning such diverse needs and problems as abortion, homosexuality, abuse of children, the working mother, divorce, single life *versus* marriage, sexual "freedom," alcoholism and drug abuse, living together without being married, discipline of children, euthanasia, neglect of parents, and numerous others? Whether the Bible speaks a relevant or significant word to us in these and related areas will depend a great deal on how we read, study, and interpret it. It is a *mistake* and will be disappointing *if we consider the Bible a rule book* to which we can turn for a chapter-and-verse answer to every question or a solution for every problem. While the basic needs of men, women, and children remain relatively the same from age to age, their specific needs and problems may vary a great deal.

We should also remember as we read and study the Bible that some *portions* of it were so thoroughly *historically conditioned* that they do not apply, in any direct way, to our day. They were written primarily to meet the needs of a particular group of people faced with some particular problems at a particular point in time. Examples of this are many of the laws of the Old Testament, particularly the ceremonial laws. The same is also true of some things in the New Testament, particularly in the Pauline Epistles. If Paul met the needs of the people to whom he wrote, he had to direct much of what he wrote to their immediate needs. This is clearly evident in 1 Corinthians which is, incidentally, the epistle in which we find Paul's fullest statements concerning family relations.

A problem that Paul dealt with in 1 Corinthians 8; 9; and 10; as well as in Romans 14, was the eating of meat offered to idols. We do not have that problem in our day. But if we examine carefully what Paul said, we may discover even in instructions that seem entirely irrelevant some principles that are abidingly relevant. For example: (1) Right for the children of God is not decided exclusively by what they consider right for them to do. They must also consider what others consider right for them. (2) An activity that may be right within itself can become positively wrong or sinful because of its effect on others. (3) Also, one needs to realize that love rather than knowledge, as important as it is, is the final criteria of the right: " 'Knowledge' puffs up, but love builds up" (1 Cor. 8:1).

The preceding correctly implies that the *most relevant* portions of the Bible are *its ideals and principles.* And we might also suggest that some whose words are recorded in the Scriptures would teach us as much by what they did or by the life they lived as by anything they said or wrote. This was and is particularly true of Jesus, as seen in the four Gospels which not only recorded what he said but also portrayed the kind of life he lived: "he went about doing good" (Acts 10:38). He exemplified in his life every basic truth that he taught.

The preceding means that, if we are properly to interpret and use the Bible, we should seek as best we can to *capture its spirit,* which may be as relevant and possibly more so than its words.

Its Interpretation[3]

John Wilkinson says, "It is the simple testimony of human experience throughout the centuries that the Bible, read without even note or comment, has brought spiritual illumination to a multitude of souls."[4] Bernard Ramm feels that "everything essential in the Scriptures is clearly revealed." How grateful all of us should be for the wonderful blessings that have come and continue to come from the simple reading of and meditating upon the Scriptures.

If the foregoing is true, why is there a need for interpretation? The conversation of Philip and the eunuch is one situation which illustrates this need (Acts 8:26-40). The eunuch was reading from Isaiah. Philip questioned, "Do you understand what you are reading?" The eunuch replied, "How can I, unless someone guides ["teaches," Williams] me?" or "unless someone explains it to me" (v. 31, NIV). Will you not agree that the same is true, to varying degrees, of most of us at times?

The experience of Jesus with the two on the way to Emmaus also points up the need, at least at times, for someone to explain the Scriptures to us. They described to Jesus what had happened in recent days, including his resurrection and the empty tomb. Then the record says, "And beginning with Moses and all the prophets, he interpreted[5] to them in all the scriptures the things concerning himself" (Luke 24:27).

Objectives. Dana and Glaze briefly discuss three objectives of interpretation.[6] (1) The historical: seeks "to discover what the passage meant to the first recipients." (2) The universal result: an effort "to discover the universal principle which, though grounded in the historical result, is not limited to any particular time or place." (3) The practical: "The objective . . . is to find out and to apply the universal result growing out of a past situation to concrete situations confronting the Christian in the present." They suggest that the last objective should be the controlling interest of biblical interpretation. For them, "the Scriptures are worthy of interpretation only in so far as they minister to the moral and spiritual needs of human life." One of the great needs of the contemporary period is to hear a word from the Lord concerning many conditions and trends that threaten our homes.

Attitudes. An important factor in properly interpreting the Scriptures is our attitude toward the Bible. This attitude, in turn, is shaped and informed, to a considerable degree, by ideas and principles, such as the following:

(1) A reverence for God and a deep desire to know and do his will.

(2) Belief in the inspiration and authority of the Scriptures.

(3) Reverently read and study the Bible.

(4) Approach the study with a searching mind, not looking for proof texts to support a preconceived position but honestly searching for the truth.

(5) Realize that the Bible represents a progressive revelation becoming more clear as it nears completion. "God brings man up through theological infancy of the Old Testament to the maturity of the New Testament."[7] The Old Testament is the bud, the New Testament, the flower. Augustine said, "The New Testament lies hid in the Old, the Old lies open in the New."

(6) Understand that any translation, such as our Bibles, inevitably involves some interpretation. Otherwise, why do we have so many translations of the Scriptures?

(7) Recognize that many portions of the Scriptures have to be interpreted.

(8) Welcome the work of biblical scholars who help get us closer to the original words and meaning of the Scriptures.

(9) Critically use the interpretation of others, such as carefully and reverently written commentaries.

(10) Understand, however, that we as individual Christians have the right and the accompanying responsibility to read and interpret the Scriptures for ourselves.

Some of the preceding attitudes are developed by Dana and Glaze and by Ramm. This is also true of the following section on principles.

Principles. Some of the above attitudes might be considered principles of interpretation. At least, they are important factors in properly interpreting the Scriptures. Some of the following principles can be of help to us as we seek to interpret some things in the Scriptures concerning the home and particularly the relationships in the home.

(1) Relate as far as possible any particular Scripture to its background and its historical situation.

(2) Give proper consideration to the context.

(3) Use Scripture to interpret Scripture. Utilize clear teachings to clarify the less clear.

(4) Recognize that usually the most natural interpretation of a particular Scripture is more likely to be correct than a more involved interpretation. "Give preference to that meaning which is clearest and most evident."

(5) Christian experience is not a substitute for a knowledge of the Bible, but it can be a valuable factor in the correct interpretation of the Scriptures. If our interpretation of a particular Scripture conflicts with our experiences as Christians, we may need to reexamine our interpretation or reinterpret our experiences.

(6) In some biblical statements, the spirit of the statement should be our guide rather than its specific words. Commands or teachings in terms of one culture must be translated into our culture. Example: the statements of Jesus about cutting off a hand or plucking out an eye (Matt. 5:29-30). Also, some things that Paul said, particularly concerning women, such as the wearing of a veil and instructions concerning their hair (1 Cor. 11:6-15).

(7) A distinction should be made between what the Bible records and what it approves. "The Bible no more approves of all it records than an editor approves of all that he reports in his newspaper."[8] Example: polygamy.

(8) Commands to individuals in biblical days are not necessarily the will of God for us. Example: Abraham's offering of Isaac.

(9) Acknowledge the need for and seek the guidance of the Holy Spirit as we interpret the Scriptures.

(10) While it may not properly be called a principle, a sincere desire to live in harmony with the truth discovered in the Bible is an

important factor in understanding what our Father would say to us in and through the Scriptures.

Helps. There are many sources of help for a serious study of the Bible. Some suggestions follow, though given with considerable hesitation. You should make your own decision concerning any book that you may want to purchase. If possible, check the available books in a church, college, university, or seminary library. Also, book stores that handle Christian books can be of considerable help. Your pastor might be of help. But let any decision concerning the purchase of books be a personal decision. Books that attract and appeal to one person may not suit another.

In addition to the King James Version and the Revised Standard Version, which is basically used in this book, one or more additional *translations* can be helpful. Frequently, they may give a clearer insight into the meaning of a word, a verse, or a passage. After all, any translation from one language to another involves some interpretation. The following are some of the modern translations:

The *Good News Bible*

The *New American Standard Bible*

The *New English Bible*

The *New International Version*

The *Living Bible* (which is a paraphrase that at times reveals the translator's particular theological position)

There are several translations restricted to the New Testament:

The *New Testament in Modern English,* J. B. Phillips

The *New Testament, a Translation in the Language of the People,* by Charles B. Williams (an excellent Greek scholar who frequently brings out the meaning of the verb tenses)

Next to one or more translations, the most important tool for effective Bible study is a good *concordance* and preferably a complete or exhaustive one.

Cruden's for many years was the most widely used concordance. A number of publishers, such as Baker, Broadman, Revell, and Zondervan have published editions (21st printing, 1972). Others are:

Revised Standard Version

New American Standard Exhaustive Concordance of the Bible (Nashville: Holman, 1981).

J. Strong, *Exhaustive Concordance* (several publishers: Abingdon, Broadman, Nelson)

Robert Young, *Analytical Concordance to the Bible* (Eerdmans and Nelson)

Clinton Morrison, *An Analytical Concordance to the Revised Standard Version of the New Testament* (Philadelphia: Westminster Press, 1979)

In addition to the preceding, some of you would find very helpful:

Englishman's Hebrew and Chaldee Concordance of the Old Testament

Englishman's Greek Concordance of the New Testament[9]

There is such an abundance of *commentaries* that one hesitates to mention any. Some one-volume commentaries are:

John R. Dummelow, *Commentary on the Holy Bible* (New York: Macmillan, 1909).

Jameson, Fausset, and Brown, *Critical and Experimental Commentary* (Grand Rapids: Eerdmans) (These two are older, considered somewhat standard for years.)

M. Black and H. H. Rowley, *Peake's Commentary on the Bible* (Camden, N.J.: Nelson, 1962). Multiple authors, based on Revised Standard Version.

The Interpreter's One-Volume Commentary on the Bible (New York: Abingdon, 1971). In addition to scholarly articles, includes chapters on the books of the Apocrypha. Based on Revised Standard Version.

A one-volume commentary is an inadequate substitute for a good, multiple-volume commentary. Any purchase of the latter will usually involve a considerable sum of money. You will want to be careful about any purchase you make. If you have a pastor, teacher, or other mature Christian friends you trust, you might consult with them. Even more important, if you can do so, check personally in college, university, or seminary libraries.

The following are some of the better known and more widely used sets—some of which are complete, others that are not:

The Anchor Bible (New York: Doubleday). Both translation and commentary; scholarly

Broadman Bible Commentary (Nashville: Broadman Press). Southern Baptist; primarily expository rather than exegetical

Cambridge Bible (Cambridge: Cambridge University Press). Compact; exegetical—meaning of words, phrases, and so forth

Ellicott's Commentary on the Whole Bible (Grand Rapids: Zondervan). Old, worthwhile if you can find it

International Critical Commentary (London: T&T Clark). Old, scholarly

G. A. Buttrick, ed., *Interpreter's Bible* (New York: Abingdon, n.d.)—Two writers; one primarily exegetical, the other exposition

Layman's Bible Book Commentary (Nashville: Broadman Press). Twenty-four volumes in process [1982], vary considerably in depth and insight)

In addition to the preceding, there are some good commentaries restricted to the New Testament:

Barclay (scholarly but not technically so)

W. R. Nicoll, ed., *The Expositor's Greek Testament* (New York: George H. Doran). Can be quite helpful to one who does not use Greek; standard for many years.

Tyndale (20 volumes, brief, mostly by well-known scholars)

A. T. Robertson, *Word Pictures* (Nashville: Broadman Press, 1932). Based on Greek text but, like *Expositor's Greek,* can be helpful to one who has never studied Greek; writer, A. T. Robertson, long-time professor at Southern Baptist Theological Seminary

Many biblical scholars and teachers suggest that the wisest policy regarding commentaries is to purchase individual volumes. There is frequently considerable difference in the quality of volumes in the same set. Furthermore, there are some outstanding volumes that are not a part of multiple-volume sets.

A serious student of the Scriptures needs one or more *harmonies of the Gospels.* There are a large number available, such as:

Ralph D. Heim, *A Harmony of the Gospels* (Philadelphia: Muhlenberg Press, 1947). Revised Standard Version.

A. T. Robertson, *A Harmony of the Gospels for Students of the Life of Christ* (Nashville: Broadman Press). Based on an earlier volume by John A. Broadus.

Robert L. Thomas and Stanley L. Gundry, *A Harmony of the Gospels* (Chicago: Moody Press, 1978). Based on *New American Standard Version.*

A volume that is not a harmony but can be helpful and serves somewhat the purpose of a harmony is Fred Fischer, *A Composite Gospel* (Nashville: Broadman Press, 1948).

There are a few *additional helps* such as

G. Kittel and G. Friedrich, eds., *Theological Dictionary of the New Testament* (Grand Rapids: Eerdmans, 1965). Scholarly. "There is no equal as a source of information on significant New Testament words."

W. E. Vine, *Expository Dictionary of New Testament Words* (Old Tappan, N.J.: Revell). Much simpler than Kittel. Does not require a knowledge of Greek.

William Barclay, *New Testament Words* (Naperville, Ill.: Allenson, n.d.).

William Barclay, *More New Testament Words.*

Some of you will find these little books by Barclay quite helpful.

Two other volumes personally found to be helpful are: A. Richardson, *A Theological Word Book of the Bible* (New York: Macmillan, n.d.); J. J. Von Allmen, ed., *A Companion to the Bible* (Oxford: Oxford University Press, n.d.).

Notes

1. This chapter, except the last section on "Its Interpretation," will be closely related to chapter 4 of T. B. Maston, *Why Live the Christian Life?* (Nashville: Broadman Press, 1974). There is some excellent material in Volume 1 of *The Broadman Bible Commentary* (Nashville: Broadman Press, 1969), pp. 1-33, by Clifton J. Allen, Robert Bratcher, and John Newport.

2. See Maston, chapter 11.

3. There is an abundance of books on principles of interpretation or biblical hermeneutics.

Hermeneutics in general is much broader than the strictly biblical. The study has been quite prevalent in philosophy. One of the most helpful books on biblical hermeneutics is H. E. Dana and R. E. Glaze, Jr., *Interpreting the New Testament* (Nashville: Broadman Press, 1961). This is an update of Dana's *Searching the Scriptures* (1933). Scholarly but very readable. Another is A. Berkley Mickelsen, *Interpreting the Bible* (Grand Rapids: Eerdmans). There has been a third printing of this book in 1963. It is a very thorough book. Bernard Ramm, *Protestant Biblical Interpretation*, 3rd rev. ed. (Grand Rapids: Baker Book House, 1970). It is a very helpful book by one of the top scholars in the area. He defines *hermeneutics* as "the science and art of Biblical Interpretation. It is a science because it is guided by rules within a system; it is an art because the application of the rules is by skill, and not by mechanical imitation" (p. 1). John T. Wilkinson, *Principles of Biblical Interpretation* (London: Epworth Press, 1960). A brief book of a thoroughly documented lecture (sixty pages).

There are other books that are somewhat more technically scholarly. Among these are: Rene Marle, *Introduction to Hermeneutics*, trans. E. Froment and R. Albrecht (New York: Herder & Herder, 1960); James M. Robinson and John B. Cobb, Jr., eds., *The New Hermeneutics* (New York: Harper & Row, 1964). This is a scholarly discussion among a couple of continental scholars and three or four American scholars.

4. Wilkinson, p. 8.

5. The word translated "interpreted" is a form of *hermeneuo* from which *hermeneutics* is derived. Some form of the word is found approximately twenty times in the New Testament. In the King James Version, it is translated "interpret" or "interpretation." In the Revised Standard Version, it is usually translated "means." Some references are: Matthew 1:23; Mark 5:41; 15:22,34; John 1:42; 9:7; Acts 4:36; 13:8. Particularly interesting may be 1 Corinthians 14:28, where Paul said that if there were no interpreter present there should be no speaking in tongues.

6. Dana and Glaze, pp. 123-125.

7. Ramm, p. 102.

8. Ibid., p. 190.

9. Baker Book House has published an edition (1980) of *Englishman's* Greek Concordance of the New Testament that is "coded" to Strong's *Exhaustive Concordance*. Once you learn how to use these, you will discover that you do not have to have a technical knowledge of the original languages to find them very helpful.

2

The Family

This chapter will sketch the perspective and teachings of the Bible regarding the family in general.[1] Later chapters will deal with specific members of the family (part 2) and with the relations of those members to one another (part 3).

In the beginning of this chapter and this study, it should be recognized that the Scriptures do not provide a systematic discussion of the family. After all, the Bible is not a textbook on sociology, psychology, or on any other subject. This does not mean, however, that it does not contain some important insights and even some rather specific teachings regarding the family. We may discover that some of its more or less incidental teachings are quite important. It is even possible that some of the most significant lessons in the Bible concerning the family may be learned from the observation of the mistakes of some whose lives are recorded in the Scriptures. This is particularly true of such Old Testament personalities as Abraham, Jacob, David, and Solomon.

There are places, however, even in the Old Testament, where some very important truths are set forth more or less specifically. This is particularly true in the first chapters of Genesis. These chapters are of major importance in a study of the family, as they also are for a study of Christian theology and the Christian life in general.

Its Source

The first chapters of Genesis provide insights regarding the source of the home or family.

The family is grounded on or evolves from *the nature of the man and woman* God created. The Bible clearly reveals that the creation of man and woman was the crowning act of God's creative work. It is also evident that there was a unique element in their creation. The record says, "Then God said, 'Let us make man in our image, after our likeness;' . . . So God created man in his own image, in the image of God he created him; male and female he created them" (Gen. 1:26-27). "The male is never the male in the abstract nor the female the female in the abstract. That is why the Scripture does not say that God created Man male *or* female—though in a sense that is true—but male *and* female."[2]

There is considerable significance for a study of the family in the fact that both male and female were created in the image of God. Paul said that in Christ "there is neither male nor female; for you are all one in Christ Jesus" (Gal. 3:28). But we are not only one in Christ but we are also one in creation. This oneness in creation and in Christ has great importance for the relationship between husbands and wives, parents and children. It should also deeply affect the attitudes of our churches and society in general toward women, children, single adults—including the widowed and the divorced, and older adults.

What is meant by "the image of God"? A proper understanding of its meaning will tend to underscore its importance for human relations in general and family relations in particular. Through the Christian centuries there have been varied and at times conflicting interpretations of "the image of God." God, in the Old Testament, is sometimes described in anthropomorphic or human terms (see Pss. 33:6; 119:73; Isa. 60:13; Zech. 14:4). This has caused some to interpret "the image" to refer to physical likeness.

It seems more likely, however, that "the image" referred to something of a deeper and spiritual nature. God is a Person; man and woman created in the image of God are persons. A person can think, feel, will. A person is conscious of self and of other selves or persons. Possibly most important from the perspective of our study of the family is the fact that a person has the capacity and even the necessity for communication with other persons. In other words, his or her nature requires communication. In the truest sense there is no person without other persons. Even our God is three in one: Father, Son, and Holy Spirit.

Man and woman, on the highest level, find their fulfillment in communication with God, the one who created them in his image. On the human level, men and women usually find their fullest and most meaningful communication with each other as husbands and wives.

The second chapter of Genesis contains some material equally important to chapter 1 for our study of the family. There are two major viewpoints concerning this chapter. One is that beginning with the fifth verse of chapter 2 there is simply a more detailed account of the creation. The other viewpoint is that chapters 1 and 2 represent different perspectives concerning the creation, particularly of woman, and that the chapters came from different sources. The latter is the position of those who believe in the documentary theory regarding the Old Testament—that much of it was compiled from different documents or sources.

From our perspective, it makes little difference which of the preceding viewpoints is accepted. Whichever one accepts, Genesis 2:4 is a transitional verse. It can properly be considered a conclusion for Genesis 1:1 to 2:3 or an introduction to Genesis 2:5-25.

Particularly important for a study of the family are the last verses of chapter 2 (18-25). Chapter 1 simply says that God created male and female. It does not say how he created them or how long he took to do his creative work. Really, the most important words in those first chapters are the first four words: "In the beginning God."

Chapter 2, verse 18, is as follows: "Then the Lord God said, 'It is not good that the man should be alone; I will make him a helper fit ["suitable," NASB] for him.'" The animals were not suitable or fit for him. They could not give him what he needed to become truly man since they were not like him in any essential way. "Hence the creation of the woman was the one who alone can give man what he must have, being essentially like him and yet mysteriously unlike him."[3] In what way was this helper fit or suitable for the man? The old American Standard Version, in a marginal reading, says, "answering to him." How are men and women made suitable to or with the capacity to answer to one another? Certainly this is true of their biological natures. They are suitable to one another for physical intimacy and for the propagation of the race. They are not only suitable to one another physically but also, to a considerable degree, emotionally and psychologically. If we ignore the latter, we will miss much of the potential richness in the husband-and-wife relationship.

Whatever may be the best translation of Genesis 2:18, it clearly suggests that man and woman belong together, that they will find their fulfillment in one another. Just as two cogs of a machine are made to mesh into one another and turn the machine, so men and women are made for one another. And just as a violin and a bow find fulfillment of their purpose in one another, so a man and woman as husband and wife are created for one another.

Man, being created in the image of God, was a person and needed someone with whom he could communicate. "So the Lord God caused a deep sleep to fall upon the man, and while he slept took one of his ribs . . . and the rib which the Lord God had taken from the man he made ["fashioned," NASB; "built," NEB] into a woman and brought her to the man" (Gen. 2:21). "Fashioned" or "built" implies that God may have taken some time and care in providing the woman for the man. Whatever may be the best translation, the verse clearly suggests that woman came from the side of man and that they belong together. Paul, after he had said that woman was created for man, added: "(Nevertheless, in the Lord woman is not independent of man nor man of woman; for as woman was made from man, so man is now born of woman)"; he then said, "(And all things are from God)" (1 Cor. 11:11-12).

When God brought the woman to man, the latter's response was: "This at last is bone of my bones and flesh of my flesh; she shall be called Woman, because she was taken out of Man" (Gen. 2:23). The word for "man" here is *ish,* for woman *ishsha.* In other words, the man gave his own name to the woman. Previously, the word for man was *adam.* The latter *(adam)* is generally used for the human race as such, including male and female. However, it is used as a proper name in Genesis 5:3. *Ish* usually refers to a particular man or individual.

There follows a statement not by the man but by the writer: "Therefore a man leaves his father and his mother and cleaves to his wife, and they become one flesh" (Gen. 2:24).

We may and should be concerned about some of the challenges to the home in the contemporary period, but we can be assured that the home will persist in some form as long as men are men and women are women. In other words, the home is written into their natures.

Its Purposes

The Bible not only reveals the source of the family or home but it also clearly reveals its purposes. The first stated purpose of the home, although not necessarily the most important one, was the *propagation of the race*. After God had created male and female, he "blessed them, and said to them, 'Be fruitful and multiply, and fill the earth and subdue it" (Gen. 1:28). Husbands and wives can be "God's deputy creators." What a sacred privilege and responsibility!

The propagation of the race is a continuing purpose of marriage and the home. Although there is not the same need for the multiplying of children in the contemporary period as formerly, a husband and wife who can and should have children (and there are a few who should not have any children) and deliberately choose not to do so are violating a basic purpose for their marriage. If the latter is correct, then they will—sooner or later—pay a price for that violation.

A more serious violation of the purposes of God for the home is the fact that many children come into the world outside of an established family. Every child has a right to have a father and mother who look forward to and plan for the child's coming into the world. The child also has the right to mature in a wholesome environment where there will be understanding and love.

In a later chapter, there will be a fuller discussion of the responsibility of parents to teach, train, and discipline their children. There are entirely too many parents who seem to have little sense of responsibility for their children. Many of the problems of our contemporary world stem from those neglected children.

Another purpose for marriage or the family is *the provision of a place of understanding, love, and companionship.* As implied earlier, a husband and wife can find the fulfillment of their deeper hungers and needs as creations of God in the intimate relations in the home. This purpose of the home is implied in Genesis 2. It is also emphasized in other portions of the Scriptures. Genesis 2:18 simply states, "It is not good that the man should be alone" or for woman.

The preceding—the relational or companionship purpose or aspect of the family—is particularly emphasized in the New Testament. For example, Jesus and Paul, so far as our records reveal, did not refer specifically to Genesis 1:27-28 but did cite Genesis 2:24 (See Matt. 19:5; Mark 10:7; 1 Cor. 6:16; Eph. 5:31). The propagation of the race was evidently assumed, but the emphasis was on the relational aspects of marriage and the home.

Another function or purpose of the home, which may have been implied by what has been said, was and is its service as a *channel for the legitimate expression of sexual urges.* Paul, in 1 Corinthians where he seems to prefer celibacy to marriage, had a specific word to the unmarried or the widows. His word was, "I say that it is well for them to remain single as I do. But if they cannot exercise self-control, they should marry. For it is better to marry than to be aflame ["burn," NEB] with passion" (1 Cor. 7:8-9). Some may think of this as a rather low purpose for marriage. "We may be convinced, however, that such is not necessarily true if we will consider properly the strength of the sex urge, the lift and enrichment that it can and does bring to human personalities when expressed within proper limits, with proper motive, and in the right spirit; and its terribly degrading effect when expressed wrongly or on a low level."[4]

There is at least one distinctly Christian purpose for the home: *the promotion of the kingdom of God.* This purpose may never be specifically stated in the Scriptures, but it is strongly and frequently implied. There is a sense in which the home, even the Christian home as is also true of the Christian church, is not an end within itself but a means to a broader and more important end in the promotion of the kingdom of God. "If the Christian husband and wife will let this conception of the home grip their lives, it will tend to purify and glorify every relation within the home and will deepen and make more meaningful every natural purpose of the home. It will give an added quality to every phase of their lives together. They will recognize themselves as co-laborers with God in his work in the world."[5]

The preceding means, among other things, that a Christian's supreme loyalty should not be to his home or to any member of his family but to Christ and his cause. It was Jesus himself who said, "He who loves ["cares more for," NEB] father and mother more than me is not worthy of me; and he who loves son or daughter more than me is not worthy of me" (Matt. 10:37). A possible background for this statement was and is the fact that Christ may cause divisions in families: son against father, daughter against mother, and daughter-in-law against her mother-in-law (Matt. 10:34-36). This continues to be the experience of many children of God who have to break with their families to follow the call or purpose of God for their lives.

There came a time in the life of Jesus when he had to break with his family in response to the Father's call and will. On one occasion when his mother and his brothers came and wanted to speak to him, he asked, "Who is my mother, and who are my brothers?" He answered his own question: "Here are my mother and my brothers! For whoever does the will of my Father in heaven is my brother, and sister, and mother" (Matt. 12:46-50).

And we know that the original followers of Jesus had to leave not only their places of business but also their families. Their Master and Teacher was an itinerant or traveling teacher. He taught as he walked with them from place to place. Many of his greatest teachings seemed more or less incidental. Some of the disciples may have occasionally gotten back to their homes. We know this was true of Peter, since Jesus on one occasion was in his home and healed his mother-in-law (Luke 4:38-39).

It was Peter who, on another occasion, said to Jesus, "Lo, we have left our homes and followed you." The Master's reply not only to Peter but to all and to us was and is, "Truly, I say to you, there is no man who has left house or wife or brother or parents or children, for the sake of the kingdom of God, who will not receive manifold more in this time, and in the age to come eternal life" (Luke 18:28-30). Many a child of God through the centuries has found that to be literally true!

Let us repeat that the maximum fulfillment for us as husbands and wives, parents and children, and for our homes in general will come as a by-product of giving the kingdom of God first place in our lives and in our homes. It costs to follow fully the purposes of God in our lives but also, as an old song says, "It pays to serve Jesus."

Its Nature

The Bible sets forth the ideals concerning the family and family relations. It also records the failures of many homes to measure up to these ideals. It not only does this for the family but also for human relations in general.

This tension between the ideal and the real, which is a continuing problem for all of us, is one of the reasons for the continuing appeal of the Scriptures. They find and challenge us where we actually are. This is not only true in our families but also in every area of our lives—at church, in our vocation or calling, and as citizens, neighbors, and friends.

In this section on the nature of the family, we want primarily to set forth, admittedly quite briefly, the biblical ideal concerning the home in general. In the next section we shall set forth, in a limited way, some of the departures even of God's chosen people from the ideal for the home. We will discover, however, that there was some evidence even before the close of the Old Testament of a movement back toward God's ideal for the family.

Now, let us look at some biblical teachings concerning the nature of the family. First, it should be recognized that *the family belongs to the natural order* and not to a distinctly Christian order. This fact has important implications for many marriages. It means, among other things, that the basic purposes and laws of God for marriage and the home apply to all marriages: unbelievers as well as believers. God does not have different fundamental laws and purposes for Christian and non-Christian homes. And, incidentally, it will be wise for all of us, Christians and non-Christians, to remember that his laws, in every area of our lives, are for our own good; they are best for us. We will find the maximum fulfillment and happiness as individuals and as families when we find and are obedient to his purposes and laws.

Much of what we know about God's ideals concerning the nature of marriage is found in Genesis 1 and 2, particularly in chapter 2, and most especially in 2:24. There are several things implied if not specifically stated in this one verse. This verse, as suggested previously, was a summary by the narrator or author. Moffatt, in his translation, placed it in parentheses. What does it suggest or imply about marriage and the home that a marriage establishes?

It plainly says that the two—husband and wife—"become one flesh." It is *a physical union,* although it is much more than that. One translation of the New Testament omits the word *flesh* when Genesis 2:24 is quoted or referred to, although the word for "flesh" (*būsār,* Hebrew; *sarx,* Greek) is in the original. Other translations not only retain "flesh" in Genesis 2:24 but also in the New Testament references to the verse. One explanation and possible justification for the omission of "flesh" in some translations is the fact that for the Jews "flesh" included more than the strictly physical. It at times referred to the total person.

It is a marvel and, in some ways, a mystery that the physical union of husband and wife makes them one not only physically but also in other and deeper ways. One fact that gives their union its deepest meaning is the fact that two persons in their totality are involved in the relationship. This means that sexual union that is not accompanied by mutual respect and genuine love is degrading and a serious offense.

Marriage provides *the deepest known physical and spiritual unity* between a man and a woman. Two lives are, or should be, so blended in marriage that they can never be entirely unblended. In a very real sense in the conjugal union, one plus one equals one. This oneness has been described as "the most distinctive . . . fact in human existence." Paul even said that one who is joined to a harlot or prostitute "becomes one body with her ["physically one with her," NEB]" (1 Cor. 6:16). To support his statement, Paul referred to Genesis 2:24.

Jesus quoted this same verse (Matt. 19:5; Mark 10:7). He then added: "So they are no longer two but one flesh. What therefore God has joined together, let not man put asunder" (Matt. 19:6). *The New English Bible* translates the preceding statement as follows: "It follows that they are no longer two individuals: they are one flesh. What God has joined together, man must not separate." God took woman from man. They were originally one flesh. In their union as husband and wife, they again become one flesh.

Genesis 2:24 also clearly implies that God's original purpose was the union of one man and one woman for life. In other words, it was to be *a monogamous union.* Anything other than that was and is a departure from God's purpose. It should be recognized that any marriage that fails to be a lasting union of one man and one woman for life falls short of God's purpose. Since it misses the mark that he has set for the marriage, it is sin—a subject we will return to in the chapter on divorce.

God's ideal for marriage and the home also included and includes the *ideal of exclusiveness.* "Therefore ["for this cause," NASB; "this is why," NEB] a man leaves his father and mother and cleaves to his wife, and they become one flesh." What will cause a man or a woman to leave the security of the home of father and mother to take a husband or wife? The answer is found in the nature that God gave to man and woman in the beginning of time, a nature that is ours today.

The fact that they are created for one another is the basic reason why mature sons and daughters will leave the security of an ancestral home and walk what may be an uncertain path with a husband or a wife. In biblical days, it was usually the wife who left her home and became a member of the husband's family.

A striking example is Rebekah who left her home to become the wife of Isaac. This is a beautiful story. It may sound strange in the customs revealed, but it is abidingly relevant in its perspective and basic concepts (see Gen. 24). Imagine how much courage and commitment it took for Rebekah to say, "I will go" (v. 58) when she faced the decision whether to go with Abraham's steward. She was going to be the wife of a man she had never seen. When she left with the steward, it likely meant that she would never see the members of her family again. The only way one can explain her courage is the fact that she evidently sensed that it was the purpose of God for her life.

Even in the contemporary world, there will be occasions when it will be necessary or at least wise not to live close to father and mother and other close relatives. This new relationship should take precedence over every other human relationship. From the time husband and wife are joined together, his and her supreme human loyalty belongs to that companion.

We will not do any violence to the overall emphasis in the Scriptures to suggest that this idea of exclusiveness should apply to young people before marriage as well as after marriage. At least this should be true of the physical expression of affection that makes them one flesh.

The whole biblical concept of the nature of marriage and the home can be summed up by saying that it is *a God-ordained union* of one man and one woman for life; that when they have physical union they are made one in the sight of God; that this oneness should never be broken; and that the union is to exclude similar relations with anyone else which should be true before as well as after marriage.

Its Form

Genesis 2:25 is a transitional sentence. It looks in two directions: back to the one-flesh concept and forward to the temptation and fall. Before the disobedience of the man and woman, they were as innocent as children. It is impossible to know how long their state of innocence continued: it could have been for days, weeks, months, or even years. But this verse also is introductory to the story of the temptation and fall and all the tragic consequences that followed the fall.

Beginning with chapter 3, there is revealed that something drastic happened to the human race in general and to the family in particular. There is no way to know how much time elapsed, but in rapid order there is recorded not only the temptation and fall but also the judgment of God on Adam and Eve: they were driven out of the Garden of Eden—sin separated them and will also separate us from God. There followed the murder of Abel by Cain and the curse of Cain by God: again sin separated man from God. Cain's word was, "Behold, thou hast driven me this day away from the ground; and from thy face I shall be hidden" (Gen. 4:14).

Lamech was the first, so far as we know, to take more than one wife (Gen. 4:19). This was the beginning of polygamy[6] which represented a dramatic departure from God's original plan for marriage. And, incidentally, there is no record of an Israelite woman having two or more husbands at a time.

As we sketch the forms or patterns of family life found in the Old Testament, we should keep in mind some relevant principles of interpretation suggested in the preceding chapter. None is more important than the fact that the Scriptures frequently record what they do not approve.

Polygamy is one example of the preceding statement. Polygamy was practiced by such heroes of the faith as Abraham, Jacob, Moses, David, and Solomon. However, it was never as common as a casual reading of the Scriptures might imply. It was evidently restricted to kings and the well-to-do. The most common form of marriage throughout the Old Testament continued to be monogamy.

Along with polygamy there arose *concubinage,*[7] a practice evidently largely restricted to a relatively few leaders. A concubine was not a prostitute or a mistress. Rather, she was "a secondary wife." The children born to her did not have all the rights of the children of the wife or wives. The Scriptures record that David had at least ten concubines (2 Sam. 15:16; 20:3), that Solomon had three hundred concubines in addition to seven hundred wives (1 Kings 11:3), and Rehoboam had eighteen wives, sixty concubines, along with twenty-eight sons and sixty daughters (2 Chron. 11:21). These kings violated a plain statement in Deuteronomy: "And he [a king] shall not multiply wives for himself, lest his heart turn away" (Deut. 17:17).

Although the practice of polygamy, as suggested previously, was relatively rare among the Hebrew people, its practice, however, by many leaders seemingly was accepted without question by the people. Feucht, in the concluding chapter of a book he edited, says that polygamy, concubinage, and so forth "are expressions of Man in his fallen state, or they are intrusions from other cultures."[8]

Monogamy seemed, however, to have been assumed by the prophets although it was not specifically defended. From the days of the prophets through the captivity and return, the trend was definitely back toward an exclusive recognition of monogamy as the only acceptable form of marriage. For example, "The image of a monogamous marriage is before the eyes of those prophets who represent Israel as the one wife chosen by the one and only God . . .; (Jn. 2:2; Is. 50:1; 54:6-7; 62:4-5)."[9]

The Old Testament family was definitely *patriarchal*. Usually the oldest male member of the family was considered the head of the family, which in some cases was large enough to be a clan. The wife or wives filled a secondary place, although some of them exercised considerable influence.

The Old Testament family was frequently an *extended family*. This extended family was not restricted to a three-generation family that was more or less prevalent in our culture two or three generations ago. The extended family of the Old Testament included not only all the children but also all of their children, as well as servants and their families. At times relatives other than the immediate family were included. This was evidently true of Abraham and Lot before they separated. The extended family on occasions was referred to as the "household" (Gen. 18:19; 47:12). We know that Abraham had a large household. He had 318 trained men "born in his house" (Gen. 14:14).

The extended family developed, to some degree, out of the nature of the life lived by a nomadic people who dwelt, in the main, in tents and moved from place to place. They needed one another for protection and for companionship.

A brief statement should be made concerning *levirate marriage*.[10] The law of the levirate required that if a husband died without a son, his brother was to take the widow as his wife (Deut. 25:5-10). This law may have been, to some degree, for the protection of the widow, but it seemed to have stemmed primarily from a desire to protect the inheritance—that it might be retained in the family. The latter was achieved by the birth of a son. Only two examples occur in the Old Testament, "both of them difficult to interpret and only superficially correspond to the law in Deuteronomy: the stories of Tamar and Ruth."[11]

This section on the form of marriage and the home would not be complete without a brief statement concerning *marriage by capture*.[12] This, like most of the other forms of marriage among the Israelites, was quite similar to surrounding nations and their cultures. It is true, however, that some provisions were made in the Old Testament law for the protection of a captive who had been taken as a wife. For example, if the husband had "no delight in her," he could "let her go where she will"; but he could not sell her for money and treat her as a slave, since he had "humiliated her" (Deut. 21:10-14).

Let us conclude this section on the form of marriage, which has been largely a review of varying Old Testament perspectives, with the following quotation: "The forms of marriage and the patterns of family structure and authority in various Old Testament eras varied with changing times and circumstances, revealing not only the cultural influences of other Near Eastern nations with whom Israel came into contact but also the impact of social and economic factors in Israel's own internal development."[13] It may be wise to remember another statement by Wegner, "The fact that a certain marriage or family pattern appears at a given point in Israel's history . . . does not elevate that pattern to the status of a divine ordinance expressive of God's will for humanity in all times and places."[14]

Its Customs[15]

David Mace says, "The institution of marriage assumes in every society a certain fixed form which is maintained by the joint operation of law and custom."[16] And after all, effective laws are primarily crystallized customs. This section will be restricted to customs related to marriage. No attention will be given to customs of family living after marriage. Some significant customs have been mentioned previously.

What about the *age of marriage?* There is nothing in the Mosaic law about marriageable age. It was the custom for marriage ordinarily to take place at an early age, probably not long after puberty had been reached. "In late days, the Rabbis fixed the minimum age for marriage at twelve years for girls and thirteen for boys."[17] The Talmud considered it a disgrace or at least a disregard of custom for a man not to be married by age twenty.

It is clearly revealed in the Old Testament that the *selection of a wife* was considered a major responsibility of the parents, particularly the father. It was almost a universal practice for marriages to be arranged. It was primarily an affair for the families involved rather than the individuals. Sometimes the parents acted jointly, as in the case of Samson (Judg. 14:1-20). Hagar, acting for her son in the absence of his father, took a wife for Ishmael (Gen. 21:21). A father could ask someone to make the arrangements for the wedding, as was the case of Abraham and his trusted steward (Gen. 24:3-8). The proposal of marriage was usually presented to the family rather than to the girl or young woman. At times she was consulted (Gen. 24:58). Sometimes a daughter was given in marriage as a reward for extraordinary bravery or valor (see 1 Sam. 18:17-20; Josh. 15:16-17; Judg. 1:12-13). There is evidence in the Old Testament that the son, at times, could take the initiative regarding his marriage, as was clearly the case of Esau (Gen. 28:8-9) and Samson (Judg. 14:1-3). There are some hints of courtship such as the wise man's statement:

> Three things are too wonderful for me;
>   four I do not understand:
> the way of an eagle in the sky,
>   the way of a serpent on a rock,
> the way of a ship on the high seas,
>   and the way of a man with a maiden.
>   (Prov. 30:18-19)

There were some restrictions, or *impediments to,* concerning *marriage.* For example, there was a considerable list of relatives whose "nakedness" should not be uncovered (Lev. 18:6-18; 20:17-21; see Deut. 27:20-23). There is some question about the meaning of "nakedness," particularly in the instructions in Leviticus 18. The reference is clearly to sexual intercourse. The question is whether it prohibited "incestuous marriages" or "incestuous intercourse." Even if it was specifically restricted to the latter, it could include the former since only by sexual intercourse could a marriage be finally consummated.

Those included in the restricted list were members of the extended family. Referring to exogamy in general, Westermarck says, "The exogamous group is in most cases composed of persons who are, or consider themselves to be, related by blood or of the same kin; and the nearer the relationship, the more frequently it is a bar to inter-marriage, at least within the same line of descent."[18]

There were also restrictions concerning the marriage of the children of Israel to those of other groups (endogamy). In the Pentateuch, there are listed six (Ex. 23:23-33) or seven (Deut. 7:1-8) nations to whom God's people were not to give their sons or daughters in marriage. Ezra later extended the list to other nations or peoples (Ezra 9:1). Intermarriage with surrounding peoples was a major moral and social problem faced by Ezra and Nehemiah. Even some priests and Levites were guilty. The mixing had become so prevalent that Nehemiah said that half of the children "spoke the language of Ashdod, and they could not speak the language of Judah" (Neh. 13:24).

It should be pointed out that the restrictions concerning marriage with other peoples were based primarily on tribal, national, or religious grounds. The religious motivation is stated specifically in the law as follows: "You shall not make marriages with them, . . . For they would turn away your sons from following me, to serve other gods" (Deut. 7:3-4).

Solomon's life underscored in a striking way the truthfulness of the preceding. "Now King Solomon loved many foreign women.

. . . Solomon clung to these [foreign wives] in love. . . . and his wives turned away his heart" (1 Kings 11:1-3). Nehemiah referred to the effect on Solomon of his foreign wives, when he remonstrated with the children of Israel about their marriages to the women of Ashdod, Ammon, and Moab. He said, "Did not Solomon king of Israel sin on account of such women? . . . there was no king like him, and he was beloved by his God, . . . nevertheless foreign women made even him to sin" (Neh. 13:23-26).

A Hebrew marriage was preceded by a *betrothal,* which was different from a contemporary engagement. It was almost the equivalent of marriage. The major difference was that the marriage had not been consummated. Jacob, after he had served Laban seven years for Rachel, said, "Give me my wife that I may go in to her, for my time is completed" (Gen. 29:21). Notice that he called her "my wife," although he had not gone "in to her." Sexual relations with a betrothed virgin was punishable by death "because he violated his neighbor's wife" (Deut. 22:23-24).

There is no complete set of rules in the Scriptures governing the betrothal, but enough is known to establish it as a common and well-recognized practice. It did, however, exist by force of tradition and custom rather than by law. A man who had betrothed a wife and had not "taken her" was excused from service in the army "lest he die in the battle and another man take her" (Deut. 20:7; see 24:5). Special protection was also provided for the betrothed (Deut. 22:23-27).

A prominent element in the betrothal was the payment of the *mōhar* (Gen. 34:12), translated "marriage present and gift" (RSV), "dowry" (KJV), "bridal payment" (NASB). The payment of the *mōhar* was much more prevalent than the limited usage of the word (Gen. 34:12; Ex. 22:16; 1 Sam. 18:25) would imply. A striking example, where the word is not used, is the occasion of the presentation of gifts by the steward of Abraham to the family of Rebekah. The *mōhar,* which was compensation to the family, ratified the engagement and seemingly sealed the covenant between the two families. Jacob, who had no present from his family and had nothing personally to give, paid the *mōhar* in service.

In some cases, there were other gifts in addition to the *mōhar* proper. In the case of Isaac and Rebekah, gifts were given to her by the steward (Gen. 24:22). Also, there were occasions when the bride's family gave her presents as she left her home. This was clearly evident in the case of Rebekah (Gen. 24:60-61) and also of Leah (Gen. 29:24) and Rachel (Gen. 29:29). The Old Testament concept of the betrothal evidently carried over to New Testament days. We know this was true of Joseph and Mary before the birth of Jesus (see Matt. 1:18-19).

There is little information in the Scriptures concerning the *marriage ceremony*. It seems to have been a private affair of the families that required no public ceremony—religious or otherwise. It was never, from the Old Testament perspective, in the hands of the priests. Then, as today, the wedding was an occasion of rejoicing (see Isa. 61:10; 62:5; Jer. 7:34; 16:9; 25:10; 33:11). Some mention is made of the bride's attire, particularly the veil (Gen. 24:65). A procession usually was an integral part of the wedding. The bridegroom was attended by friends. The final destination of the procession was the house where a feast was to be held. This feast, which could last for several days (Judg. 14:12), is referred to in Revelation as a supper (Rev. 19:9). The first recorded miracle of Jesus was when he, his disciples, and his mother attended a wedding feast at Cana of Galilee (John 2:1-11). Jesus also alluded to the wedding feast (Matt. 22:2-14; 25:1-13; Mark 2:19-20).

A formal marriage ceremony, such as we have in the contemporary period, developed rather late. It seems in the Old Testament period and possibly also in the New Testament era that, after the betrothal which may have been for a short or long period of time and after all the celebration that might attend a wedding ceremony, the actual marriage was not final until its consummation by means of sexual intercourse on the first night (Gen. 29:23).[19] This was the final step in whatever ceremony they had. It was when Isaac brought Rebekah "into the tent" that "she became his wife" (Gen. 24:67). Was it just because she took over the tent of Sarah, or was it what was assumed went on in the tent that made them husband and wife? There is no way to know for sure.

Its Symbolic Use

The importance of the family is underscored by its symbolic or figurative use in the Scriptures. The family and family relations are frequently used to describe God's relation to his people and their relations to him. This is true in both Testaments.

In the Old Testament, the *relation of God to Israel* is frequently described in terms of the family and family relations. For example, Moses was instructed to say to Pharaoh, "Thus says the Lord, Israel is my first-born son, and I say to you, 'Let my son go that he may serve me'" (Ex. 4:22). Later, Moses reminded the people that, while they were in the wilderness, God had carried them "just as a man carries his son" (Deut. 1:31, NASB). He also reminded the children of Israel "that, as a man disciplines his son, the Lord your God disciplines you" (Deut. 8:5). The idea that God is the Father of his people is prominent elsewhere in the Old Testament (see Ps. 103:13; Isa. 63:16; 64:8; Jer. 3:19). Also, he is revealed as the Father of the fatherless (Ps. 68:5-6).

One of the tenderest passages in the Old Testament is the opening verses of Hosea 11:

> When Israel was a child, I loved him,
>   and out of Egypt I called my son.
>
> ....
> Yet it was I who taught Ephraim to walk,
>   I took them up in my arms;
>   but they did not know that I healed them.
> I led them with cords of compassion,
>   with the bands of love,
> and I became to them as one
>   who eases the yoke on their jaws,
>   and I bent down to them and fed them.
>   (Hos. 11:1,3-4)

But God is also portrayed in the Old Testament as the Husband of his people—the children of Israel. This emphasis is particularly prevalent in the prophets. For example, Hosea used "the marriage relationship as a symbolic portrait of the covenant relationship between Yahweh and His bride, Israel" (see Isa. 54:5-8; 62:1-5; Jer.

2:2; Ezek. 16:32). Israel's unfaithfulness was considered "adultery" (Jer. 3:8-9; Ezek. 23:37-38). Jeremiah, in pathetic tones, spoke for God:

> And I thought you would call me, My Father,
> and would not turn from following me.
> Surely, as a faithless wife leaves her husband,
> so have you been faithless to me, O house of Israel
> (Jer. 3:19-20).[20]

When we turn to the New Testament, we discover that the idea of God as Father is much more prevalent. There are approximately 275 references to God as Father in the New Testament, with over 100 of those in John's Gospel and an additional dozen in 1 John. "It is primarily the Johannine writings that have made 'Father' the more or less natural name for God for Christians, although it is used in the synoptic gospels and frequently in Paul's epistles."[21]

Jesus referred to *God as* "my *Father*," "your father," with fifteen such references in the Sermon on the Mount. It was in the Model Prayer that Jesus used the all-inclusive "Our Father" (Matt. 6:9), and it possibly should be added that God cannot really be *my Father* unless I can accept him as *your Father* and hence as *our Father.*

Jesus also told the parable of the prodigal son or of the loving, forgiving father (Luke 15:11-32). This, certainly one of his most memorable parables, was a parable of parental compassion. On another occasion Jesus compared our Heavenly Father with an earthly father who gave good gifts to his children (Matt. 7:9-11). He also exemplified in his relation to people the love and compassion of the Father. When he was preparing his disciples for his departure, he said, "There are many dwelling-places in my Father's house" (John 14:2, NEB). Notice that they and we are to be with him in his Father's "house."

Family terminology, particularly the idea of God as Father, is not as prevalent in Paul's Epistles as in the life and teachings of Jesus. Paul, however, did frequently use family terms in speaking of spiritual relationships. For example, Christians are sons and daughters or children of God through faith (Rom. 8:14-17; 2 Cor. 6:16-18; Gal. 3:26). It is the Spirit within that causes us to say

"Abba! Father!" (Rom. 8:15-16; Gal. 4:6-7). Paul referred to Timothy as "my son" (1 Tim. 1:18; 2 Tim. 2:1). Also, Paul over and over again referred to fellow Christians as brothers (Rom. 14:10,13; 1 Cor. 8:11-13; Eph. 6:21). Then in the beautiful passage that we will examine more thoroughly in a later chapter, Paul compared the relation of a husband and wife to the relation of Christ and his church (Eph. 5:21-33).

Through the Epistles and the Book of Acts, the *church* is portrayed as *a family* that shares with one another. This is clearly evident in the church at Jerusalem and in the sharing of the broader Christian fellowship with the fellow Christians in Jerusalem. Family terminology is also evident in the Revelation. For example, the church is portrayed as the Lamb's bride (Rev. 19:6-9; 21:2,9; 22:17).

Conclusions

1. It is clearly seen in Genesis 1 and 2 that marriage and the family were ordained of God. He also ordained the purposes of the marriage and the form or structure of the family.

2. Following the temptation and fall, it is said that the man or husband was to rule over the woman or his wife. Through the centuries and even today there is some difference of opinion whether the statement was and is to be considered prescriptive or descriptive. G. Ernest Wright says that "the equality of the sexes is within the order of creation . . . the subservience of woman to man belongs to the 'fallen world.'" He further says that the verses of judgment in Genesis 3, including verse 16, "are simply descriptions of the way things are in the world as it is."[22]

3. The actual situation concerning the family in the Old Testament fell far below God's original plan and purpose for marriage and the home: polygamy, concubinage, divorce, and so forth. This was due to the direct and indirect impact of surrounding peoples with their competing cultures.

4. The prophets challenged the prevalent forms of marriage and the family, as well as other practices, that represented a departure of the children of Israel from God's original purposes for them.

5. Christ, when he came, breathed a newness into every aspect of life including the family and family relationships. He went back to Genesis for God's purpose for the home. Jesus also honored the family or the home by his relation to his own home and the homes of others. (Among the latter was not only the home of Levi or Matthew [Luke 5:29-32] and Peter [Matt. 8:14-15] but also Simon the leper [Matt. 26:6-13] and Simon the Pharisee [Luke 7:36-50]. Jesus was a self-invited guest in the home of Zacchaeus, the publican [Luke 19:1-10]. The home of Lazarus, Martha, and Mary in Bethany was evidently a special blessing to Jesus [Luke 10:38-42; John 11:1-44; 12:1-8].)

6. Paul, like Jesus, emphasized the relational aspects of marriage and the home. He did this in 1 Corinthians in response to some questions the church, or at least a group in the church, had asked him. But he also set forth, in a beautiful way, his ideal concerning the relation of husbands and wives, parents and children in Ephesians 5:21—6:4. A more compact statement is found in Colossians 3:18-21.

7. We need very much in the contemporary period to re-discover and take seriously the biblical ideal for the family and family relations: one man and one woman joined together as husband and wife for life, fulfilling the purposes of God for their home and sending out into the world individuals—husband, wife, and children—who will put first in their lives the kingdom or reign of God and who will be channels for God's love and compassion as he seeks to reach out to those in need.

The home is God's first institution: first in time and first in importance. All the basic institutions—the home, the church, the state—come from God, but the first one was the home. *The state:* Paul said, "Let every person be subject to the governing authorities. For there is no authority except from God, and those that exist have been instituted by God" (Rom. 13:1). *The church:* at Caesarea Philippi, Jesus said to Peter and the other disciples, "and on this rock I will build my church" (Matt. 16:18). It was and is his church, and he is the Builder. *The home:* for the beginning of the home, we have to go back to the first chapters of the first Book of the Bible where it is revealed that God wrote the home into the basic nature of the man and woman he created. They were and still are made to find their fulfillment in one another.

And we might add that the home or family is not only God's first institution in time but also in importance. It is a more important educational institution than the school, a more important institution for law and order than the state, and even a more basically important religious institution than the church. There is no surer barometer of the condition of a culture than the health or sickness of its families. As the home goes, so goes everything else: school, church, and civilization itself.

Notes

1. Some of the best books on the family in general, and particularly on the history of marriage and the family, were written several years ago. There is no better example of this than Edward Westermarck's three volumes, *The History of Human Marriage* (New York: The Allerton Book Company, 1922). This work has gone through several printings and is still in print. Based on the fifth edition of the three volumes, Westermarck wrote *A Short History of Marriage* (New York: Humanities Press, 1968). There is also the three-volume work of Robert Briffault, *The Mothers* (New York: Macmillan, 1927). Similar to Westermarck, it has gone through several printings. The title of Briffault's monumental work is somewhat misleading. He touches on practically every phase of marriage and the family. In 1977, there appeared an abbreviated edition of Briffault, edited by Gordon R. Taylor, published by Doubleday.

A couple of other books, not as exhaustive nor quite as old as those by Westermarck and Briffault, but related more directly to our study are E. Neufeld, *Ancient Hebrew Marriage Laws* (New York: Longman, Green and Co., 1944) and one of David Mace's earliest books, *Hebrew Marriage: A Sociological Study* (London: Epworth Press, 1953). Both of these books are scholarly, with Neufeld somewhat more technical. Also Neufeld compares Hebrew marriage laws and customs to those of other Semitic peoples. Mace, as should be expected, is more biblically oriented. These two books will be helpful on practically every phase of our study. Another scholarly book—with a very compact, helpful section of less than fifty pages on "Family Institutions" is Roland de Vaux, *Ancient Israel: Its Life and Institutions*, John McHugh, trans. (New York: McGraw-Hill Book Co., Inc., 1961).

Many books have been written on the family from the rather strictly sociological viewpoint. Some of these, such as those by Henry Bowman and by Judson and Mary Landis, to varying degrees are defenders of the traditional Christian ideals for the home.

2. Paul K. Jewett, *Man as Male and Female: A Study in Sexual Relationships from a Theological Point of View* (Grand Rapids: Eerdmans, 1975), p. 38.

3. Ibid.

4. T. B. Maston, *Christianity and World Issues* (New York: Macmillan, 1957), p. 70.

5. Ibid., p. 71.

6. Neufeld has a chapter (7) on "Polygamy and Concubinage." Mace, in *Hebrew Marriage*, includes a chapter on "Monogamy and Polygamy" (pp. 121-141).

7. The first mention of a concubine is Genesis 22:24, the concubine of Nahor, Abraham's brother.

8. Oscar E. Feucht, ed., *Family Relationships in the Church* (St. Louis: Concordia Publishing House, 1970), p. 219.

9. de Vaux, p. 26.

10. See part I, chapter 1 of Neufeld. The law of the levirate was the background for an interesting conversation of Jesus with some Sadducees (Matt. 22:23-33).

11. de Vaux, p. 37.

12. Chapter 4 in Neufeld's book is "Marriage by Capture."

13. Walter Wegner in Feucht, p. 50.

14. Ibid.

15. The following are some of the numerous publications available for those who want additional material on the Jewish family and family relations and customs: Earl Bennett Cross, *Hebrew Family* (Chicago: University of Chicago Press, 1927), an old but compact, helpful survey of most aspects of ancient Hebrew life; Louis M. Epstein, *Marriage Laws in the Bible and the Talmud* (Cambridge, Mass.: Harvard University Press, 1942), covers thoroughly such subjects as polygamy, concubinage, the levirate marriage, and incest. There is a companion volume by Epstein, *Sex Laws and Customs in Judaism* (New York: Block Publishing Co., 1948). Still another book by Epstein is *The Jewish Marriage Contract*, with the lengthy subtitle: *A Study in the Status of the Woman in Jewish Law*, reprint ed. (New York: Arno Press, 1973). A book that some may find interesting is by Rabbi K. Kahana, *The Theory of Marriage and Jewish Law* (Leiden: E. J. Brill, 1966). This, a relatively brief book of one hundred pages, includes an index and is based largely on the Talmud.

16. Mace, p. 165. There are several books that deal with marriage and the family in other cultures. A few of these are: David Mace and Vera Mace, *Marriage—East and West* (Garden City, N.Y.: Doubleday and Co., 1963); Thomas Price, *African Marriage* (New York: SCM Press, 1954), a book of approximately seventy pages, which compares the African family and the Jewish family of Old Testament days. Other books that may be of interest are Ahmed Shukri, *Muhammedan Law of Marriage and Divorce* (New York: AMS Press, 1966), a Ph.D. Dissertation at Columbia University, and John S. Mbiti, *Love and Marriage in Africa* (London: Longmans, 1973) which covers practically every aspect of family life.

17. de Vaux, p. 297.

18. Westermarck, *A Short History of Marriage*, p. 66.

19. de Vaux says, "The blood-stained linen of the nuptial night was preserved; it proved the bride's virginity and would be evidence if she were slandered by her husband (Dt. 22:13-21)" (p. 34).

20. See Phyllis Trible, *God and the Rhetoric of Sexuality* (Philadelphia: Fortress Press, 1978), for a scholarly discussion of family terms applied to God with a particular emphasis on "female imagery for God in the Hebrew Scriptures."

21. Maston, *Why Live the Christian Life?* (Nashville: Broadman Press, 1974), p. 24.

22. James I. Cook, *Grace upon God: Essays in Honor of Lester J. Kuyper* (Grand Rapids: Eerdmans, 1975), p. 68.

PART II
FAMILY MEMBERS

Some members of the family are of particular interest and importance in the contemporary world. This is true of women, with what some have considered in recent years as a "women's revolution." Also, there is an increasing interest in single adults—the divorced, the widowed, and the never married. There has been considerable discussion of a more or less permanently single life as a legitimate competitor to the traditional family of father, mother, and children. With the marked increase in the number of older adults, some attention needs to be given to them. There is a fourth group which is of abiding interest and sometimes of deepening concern. They are the children, most of whom come into the world and spend their most formative years in an established home, but with an increasing number born to unwed mothers. A chapter will be devoted to each of the preceding four groups.

It will be noted that there is no chapter on men. It was felt that such was unnecessary. There was some discussion of the man's place in the home in the chapter on "The Family." Also, a man's relationship to his wife and children will be discussed in subsequent chapters.

3

Women

It does not take a prophet or the son of a prophet to know that we live in a revolutionary age. And one of the most vocal expressions of that revolution has been and still is by women and about women. This is evident in society in general and to varying degrees in our churches. Some men and an increasing number of women have become conscious of the inequities suffered by women. For example, women usually outnumber men in our churches, and yet in most churches they have relatively little voice in determining programs and policies. They seldom hold places of significant leadership. When placed on a committee it is usually a committee of minor importance or as a minority member of a major committee. The work of many churches is impoverished by failure to utilize the distinctive contributions that women could make. It has been said, "Woman has always been the best friend religion has ever had, but religion has by no means been the best friend woman has had."

One writer has said that "the debate on women and religion is the single most important and radical question for our time and the foreseeable future." This is true "because it concerns religion and because it affects all possible people and peoples."[1] The same author also says that the subject of women affects more people than any other issue and refers to it as "a new, radical, and fundamental question."[2] Even if these statements should be only relatively correct, they justify if they do not necessitate this chapter. It will be tragic if churches and Christian leaders are among the last to face up to the contemporary challenge concerning women and their place in the home, church, and society in general.

It should be noted that the concern of this chapter is not

"women of the Bible"[3] but the teachings and perspective of the Bible concerning women. In this discussion we will first consider the Old Testament, to be followed by sections on Jesus and Paul. We will close with some concluding remarks, including some statements concerning the ordination of women.[4]

Old Testament

The Old Testament is predominantly a *"man's book."* Women, in the main, were second-class citizens, mere adjuncts to men and their world. "The wife called her husband ba'al or 'master'; she also called him *ados* or 'lord' (Gn. 18:12; Jg. 19:26; Am. 4:1."[5] Even the images or figures used to describe God were predominantly, but not exclusively, masculine. A woman, with rare but striking exceptions, was subservient to the men in her life: father, husband, brother, and even her husband's brother. Her father arranged for her marriage; she could be divorced but did not have the right of divorce. Stagg concludes that "in regard to marriage, divorce, and penalties for adultery, it is difficult to excape the conclusion that the subordination of women . . . prevailed."[6] This was also true regarding such matters as slavery (Ex. 21:1-11) and inheritance (Num. 27:8).

The inequity between men and women is even evident in the Ten Commandments. Except for the command to honor father and mother, the Decalogue is male oriented. For example, the wife is listed with the possessions of the man (Ex. 20:17); in Deuteronomy she is listed first (Deut. 5:21). Also, there is no command for the wife not to covet another woman's husband.

This inequity is rather strikingly evident in the Book of Proverbs. There are warnings against the "loose woman" (Prov. 2:16; 7:5) but none against the "loose man." Also, a recurring emphasis is that

> It is better to live in a corner of the housetop
> than in a house shared with a contentious woman
> (Prov. 21:9; see 21:19; 25:24).

In a particularly graphic statement, the wise man said,

> A continual dripping on a rainy day
> and a contentious woman are alike;

to restrain her is to restrain the wind
or to grasp oil in his right hand
(Prov. 27:15-16).

But on the other hand, "A good wife is the crown of her husband" (Prov. 12:4). Also, Proverbs includes the great chapter (31) on the good or industrious wife; Toy, in his excellent commentary, refers to it as "The Alphabetic Ode or 'Golden ABC' of the perfect wife."[7]

Let us examine briefly some of the additional evidences of the *twofold perspective* in the Old Testament *concerning women* and the further fact that the Old Testament was not and is not antifeminist. One example is the fact that "wisdom," which held a prominent place in Hebrew literature and was frequently personified, was referred to as "she" (Prov. 1:20; 7:4; 9:11; see Matt. 11:19*b*; Luke 7:35).

There are some special provisions in the Mosaic law for the protection of women. For example, a captive woman who was taken as a wife was to have a time of mourning before her captor could go in to her and become her husband. Furthermore, if he had "no delight in her," he could not sell her or treat her as a slave (Deut. 21:10-14). Also, a wife who was falsely accused of not being a virgin when taken as a wife could not be put away or divorced (Deut. 22:13-21).

There are also some provisions in the Old Testament law that reveal a respect and a concern for females, both children and women. While a female child or an adult woman did not have as much monetary value as men (Lev. 27:1-8), they could, with some limitations, make the same kind of vow as men (Num. 30:1-15). Women, along with men, were included in the renewal of the covenant in the days of Nehemiah and Ezra. The record plainly says, "And Ezra the priest brought the law before the assembly, both men and women and all who could hear with understanding" (Neh. 8:2). Also, wives and daughters were specifically mentioned as among those who had separated themselves from the surrounding people (Neh. 10:28-31).

A complete picture of *women* in the Old Testament would require some attention to those *who rose to positions of prominence* in the life of Israel. There were no priestesses among the Israelites[8] but there were some women who were called "prophetesses." In some cases the reference may have simply been to the wife of a prophet (Isa. 8:3). But at other times the reference was clearly to women who fulfilled the prophetic role. This was true of Miriam (Ex. 15:20-21) and Huldah (2 Kings 22:14-20). The most outstanding prophetess of the Old Testament was Deborah who "used to sit under the palm of Deborah . . . and the people of Israel came up to her for judgment" (Judg. 4:5). She cooperated with Barak in the defeat of Sisera and his army. In the song that she and Barak sang, she is referred to as "a mother in Israel" (Judg. 5:7). There were other women, such as Ruth and Esther, with major achievements. The psalmist in one place said,

> The Lord gives the command;
> The women who proclaim the good tidings are a
>   great host (Ps. 68:11, NASB).

This is enough to underscore the fact that the picture concerning women in the Old Testament is not one-dimensional.

The first chapters of Genesis are the most important references in the Old Testament relative to women. Let us, in outline form, suggest some of the more significant aspects of the account of the creation in Genesis. There will be some repetition of what has been said in chapter 2. This will be done consciously for the sake of completeness and emphasis.

1. The word for *man* or *Adam*, as in Genesis 1, is found, according to Heflin,[9] 562 times in the Old Testament. It is used predominantly in the generic sense inclusive of male and female.

2. "The image of God," found here (Gen. 1:27) and elsewhere in the Scriptures, has been variously interpreted. Heflin suggests that "we will never grasp all of the significance of being in the image of God." One suggestion is that God is a person and that men and women are created persons.

3. As suggested previously, a person can think, feel, will. Also, he or she is conscious of self and of other selves or persons. Persons are not only capable of communication, but communication

with other persons is necessary. There is no person without other persons. It is no accident that our God who is one is also the triune God: Father, Son, and Spirit. Notice, "God said, 'Let *us* make man in *our* image, after *our* likeness'" (Gen. 1:26, authors italics). God further said, "Let them have dominion."

4. The most important aspect of the creation, from the perspective of this chapter on women, is the fact that male and female were both and equally created in the image of God. The Bible pointedly says, "So God created man in his image, in the image of God created he *him*; male and female created he *them*" (1:27, KJV, authors italics). Genesis 5:1-2 similarly says, "When God created man, he made him in the likeness of God. Male and female he created them, and he blessed them and named them Man when they were created."

5. The fact that all are created in the image of God, and the companion fact that Christ died for all to restore that image, marred by sin, is or should be the basis for our respect for persons, regardless of sex, race, culture, or condition of life.

6. This means, among other things, that no person, male or female, should ever be used as a mere means. Each person is an end of infinite value.

7. While male and female are equally created in the image of God, being male and female they are different and have some distinctive functions to perform. Jewett suggests that men and women are different but then adds, "There can be no fellowship where there are no differences. Differences make for mutual enrichment."[10] The complementarity of men and women is a recurring emphasis in Lois Clemens' book *Women Liberated*.[11] She correctly emphasizes that the complementarity includes much more than sex relations. It has also been unfortunate that entirely too frequently both men and women have considered the female's distinctive contributions as inferior to that by men.

Heflin's conclusion regarding Genesis 1:26-31 is as follows: "Woman in this passage is certainly no inferior afterthought; she is rather one with man in the responsibility of subduing the creation and propagating the race."[12]

Let us now suggest a few things related to Genesis 2:18-24.

1. In Genesis 1:31, God looked over all his creation, including male and female, and concluded that it was very good. In contrast, in Genesis 2:18, God said, "It is not good that man should be alone; I will make him a helper fit for him" or "a partner for him" (NEB).

2. Genesis 2:18-24 supplements the account of the creation in Genesis 1, particularly the creation of male and female.

3. The word translated "rib" (v. 21) is usually translated "side." The word for "made" (v. 22) is so translated only three times but over three hundred times "build" or "built," and is so translated here in some of the versions (NEB, Jer. B.). This may suggest that God took some time and care in making or building woman. "Man" in verse 23 is *ish* rather than *adam*. Woman is *ishshah*. *Ish*, which refers primarily to man as an individual person, really comes into being only with the creation of *ishshah*; so far as we know, man or *ish* here speaks for the first time—"*ish* comes alive in meeting *ishshah*."

4. Some who contend that woman is innately inferior and should be subservient to man defend their position on the basis that woman was created or "built" from the rib or side of man. The statement of the apostle Paul is frequently quoted. He said, "(For man was not made from woman, but woman from man. Neither was man created for woman, but woman for man)" (1 Cor. 11:8-9). There is another parenthetical statement in verses 11 and 12 of this same chapter of 1 Corinthians that the defenders of the superiority of men usually overlook. It is, "(Nevertheless, in the Lord woman is not independent of man nor man of woman; for as woman was made from man, so man is now born of woman. And all things are from God)."

5. If one argues that woman is inferior because she was taken or built from the side of man, what about man? It says, "The Lord God formed man of dust from the ground" (Gen. 2:7). Is man inferior to the dust?

6. Closely akin to the preceding is the contention of some that the fact that woman was created after man implies her inferiority. The animals were created before man. Does this mean that they are superior to man? The order of creation could be used to prove

woman's superiority. It has been suggested "that which comes second may well be the better."

7. When God brought the woman to man, the latter's immediate response was:

> This at last is bone of my bones
> and flesh of my flesh;
> she shall be called Woman,
> because she was taken out of Man (Gen. 2:23).

The latter part of this statement could be interpreted to imply the inferiority of women. The first portion, however, clearly implies partnership.

Genesis 2:24 says, "Therefore a man leaves his father and his mother and cleaves to his wife, and they become one flesh." This statement reverses the generally accepted order or policy of the times and even the general practice in the Old Testament. The wife usually left her family and became a member of the husband's family.

There should be, for a complete picture of the Old Testament and women, some consideration of the *temptation and fall* as recorded *in Genesis 3*. Those who defend the subserviency of women justify their position frequently by using God's curse on the woman following the fall:

To the woman he said,

> "I will greatly multiply your pain in childbearing;
> in pain you shall bring forth children,
> Yet your desire shall be for your husband,
> and he shall rule over you" ("shall be your master," NEB)
> (Gen. 3:16).

The desire spoken of her may have referred to desire in general, but its relation to the bearing of children suggests that the primary reference was to sexual desire. Whatever may be the correct interpretation of "desire," some claim that it provides the basis for man ruling over woman. Also some regard this as a prescriptive ordinance; others consider it a descriptive statement of actual conditions within marriage, resulting from human sinfulness. The prescriptive interpretation has continued to be quite prevalent in spite of the redeeming impact of the life of Jesus. In Christ the image of God is equally restored in both men and women through their union with him. The only person who has the right or authority to rule over woman is the Ruler of the universe, who has the right to rule over men as well as women. But even the Lord does not force his authority on anyone. It must be voluntarily accepted; when accepted, we will discover that his yoke is easy and that his burden is light (Matt. 11:30). In other words, his rule and authority is best for us. This is true in our individual lives and in our relationships as men and women, husbands and wives, parents and children.

Jesus

In the Jewish home, the woman's position was one of marked subordination. Some extremists even contended that a man should not converse with a woman, even his wife. What a contrast with Jesus! "In his public ministry . . . he spoke of women and related to women as being fully human and equal in every way to men . . . thus restoring to the woman the full humanity which was given her by the Creator when he made Man male and female."[13] We can sum it up by simply saying that Jesus *lifted the level of womanhood*, just as he did for every other oppressed, underprivileged group.[14]

And it might be wise for us to remember again that the *final* authoritative *word* from our Heavenly Father is in his Son and our Savior and Lord. The writer of Hebrews said that God, in times past, spoke "in many and various ways . . . by the prophets; but in the last days he has spoken to us by a Son," and the Son "reflects the glory of God and bears the very stamp of his nature" (1:1-3). Possibly the Father would say to us today, as he said to the disciples on the mount of transfiguration: "This is my beloved Son; listen to him" (Mark 9:7). We ought to listen to him regarding what he said concerning women but even more, we ought to examine his *attitude toward* and relation to *women*. After all, Jesus, as is true of any great spiritual teacher or leader, taught as much if not more by his spirit and attitude than by anything he might have said.

Really, Jesus gave *no specific teachings* concerning women. This was and is in marked contrast to most religious teachers. The sacred books of most of the peoples of the world include rather detailed instructions concerning the nature of women and how they should be treated or mistreated. Some of these sacred books contain specific instructions about how male and female children were to be trained. In contrast, Jesus either largely ignored women in his teachings or he believed that his teachings were equally applicable to men and women. The latter was clearly the case. Jewett concludes that Jesus *"treated women as . . . equal to men in every respect; no word of deprecation about women, as such, is ever found on his lips."*[15]

There was also a marked *contrast between the attitude of Jesus toward women and the religious leaders of his day*. The latter not only did not permit women to teach the law but also they were not taught the law. Jewish men, in their morning prayer, thanked God that he had not made them Gentiles, slaves, or women. No wonder the disciples marveled when they found Jesus talking with the Samaritan woman at the well (John 4:27). Incidentally, this is the first recorded conversation of Jesus with a woman, except with his mother. The Samaritan woman was even surprised that he talked with her. She reminded him that the Jews had "no dealings with Samaritans" (John 4:9). But Jesus never permitted any barrier—race, sex, or moral condition—to keep him from reaching out to a person in need. This was just as true of the beggar as the rich man, the Samaritan as the Jew, the sinner as the saint, and the woman as the man. We can summarize by simply saying that the attitude of Jesus toward women and his relation to them were revolutionary for his day. Also, we may conclude that it would be rather revolutionary for our day.

There is a woman in the New Testament who demonstrated the attitude that all of us, but particularly women, should have toward Jesus. The Bible states that Mary of Bethany was in the presence of Jesus three times. Each time she was at his feet: first, to listen to his matchless teachings (Luke 10:39), then to cry out her sorrow at the loss of her brother (John 11:32), and finally, she anointed his feet with a pound of pure nard and then wiped them with her hair (John 12:3).

One evidence of the attitude and relationship of Jesus to

women is the *balancing of the sexes* in Luke's account of his life. The balancing began even before his birth. Luke recorded the Magnificat of Mary (Luke 1:46-56) and the prophecy of Zechariah, father of John the Baptist (Luke 1:67-79). Luke also told us that, when Joseph and Mary presented the baby Jesus to the Lord in the Temple, Simeon took him in his arms and praised God (Luke 2:22-32). There was also present an aged prophetess, Anna, who "gave thanks to God" and spoke about him to others who were present (Luke 2:36-38). Women had a particularly prominent place in Luke's Gospel. Stagg suggests that Luke's special concern for women "seems to have been a part of a larger concern for human dignity and liberation."[16]

The balancing of the concern of Jesus for and ministry to both men and women is evident, in varying degrees, in all four Gospels. For example, in John 3, we find the remarkable conversation of Jesus with Nicodemus, the learned and respected rabbi. The next chapter records the equally remarkable conversation of Jesus with the Samaritan woman at the well. A conversation which, incidentally, was begun by Jesus.

The healing ministry of Jesus revealed a similar balancing. He healed both men and women, boys and girls. His parables likewise referred to men and women. On one hand, he spoke of the unjust servant (Matt. 18:23-35), the sower who went forth to sow (Matt. 13:3-12), and the prodigal son (Luke 15:11-32). On the other hand, he referred to the woman who put leaven in her meal (Matt. 13:33), the importunity of a widow (Luke 18:1-8), the housewife and her lost coin (Luke 15:8-10), and maidens or virgins going forth to meet the bridegroom (Matt. 25:1-13).

Some such balancing continued throughout the life of Jesus. Two sets of brothers—Andrew and Peter, James and John—were among his traveling companions. There was a pair of sisters—Martha and Mary—who performed a distinctive ministry for him.

This balancing of the sexes was also evident at the end of his life. When he was crucified, Joseph of Arimathea and Nicodemus (mentioned only in John's Gospel) requested his body, prepared it for burial, and placed it in a new tomb (John 19:38-42). But to Mary

Magdalene, Jesus first revealed himself after his resurrection (John 20:11 *ff.*).

Some of the great teachings of Jesus were to a single individual and not to a crowd. Some of the greatest truths he ever expressed were in his conversation with the woman at the well. He revealed to her that he was the Living Water. He told her that "whoever drinks of the water that I shall give him will never thirst; the water that I shall give him will become in him a spring of water welling up to eternal life" (John 4:14). He also revealed to her the great truth, so frequently quoted, that "God is spirit, and those who worship him must worship in spirit and in truth" (v. 24). Christ's first clear announcement of his messiahship was to this Samaritan woman, "Jesus said to her, 'I who speak to you am he [the Messiah]'" (John 4:26).

To Martha, after the death of her brother Lazarus, Jesus said, "I am the resurrection and the life" (John 11:25). We should also be grateful for Martha's great confession, "I believe that you are the Christ, the Son of God" (v. 27), which is practically the same as Peter's confession, "You are the Christ, the Son of the living God" (Matt. 16:16). To Mary Magdalene, the resurrected Christ entrusted the message "go to my brethren and say to them" (John 20:17).

When we remember how Jesus treated *women*, we do not wonder that many *responded* readily *to him*. On at least two occasions, a woman anointed his feet with ointment and wiped or dried them with her hair. One of these women was Mary of Bethany who "took a pound of costly ointment of pure nard and anointed the feet of Jesus and wiped his feet with her hair; and the house was filled with the fragrance of the ointment" (John 12:3). The other recorded occasion was a nameless "woman of the city, who was a sinner ["who was living an immoral life," NEB], when she learned that he was ["reclining," NASB] at table in the Pharisee's house, brought an alabaster flask of ointment, and standing behind him at his feet, weeping, she began to wet his feet with her tears, and wiped them with the hair of her head, and kissed his feet, and anointed them with the ointment" (Luke 7:37-38). What these women did was condemned by some standing by—Mary, by some of the disciples;

the sinful woman, by Simon the Pharisee. But in both cases Jesus defended what they had done.[17]

Some *women traveled with Jesus and his disciples*. Luke mentioned three by name—"Mary, called Magdalene, from whom seven demons had gone out, and Joanna, the wife of Chuza, Herod's steward, and Susanna"—and then added "and many others, who provided for them out of their means" (8:2-3). Matthew and Mark, in their reports of the crucifixion of Jesus, included the names of some women "who had followed Jesus from Galilee, ministering to him" (Matt. 27:55; see Mark 15:41). They mentioned the names of Mary Magdalene, Mary the mother of James and Joseph or Joses (Mark) "and the mother of the sons of Zebedee" (Matt.) or "Salome" (Mark). Mark added, "and also many other women who came up with him to Jerusalem."

The suggestion has been made that possibly the seamless tunic of Jesus "woven from top to bottom" had been the gift of one of the women who ministered to him and his disciples. Knowing Jesus as we do, we do not believe that the women were restricted to the provision for the material needs of his traveling company. They doubtlessly were present when he performed some of his marvelous miracles. They heard many of the challenging words which he spoke to his disciples and to people in general.

The ministry of these women emphasizes the fact that Jesus not only ministered to women but also *accepted the ministry of women*. That would have been beneath the dignity of a rabbi in that day. The fact that at least five of the women who traveled with him and his disciples are mentioned by name is rather striking (Mary Magdalene, Joanna, Susanna, Mary the mother of James the least and Joseph or Joses, and Salome the mother of the sons of Zebedee). Other than the twelve apostles, no other male followers are so specifically mentioned.

As the trial, crucifixion, burial, and resurrection of Christ approached, the presence and ministry of women became more prominent. While the men tended to slip back, the women stepped forward. Previously, the ministry of Jesus had been primarily to and with the twelve. They had been on center stage. But as Jesus was led

away for trial and ultimate crucifixion, the best his disciples could do
was to follow from afar. Judas betrayed him, and even Peter denied
that he knew him. In contrast, the women showed their compassion
and courage. As Jesus was on the way to Golgotha, the only word or
token of concern was the lamentation of some of the women as he
passed by (Luke 23:27-31).

As Jesus hung on the cross, the only one of the twelve who
evidently was nearby was John, the beloved disciple, standing with
the mother of Jesus. Also standing with them were "his mother's
sister, Mary the wife of Clopas, and Mary Magdalene" (John
19:25-27). "The women who had come with him from Galilee . . .
saw the tomb, and how his body was laid; then they . . . prepared
spices and ointments" (Luke 23:55-56). No wonder they were the
first ones to whom the resurrected Jesus revealed himself. According
to John's Gospel, Mary Magdalene recognized Jesus as the "Master"
or "Teacher" when he spoke to her, calling her by name, "Mary"
(John 20:16). This recognition could have been because of the
distinctive inflection of his voice or the way he pronounced "Mary."
A. T. Robertson wrote, "Clearly the old familiar tone of Jesus was in
the pronunciation of her name" (W.P.). What a glorious thing to
remember—that he knows us by name! Of course, it could have
simply been the fact that he knew her name; the gardener would not
have known.

Similar to biblical visions,[18] Mary was instructed to do
something about the revelation that had come to her. She, who has
been called "a female Paul," was told to go to the disciples whom
Jesus referred to as "my brethren" and deliver to them his message
for them (John 20:17).

Paul

Some portray Paul as a chauvinist, a woman hater. This is a
gross misrepresentation and misinterpretation of Paul. In seeking to
interpret correctly and to evaluate fairly Paul's teachings concerning
women, the following should be kept in mind:

1. Most of Paul's Epistles were written to particular churches,
in particular locations, faced with some particular problems.

2. This means, among other things, that some portions of some of his Epistles are not directly relevant for our day. One striking example is what he said concerning the eating of meat offered to idols (Rom. 14; 1 Cor. 8; 9; 10). This is also true of some things he said concerning women, particularly in 1 Corinthians.

3. If we examine carefully and look deeply enough, we will discover some basic principles that are relevant for every age. This is true even in some of the most irrelevant sections of his Epistles. For example, from a study of what Paul said concerning the eating of meat offered to idols, there evolves the following abiding principles: (1) A Christian should not only consider what he thinks is right for him to do but also what others may consider right for him. (2) An activity that may be right within itself may become wrong if it is a cause of stumbling to others (1 Cor. 8:13). (3) A Christian is not to seek his own good but the good of others (1 Cor. 10:24). (4) Also, a child of God should do all things to the glory of God (1 Cor. 10:31), which means that the Christian should give "no offense to Jews or to Greeks or to the church of God" (v. 32). The preceding principles could apply to women in church and society in Paul's day and even in our day.

4. In regard to women, slavery, and in general, Paul was radical or revolutionary in the ideal he proclaimed. His radical ideal is stated most pointedly in Galatians 3:28, "There is no such thing as Jew and Greek, slave and freeman, male and female; for you are all one person in Christ Jesus" (Gal. 3:28, NEB). "There is no room for Jew or Greek, no room for slave or freeman, no room for male or female, for you are all one through union with Christ Jesus" (Williams).

"In ["with," Williams] Christ Jesus" refers to one's personal relation to Christ, but it also implies one's being in the church or the family of Christ (see 1 Cor. 12:12 ff.). For one who is in Christ or in his church, it is irrelevant whether he or she is Jew or Gentile, free or slave, male or female. This great verse (Gal. 3:28) has been referred to as "Freedom's Manifesto" and the "Magna Charta of Humanity." Paul not only wrote this to the Galatians but also spoke the same word loud and clear by the life he lived. After all, he was "the apostle to the Gentiles"; a visitor to Lydia's house; and the friend of Onesimus, a runaway slave.

5. It does seem at times that Paul was concerned that some who had discovered a new freedom in Christ would go too far too fast in exercising the new liberty that was theirs. That seemed to have been particularly true of slaves and women. This may help to explain some things he said in 1 Corinthians, statements that are hard if not impossible to reconcile with the freedom he proclaimed, particularly in Galatians.

6. A general principle of interpretation that may help with some of the difficult passages in Paul is the fact that any particular Scripture should be interpreted and particularly evaluated in the light of the total impact of the Scriptures. This at least means that we should not exclusively judge Paul's attitude toward women by one or two more or less isolated statements.

7. In interpreting Paul's attitude toward women, we should give proper consideration not only to his specific teachings but also to his relation to women. After all, as suggested previously, a great teacher usually teaches as much, if not more, by his attitudes and relationships as by anything he says.

Lockyer correctly says that "gifted and consecrated women figure prominently in the labors of Paul."[19] Luke referred rather frequently to Paul's relation to women: Lydia (Acts 16:11-15), a slave girl who had "a spirit of divination" (Acts 16:16-18), "the leading women" (Acts 17:4), "a few Greek women" (Acts 17:12), and the four unmarried daughters of Philip "who prophesied" (Acts 21:8-9). Women filled an important place in the ministry of Paul.

Also, he frequently referred to women in his Epistles. He entreated Euodia and Syntyche "to agree in the Lord" and said that they had "labored side by side with me in the gospel" (Phil. 4:2-3). In the letter to the Colossians, he sent greetings "to Nympha and the church in her house" (Col. 4:15). In the little letter to Philemon, Paul not only sent greetings to Philemon but also to Apphia, evidently the wife of Philemon (Philem. 2).

Paul closed his letter to the Romans with greetings to twenty-nine individuals—twenty-six by name. At least seven and possibly nine of these were women. There is little comment about any of them except Phoebe and Prisca and Aquila. Phoebe may have delivered the letter. She, the first one mentioned by Paul, was referred to as "our sister . . . a deaconess[20] of the church at Cenchreae" (v. 1) and asked the Roman church to "receive her in the Lord as befits the saints, and help her in whatever she may require from you." Paul then added, "for she has been a helper of many and of myself as well" (Rom. 16:1-2). In other words, Phoebe was not only a servant of the church at Cenchreae but of the kingdom in general. We do not know how she had been a helper of Paul.

Next, Paul sent greetings to that wonderful couple, Prisca and Aquila, whom Paul referred to as "my fellow workers in Christ Jesus, who risked their necks for my life, to whom not only I but all the churches of the Gentiles give thanks." He then added, "greet also the church in their house" (Rom. 16:3-5), which was not the only place that they had a church meeting in their house (see 1 Cor. 16:19). Aquila and Prisca are mentioned by name six times in the Bible—three times in Acts (18:2,18,26) and three times in Paul's Epistles (Rom. 16:3; 1 Cor. 16:19; 2 Tim. 4:19). Four of the six times, Prisca's name is mentioned first. Paul said this couple had "risked their necks" for him. When and where? There is no way to know for sure but possibly during the riot at Ephesus (Acts 19).

The preceding should be sufficient to prove that Paul was no woman hater.

Before we give some attention to two or three specific references in Paul's Epistles that are frequently used to defend the subordination of women to men, let us state briefly Paul's position on freedom or liberty. His concept of freedom or liberty was a formative factor in his thought. Those who have been made new creations through their union with Christ were free men and women. He pointedly and plainly said, "Where the Spirit of the Lord is, there is freedom" (2 Cor. 3:17), and again, "For freedom Christ has set us free" (Gal. 5:1), or "Christ set us free, to be free men" (NEB).

One evidence of the Christian's maturity is what he or she does with the freedom he or she has in Christ. Nowhere did Paul state his viewpoint more clearly than in Galatians 5:13: "For you were called to freedom, brethren; only do not use your freedom as an opportunity for the flesh, but through love be servants of one another."

Paul applied the principle of the voluntary surrender of the Christian freedom to various areas and relationships. Among these was the relation of a woman to a man. In Christ she was and is equal to man (Gal. 3:28). However, just as was true of the slave, who was also free in Christ, for the sake of order in society the Christian woman was to be submissive. It should be remembered that the same basic principle applied to all Christians—men as well as women. For example, Christians were free in Christ; but they were to be obedient to the powers that be or "the governing authorities" (Rom. 13:1). The great apostle of freedom was also the apostle of order.

This voluntary surrender of freedom for the sake of order is spelled out in a particular way in Paul's First Epistle to the Corinthians, although it is found elsewhere as we have just indicated. The fact that much that is in the Corinthian letter was in reply to a letter Paul had received from the Corinthians means that they determined, to a large degree, the issues and problems discussed in the epistle. Stagg suggests that the letter was concerned primarily with a specific situation, "about as much pagan as Christian." Paul did not have "the luxury of setting forth an ideal; he was hard pressed to bring some order out of near chaos."[21]

Furthermore, Paul faced a serious problem at Corinth; there was an effort by some at Corinth to throw off all restrictions. They considered themselves "spiritual" (1 Cor. 3:1-3).

> These "pneumatics" seized upon Paul's doctrine of freedom, but they applied it in ways which Paul disapproved. Apparently seeing themselves as above sin, they could even accept incest without shame (5:1-2). They apparently boasted that for themselves all things were "lawful" (6:12). . . . They insisted upon personal freedom and rights even to the hurt of weaker brethren (chs. 8-10). In their exercise of what they considered their personal rights and freedom, they caused confusion and disorder in their public service (chs. 11-14).

Stagg sums up the situation as follows: "Apparently Paul saw at

Corinth a misapplication of freedom and sought to curb it."[22]

Stagg further says that Galatians and 1 Corinthians "are probably best understood as struggles on two different fronts, Galatians concerned for freedom and 1 Corinthians for order.[23] It should also be remembered, as suggested previously, that much of 1 Corinthians was in reply to specific questions that were asked in the communication Paul had had from the Corinthian church (see 1 Cor. 7:1; 8:1; 12:1; 16:1). Also, he had had reports from some who had come from Corinth (1 Cor. 1:11). Evidently he had reports about disorder in the public meetings of the church.

The preceding should give us some help as we seek to interpret and evaluate properly what Paul said concerning women in 1 Corinthians 11:2-16 and 1 Corinthians 14:33-40, also in 1 Timothy 2:8-15. No attempt will be made to interpret these passages in detail.

In 1 Corinthians 11:3 Paul said, "The head of every man is Christ, the head of a woman is her husband, and the head of Christ is God." "Head" could mean "either superior rank or source of authority" (Broadman). As a man contemplates his headship, he should remember that Paul had reminded masters of slaves that they had a master (1 Cor. 7:22). In other words, the man may be the head of a woman or his wife, but Christ is not only his master but also her master. However, a whole theory of "God-approved" relations in the home and in society in general has been built, to a large degree, on this Scripture. To properly evaluate this verse and other statements by Paul concerning women, we should remember, among other things, Paul's emphasis on the mutuality of the relations of husbands and wives to each other, an emphasis that is particularly prevalent in an earlier chapter of this epistle to the Corinthians (chap. 7). This mutuality will be spelled out in more detail in a later chapter on husbands and wives.

There is some evidence of this mutuality in the relation of men and women in general in chapter 11. After Paul had said that a woman who prophesied with her head unveiled "dishonors her head" and after he had said that man was the glory of God and woman the glory of man, he made the following parenthetical statement, which is as significant as anything in the entire passage, "(Nevertheless, in the Lord woman is not independent of man nor man of woman; for as woman was made from {ek} man, so man is now born of {dia} woman. And all things are from God.)" (1 Cor. 11:11-12). This statement is frequently neglected or overlooked, particularly by the defenders of woman's subordination and the advocates of the hierarchical view of family relations and the relations of men and women in general. Paul may have said that woman, for the sake of order, was subordinate to man; but he never said or implied that she was inferior. The statement in verses 11 and 12 approximates Paul's radical or revolutionary ideal that in Christ there is neither male nor female. "Though there is in the Church a perfect spiritual equality (as taught in Gal. iii.28), yet . . . it is an equality which is of order and not of disorder" (Ell.). It is at least possible that the statements of Paul in 1 Corinthians 11 and also in chapter 14, verses 34-36, represent an adjustment of the ideal to the actual situation at Corinth and in the society of that day. Stagg concludes that Paul was "not comfortable" with his statement concerning the subordination of women, and hence he added verses 11 and 12 of chapter 11.[24]

In chapter 11, verses 3-10, Paul was concerned about the dress of women when they prayed or spoke in public meetings. He evidently did not want them to violate the customs of that day and bring some reproach on the cause of Christ. In chapter 14 his concern was the actual speaking by women in the public worship services. Incidentally, most of those who defend the subordination of women to men as an expression of God's ultimate will are not consistent in the use of the verses from 1 Corinthians 11. Paul's major concern was the wearing of the veil by women who prayed in public or prophesied. If she did go unveiled, she dishonored her head—"her physical head" (v. 4) or some suggest "her husband" (TEV). If a part of Paul's instructions is to be taken literally and considered applicable in the contemporary world, why not all of it—the veil and long hair, as well as the speaking in public? A. T. Robertson's comment is helpful for all of us who seek to interpret 1 Corinthians 11, as well as 1 Corinthians 14, in the light of contemporary movements among women. Robertson's word is, "We need to be patient with each other as we try to understand Paul's real meaning here" (W.P.).

In 1 Corinthians 14:34-36, Paul said that women should be silent in the churches. In 1 Timothy (2:8-12) after he said that "women should adorn themselves modestly and sensibly in seemly apparel, not with braided hair ["not with elaborate hair-styles," NEB] or gold or pearls or costly attire," Paul added, "let a woman learn in silence with all submissiveness. I permit no woman to teach or to have authority over men; she is to keep silent." It seems that the silence referred to here was in the public worship services. *The New English Bible* says, "As in all congregations of God's people, women should not address the meeting. . . . It is a shocking thing that a woman should address the congregation" (1 Cor. 14:34-35).

The idea that women should not speak in public or address the entire congregation may have stemmed from the practice in the synagogues. It is even possible that it was related to the fact that some of the early church groups started in synagogues. Whether this was true, it was more or less inevitable that the synagogue pattern would influence the early church. Jewett suggests that Paul's "remarks in 1 Corinthians 14:34-35 reflect the rabbinic tradition which imposed silence on the woman in the synagogue as a sign of her subjection."[25]

It is also possible, though not probable, that in both 1 Corinthians 11 and 14 Paul was answering some specific *questions*. It seems more likely, however, that he was simply dealing with some *problems* in the Corinthian congregation that had been reported to him.

What can we conclude about Paul and women? Stagg says, "His openness toward woman is far beyond that of his probable upbringing. The fact that he can worship in public service with women; . . . his recognition of woman's equality in conjugal and other rights; and his willingness to address women directly as responsible persons in the church are all factors on the positive side of one moving in the direction of the implementation of a revolutionary vision, that "in Christ there is no male or female."[26]

Summary and Conclusions

Biblical

1. The Old Testament Scriptures should be evaluated in the light of the full revelation of God in Christ.

2. Some things in the Old Testament did not and do not express the original purpose and the final will of God. This was true regarding the law of divorce (Deut. 24:1-4). Jesus said, "but from the beginning it was not so" (Matt. 19:8).

3. The prevailing attitude toward women in the Old Testament was not the ultimate will of God. If we want to know the Father's will concerning women, we need to go back to the beginning as Jesus did regarding divorce.

4. The clearest statement of God's plan and will for women in the Old Testament is found in the creation accounts (Gen. 1 and 2). The major emphases are that woman, as well as man, was created in the image of God; that either is incomplete without the other; and that they are to be partners that supplement or complement each other. The latter is not just true in the marriage state but in their relationship in general.

5. The perspective concerning women in the Old Testament, as was true to some degree in all the Bible, was not uniformly the same.

6. The final and complete revelation of God, including his will for men and women, is found in the life and teachings of Jesus. He was deeply concerned about people, particularly the neglected and underprivileged, including women and children.

7. The only clear restriction concerning women by Jesus was the fact that he did not include any of them in the twelve. That doubtlessly would have created some serious problems for him and for his whole ministry in the culture in which he operated.

8. Paul, who has been grossly misinterpreted if not maligned regarding some things he said concerning women, needs to be restudied in the light of his relation to women and the nature of his ministry, as well as some specific things he said concerning women.

9. Writing in the main to specific churches, Paul had to face

up to and deal with many pastoral problems. As a pastor-writer, he set forth the ideal in human relations; but he had to minister to people who were imperfect and who were living in an imperfect world. This and other things seemed to necessitate at times some adjustment of the ideal to the realities of the situation faced by those to whom he wrote.

Application

1. Because of the contemporary interest in the women's movement and in the light of the teachings of the Scriptures, many churches and church leaders need to reconsider the attitude of the churches toward women and the place they give to them in their program and work.

2. Because of the considerable church load carried by women in many churches and because of their possible distinctive contributions to the work of the churches, women should be given more of a voice in the programs and structures of many of our churches. "It would mean bringing into focus a more complete human view of things by adding woman's particular perspective to man's."[27]

3. Some churches, pastors, and other church leaders may be hesitant about doing anything about giving women more of a voice because of a fear that it will disturb the peace of the church and church family.

4. Such hesitation may in some cases be justified. However, it should not be defended as God's ultimate will concerning women in our churches. In many, and possibly most, of our churches, women are not treated as Jesus would treat them or as our Father would have them treated.

5. As a part of our effort to struggle through to some answer in the ordination of women, we need to restudy the whole matter of New Testament ordination. It seems to have been a relatively simple service of dedication by a church of an individual or individuals God had called to a particular task. If this simple type of ordination were followed, then the only concern of a church should be whether God had called the individual to some phase of specialized ministry. The so-called "ordination service" would be primarily a dedication

service. If our churches continue to use the rather elaborate type of ordination with examination of the candidate, etc., then they should consider carefully before expanding it to members of church staffs (men or women) other than the pastor.[28]

6. Ordination should not be sought personally by a man or a woman. The initiative should come from others unless ordination is necessary to perform some functions of the particular type of ministry.

7. In the case of ordination to the ministry, there can properly be some question about the advantages or the disadvantages of being ordained.

8. In this whole awakening of interest in women and their place in the home, the church, and society, it will be tragic if we ever belittle the traditional role of the woman as wife and mother. Even in the contemporary world with all the freedom that women have, this role should be given priority.

9. "Men and women are properly related [in church and society] when they accept each other as equals whose difference is mutually complementary in all spheres of life and human endeavor."[29]

Notes

1. Patricia M. Doyle in *Religion and Sexism*, Rosemary Radford Reuther, ed. (New York: Simon and Schuster, 1974), p. 15.
2. Ibid., p. 16.
3. Among the more popular books on women in the Bible are: Edith Deen, *All the Women of the Bible* (New York: Harper & Row, 1955); Herbert Lockyer, *The Women of the Bible* (Grand Rapids: Zondervan Publishing House, 1967); Eugenia Price, *The Unique World of Women in Bible Times and Now* (Grand Rapids: Zondervan Publishing House, 1969); and Shirley Stephens, *A New Testament View of Women* (Nashville: Broadman Press, 1980).
4. Two books that have been unusually helpful in the preparation of this chapter are Paul K. Jewett, *Man as Male and Female: A Study in Sexual Relationships from a Theological Point of View* (Grand Rapids: Eerdmans, 1975), a scholarly book by a professor of systematic theology at Fuller Theological Seminary; and Evelyn Stagg and Frank Stagg, *Women in the World of Jesus* (Philadelphia: Westminster Press, 1978), another thoroughly scholarly work by a former

professor (and his wife) of The Southern Baptist Theological Seminary. Two other books of major importance are Elizabeth Clark and Herbert Richardson, *Women and Religion: A Feminist Sourcebook of Christian Thought* (New York: Harper & Row, 1977). In addition to chapters on Old Testament and New Testament, there are chapters with brief introductions followed by readings from many creative Christian leaders and scholars, such as Clement of Alexandria, Jerome, Augustine, Aquinas, Luther, and Barth. The other book, with a somewhat distinctive contribution, is Letha Scanzoni and Nancy Hardesty, *All We're Meant to Be: A Biblical Approach to Women's Liberation* (Waco, Texas: Word Books, 1974).

5. Roland de Vaux, *Ancient Israel: Its Life and Institutions*, trans. John McHugh (New York: McGraw-Hill Book Co., Inc., 1961), p. 39.

6. Stagg and Stagg, p. 23.

7. ICC, p. 542. It is labeled "the Alphabetic Ode" because each of its twenty-two verses (vv. 10-31) begins, in order, with the letters of the Hebrew alphabet. Psalm 119 is a more elaborate alphabetic poem (NASB and NIV clearly indicate the divisions).

8. See Stagg and Stagg, pp. 29-32, for some possible reasons for the lack of female priests.

9. A research paper on Genesis 1, 2, and 3 by Boo Heflin, a professor of Old Testament at Southwestern Baptist Theological Seminary, has been very helpful.

10. Jewett, p. 69.

11. Lois Clemens, *Women Liberated* (Scottdale, Pa.: Herald Press, 1971), see particularly pp. 57-58.

12. Heflin.

13. Jewett, p. 86.

14. Chapter 5 of the book by Scanzoni and Hardesty is "Woman's Best Friend: Jesus."

15. Jewett, p. 94.

16. Stagg and Stagg, p. 219.

17. For another occasion when Jesus defended a woman who was being condemned by her accusers, see John 8:3-11. This incident will be discussed to some degree in chapter 8.

18. For visions that included a word of command, see Moses (Ex. 3:1-12), Elijah (1 Kings 19:9-16), Isaiah (Isa. 6:1-8), Paul (Acts 9:1-6), and Peter (Acts 10:1-33).

19. Lockyer, p. 20.

20. The word is *diakonon*, which basically means servant. Paul frequently used the word to refer to himself and his work. It was also used to refer to Apollos, Stephanas, and Timothy. It is translated "deaconess" here by the Revised Standard Version and by Williams. It is translated "servant" by the *New American Standard Bible* and by the *New International Version*, and *The New English Bible* refers to Phoebe as one "who holds office in the congregation at Cenchreae." A. T. Robertson says, "The only question here is whether it *(diakonon)* is used in a general sense or in a technical sense as in Phil. 1:1 and 1 Tim. 3:8-13." At least, "in some sense Phoebe was a servant or minister of the church in Cenchreae" (W.P.).

21. Stagg and Stagg, pp. 168-169.

22. Ibid.

23. Ibid.

24. Ibid., p. 177.

25. Jewett, p. 114.

26. Stagg and Stagg, p. 179.

27. Clemens, p. 79.

28. Both Jewett and the Staggs discuss the ordination of women at some length. After a rather thorough examination, Jewett concludes, "We conclude that women have full title to

the order of Christian ministry as God shall call them" (p. 170). The Staggs, after carefully examining the words in the Greek that are translated "ordain" and the Scriptures in general regarding the ministry, come to a conclusion somewhat comparable to Jewett, although it is not stated as positively: "The basic criterion for ministry in any form is having the gift for it by God's grace" (p. 186).

29. Jewett, p. 114.

4

Children

"Civilizations march forward on the feet of little children." This may be true, but all civilizations do not march forward. Some decline and ultimately die. One of the surest signs of the health or sickness of a civilization is the prevailing attitude toward and treatment of its children, along with the handicapped, the old, and the underprivileged in general.

If the preceding is correct, what about Western civilization in general and the United States in particular? There are some conditions regarding children that should give us considerable concern. Many children do not have the privilege of maturing in a healthy environment. Almost one-third grow up in one-parent families. Many others have parents who have little time for them. One study revealed that almost two-million children in the United States return home from school each day to empty houses.

One of the most serious conditions regarding children in our society is the increasing prevalence of child abuse. It is variously estimated that one to four or five million children in the United States are abused each year and that two thousand or more die each year as a result of such abuse. If we had as many children with some contagious disease as are abused each year, it would be considered a major epidemic.

There is definitely a need for a reexamination of what the Bible says about and the attitude it reveals toward children. This chapter will be limited primarily to the Bible and children in general. There will be a later chapter on parents and children so many biblical references to children will not be included in the present chapter.

Some of the material in this chapter will be examples or

illustrations. Some of these examples might even be considered case studies. They may indirectly teach some important lessons concerning children.

Desire for Them

There was a strong desire for children, particularly for sons, among the Hebrew people. Through a son, the family line could be perpetuated and the ancestral inheritance preserved. The desire for children was shared by other Semitic people. The Scriptures, in several instances, record the deep desires of barren women to become mothers. Barrenness was considered a reproach. The barren wife was, at times, an object of ridicule by another wife or even by a maid or concubine.

Let us first take a look at *Sarah*. The Bible simply says that she bore Abram, or Abraham, no children (Gen. 16:1). She wanted a child so desperately that she insisted that Abraham have sexual relations with Hagar, her maid. She said, "It may be that I shall obtain children by her" (Gen. 16:2). But then what happened? After Hagar conceived, "she looked with contempt on her mistress" (v. 4). Later, Sarah's reproach was removed; and she had Isaac, truly a child of promise.

Then there is the story of *Rachel*, a story that is full of intrigue. Jacob had no gift with which to bargain for a wife. He agreed to serve Laban seven years for Rachel, the younger of Laban's two daughters. The Bible simply says, "Jacob loved Rachel; and he said, 'I will serve you seven years for your younger daughter Rachel'" (Gen. 29:17-18). Then it beautifully says, "So Jacob served seven years for Rachel, and they seemed to him but a few days because of the love he had for her" (Gen. 29:20).

But Laban tricked Jacob and gave him Leah instead of Rachel. When Jacob protested, Laban said to him, "Complete the bridal week of this one, and we will give you the other also for the service which you shall serve with me for another seven years" (v. 27, NASB). The "bridal week" was a "seven days' feast" (NEB). Leah bore Jacob children, "but Rachel was barren" (v. 31). "When Rachel saw that she bore Jacob no children, she envied her sister; and she said to

Jacob, 'Give me children or I shall die'" (Gen. 30:1).

Then Rachel did what Sarah had done; she said to Jacob, "Here is my slave-girl Bilhah. Lie with her, so that she may bear sons to be laid upon my knees, and through her I too may build up a family" (v. 3, NEB). The children of a slave-girl or maid were considered children of her mistress. Needless to say, we should judge Laban, Jacob, Rachel, and this whole procedure in the light of the day in which they lived.

There is at least one other outstanding illustration in the Old Testament of a woman who desperately wanted a child. This was *Hannah*. Her husband, Elkanah, an Ephraimite, had two wives— Hannah and Peninnah, but Hannah had no children (1 Sam. 1:2). When Elkanah went up to sacrifice, "he would give portions to Peninnah his wife and to all her sons and daughters; and, although he loved Hannah, he would give Hannah only one portion, because the Lord had closed her womb. And her rival used to provoke her sorely, to irritate her, because the Lord had closed her womb. So it went on year by year" (1 Sam. 1:4-7).

On one occasion when Hannah was "in tears and would not eat," Elkanah said to her, "Hannah, why are you crying and eating nothing? Why are you so miserable?" He evidently knew why because he said to her, "Am I not more to you than ten sons?" (v. 8, NEB). But she cried to the Lord for a son, and the Lord heard and responded, "and she called his name Samuel, for she said, 'I have asked him of the Lord'" (1 Sam. 1:20). The name *Samuel* means "asked or heard of God."

It is impossible to know how much of a factor ridicule was in the desire of Sarah, Rachel, and Hannah for children. The very fact that it is mentioned implies that it was a factor of considerable significance. It is rather interesting to note that in the case of two of the women—Rachel and Hannah—their husbands loved them. In other words, the fact that they were barren had not adversely affected their relationship with their husbands.

It has been suggested that a Jewish woman had a distinctive reason for a desire for a son. It is claimed that she felt that she might be an ancestress or even the mother of the Messiah. There is no way to judge how much of a factor this was in women's desire for children. Really, it seems that God, who created us male and female, built into both men and women a desire for children. This desire may be restrained or even lost to a considerable degree in the contemporary period. However, underneath much seeming indifference to children, the desire to have children we can call our own seems to remain.

Source of Them

After God had created male and female, he blessed them and said to them, "Be fruitful and multiply, and fill the earth and subdue it" (Gen. 1:28). Genesis 4:1 says, "Now Adam knew Eve his wife, and she conceived and bore Cain, saying, 'I have gotten a man with the help of the Lord.'" After Cain killed Abel, the Record says, "And Adam knew his wife again, and she bore a son and called his name Seth, for she said, 'God has appointed me another child instead of Abel, for Cain slew him'" (Gen. 4:25). Notice that in both cases the conception was attributed to God.

The preceding perspective is repeated over and over again in the Scriptures. At times this may simply have been a result of attributing everything more or less directly to God. This should not surprise us because a prevalent contemporary viewpoint is to consider every natural phenomenon, such as storms, as a direct expression of the will of God. This is not bad if a distinction is made between the perfect and the permissive or the intentional and the circumstantial will of God. Such a distinction, however, is frequently not made.

But it does seem, at least at times in the Bible, that the birth of a child or children was credited, in an unusual or a unique way, to the intervention of the Lord. This was especially true of a number of individual cases that will be mentioned later.

But first, let us look at the *biblical perspective in general*. When Job learned about the death of all his sons and daughters, he said, "the Lord gave, and the Lord has taken away; blessed be the name of the Lord" (Job 1:21). We might like to ask, But did the Lord give and did he take away? If so, how? Was it in harmony with his intentional or perfect will or simply with his permissive or circumstantial will? Or, was both the giving and the taking away a natural phenomenon in harmony with and a result of the operation of natural laws?

When Esau met Jacob, after the latter had been away many years, he asked about the large number traveling with Jacob. The response was, "The children whom God has graciously given your servant" (Gen. 33:5).

Then there is that frequently quoted statement by the psalmist:

> Lo, sons are a heritage from the Lord,
> the fruit of the womb a reward (127:3).

The psalmist also said,

> He [God] gives the barren woman a home,
> making her the joyous mother of children
> (113:9; see 128:3).

Also, there is the rather striking statement:

> For thou didst form my inward parts,
> thou didst knit me together in my mother's womb
> (Ps. 139:13; see Job 31:15; Isa. 43:7; 44:2).

To the young Jeremiah, who said he did not know how to speak because he was "only a youth" (Jer. 1:6), God said:

> 'Before I formed you in the womb I knew you,
> and before you were born I consecrated you;
> I appointed you a prophet to the nations'
> (Jer. 1:5).

We have sought to point out that God is the source for children in general. This is true even if we consider children the result of the operation of certain basic laws that have been written into the nature of male and female. But God who is the source of those basic laws may sometimes make those laws function when otherwise they would not. In this sense, we can properly speak of God closing or opening the womb. And, after all, the whole birth process is so complex that much of it cannot be explained apart from the presence and power of God.

Regardless of the preceding, there was in the past and doubtlessly still are individuals for whom our Father has a special purpose. Herbert Lockyer says, "While it is true that God created man for the purpose of multiplying himself, and created the earth as the dwelling place of all the children springing from our first parents, there were occasions when he gave specific promises concerning certain children who would be born to accomplish specific purposes."[1]

These special *children of promise* began, so far as the Record reveals, with Isaac and continued until the miraculous birth of Jesus. When Abraham was one hundred years old and Sarah was ninety, God said to Abraham: "I will bless her, and moreover I will give you a son by her; I will bless her, and she shall be a mother of nations; kings of people shall come from her" (Gen. 17:16). Later, "by the oaks of Mamre" (Gen. 18:1) it was revealed again to Abraham that Sarah would have a child, although "it had ceased to be with Sarah after the manner of women" (Gen. 18:11). Through Isaac God maintained and fulfilled his covenant with Abraham—that he was to be a blessing to the nations of the world.

Isaac was forty years of age when he married Rebekah. "And Isaac prayed to the Lord for his wife, because she was barren; and the Lord granted his prayer, and Rebekah his wife conceived" (Gen. 25:21). Isaac and Rebekah received a double answer to their prayer: to her were born twins, Esau and Jacob. But it was through Jacob that God continued to fulfill his covenant and purpose.

Jacob's beloved wife, Rachel, had no children. But "God remembered Rachel, and God hearkened to her and opened her womb." Her comment was, "God has taken away my reproach" (Gen. 30:22-23). That first son, another child of promise, was named Joseph. He was one mightily used by the Lord.

The next example of a child of promise is found in the wonderful story of Hannah and Samuel. She pleaded with the Lord for a son and made a vow to give him to the Lord if the Lord would respond to her request. When she, her husband, and the rest of the family returned to their home after worshiping at Shiloh, "Elkanah knew Hannah his wife, and the Lord remembered her; and in due time Hannah conceived and bore a son, and she called his name Samuel, for she said, 'I have asked him of the Lord'" (1 Sam. 1:19-20).

Here is plainly underscored what is implied in other places: the relation of the natural and the supernatural in the birth of Samuel. There would have been no birth without Elkanah having relations with Hannah. And there would have been no Samuel if the Lord had not "remembered" Hannah and her earnest prayer for a son.

There are others in the Old Testament who were children of promise, such as Samson (Judg. 13:2-7).[2]

Then there was the forerunner of Jesus. John the Baptist was born to a woman who had been barren, and both she and her husband were "advanced in years." In this case, a special revelation was given to the husband, Zechariah. The angel of the Lord told him that his prayer had been heard and that Elizabeth would bear a son. This son would be "great before the Lord" and would be "filled with the Holy Spirit,/even from his mother's womb" (Luke 1:15). Although Elizabeth was far beyond the childbearing stage, "the God who created the body and can reverse its laws, took away the reproach of Elizabeth among men, and made her the glad and honored mother of John the Baptist, the dynamic forerunner of the Lord Jesus."[3]

Certainly there is no question about the Holy Spirit as the source of the birth of Jesus to the virgin Mary. The word of the angel Gabriel to her was, "Do not be afraid, Mary, for you have found favor with God. And behold, you will conceive in your womb and bear a son, and you shall call his name Jesus" (Luke 1:30-31). Lockyer says that "as a child Jesus was *born*, but as a Son he was *given*, indicating the union of deity and humanity in the holy One born of Mary."[4]

Paul did not claim to have been miraculously conceived or born, but he did say that God had set him apart for a special purpose before he was born (Gal. 1:15).

Many, possibly most, contemporary homes would be different

if children were recognized as gifts from God. There is no gift without a comparable stewardship responsibility for what is done with the gift. Christian parents should be sensitive to the touch of the Divine Spirit on one of their children. The Heavenly Father may have a unique mission for one or more of them.

Concern for Them

We assume that the mothers and fathers of the special children we have referred to had a deep concern for their children of promise. This certainly would have been true of Sarah and Abraham for Isaac; Rebekah and Isaac for Jacob and Esau, but Rebekah particularly for her favorite—Jacob; Rachel and Jacob for Joseph; Hannah for Samuel; Elizabeth and Zachariah for John. It is true that the Scriptures do not spell out the concern and care of the mothers of these special gift children. After all, the Bible could not record everything (see John 21:25).

There is a beautiful Old Testament story about another child. He was not called a child of promise, but Moses stood tall in God's purpose for his children. We do know that Moses' mother, his sister, and we assume his father as well, were concerned for the preservation of his life. There may even be an element of humor in the story. When the sister of Moses observed that Pharaoh's daughter had discovered the baby in the basket that had been so carefully constructed for his safety, she asked Pharaoh's daughter, "'Shall I go and call you a nurse from the Hebrew women to nurse the child for you?'" And she went and got her own mother. And Pharaoh's daughter said to the mother, "Take this child away, and nurse him for me, and I will give you your wages." (Ex. 2:1-10). Imagine a mother being paid to nurse her own child!

We can imagine the deep concern and possibly even the perplexity of Mary and Joseph as they watched *Jesus* increase or grow "in wisdom and in stature, and in favor with God and man" (Luke 2:52; see 2:40).[5] Then there was the occasion when Jesus lingered behind when the rest of the family and friends had left Jerusalem. When they found him in the Temple after a three-day search, his mother said to him, "Son, why have you treated us so? Behold, your father and I have been looking for you anxiously." Then there are the familiar words of his, "Why did you have to look for me? Didn't you know that I had to be in my Father's house? But they did not understand his answer" (Luke 2:48-50, TEV). No wonder "his mother kept all these things in her heart" (v. 51). How she must have pondered this and many more experiences that she had with her special son!

Mary's concern for Jesus did not end when he was no longer a child. She must have continued to wonder about him as she saw him helping Joseph in the carpenter shop and as he evidently took over as head of the family when Joseph died, which was the custom of the day. Also, she could not help but sense that he had a deepening conviction of a special mission for the Father. She was present with him and some of his disciples when he performed his first recorded miracle at a wedding feast (John 2:1-11).

Although Mary could never forget the visit of Gabriel and the miraculous birth of Jesus, it was natural that she could not fully comprehend his nature and his mission. After all, he evidently grew and developed very much like other children.

On one occasion after Jesus began his public ministry, Mary, along with his brothers, "stood outside, asking to speak to him" (Matt. 12:46). The Bible does not tell us why they wanted to speak to him. One suggestion is that they may have thought he was "beside himself" or mentally and emotionally disturbed. Whatever the reason, Mary demonstrated a continuing concern for her special son.

We do not know when his mother and at least two of his brothers—James and Jude—came to believe in Jesus as the promised Messiah. Mary's concern and compassion caused her to follow him to the cross. And how grateful we ought to be and how deeply touched she must have been when, from the cross, he spoke to her and provided for her: "When Jesus saw his mother, and the disciple whom he loved standing near, he said to his mother, 'Woman, behold, your son!' Then he said to the disciple, 'Behold, your mother!'" And we should be grateful for the words that follow, "And from that hour the disciple took her to his own home" (John

19:26-27). Concern and compassion were reciprocated. This is what every mother and father who has a deep concern for a child as he matures longs for in later years when they are the ones in need of concern and ministry.

Jesus, during his busy earthly *ministry*, had occasion to minister *to fathers and mothers who were concerned* for a son or a daughter. He showed his compassion and concern by responding to their appeals for help. Let us call attention to two outstanding cases, one a father who appealed for help and the other a persistent mother.

The father was *Jairus*, a ruler of the synagogue. Jesus had just come back from a trip to the east of the Sea of Galilee (Luke 8:26). A crowd met him (Luke 8:40). Crowd or no crowd, Jairus made known to Jesus his request. "He had an only daughter, about twelve years of age, and she was dying" (v. 42), "is at the point of death" (Mark 5:23), or "has just died" (Matt. 9:18).

You remember the rest of the story. On the way to Jairus's house, a woman "who had had a flow of blood for twelve years and could not be healed by any one" reached out and touched the fringe of Jesus' garment and was immediately healed (Luke 8:43-44). Even the more or less incidental ministry of Jesus was frequently tremendously significant.

A report came to Jairus that his daughter was dead. But, thank the Lord for the compassionate Christ who simply said, "Do not fear; only believe, and she shall be well." And when he came in the room where she lay, he took her hand, and I think rather quietly in a tender voice said, "Child, arise" (Luke 8:54) or "'Talitha cumi'; which means, 'Little girl, I say to you, arise'" (Mark 5:41).

On another occasion a miracle relieved the concern of *a persistent mother*. She had a "little daughter" who was possessed by an unclean spirit. The mother fell at the feet of Jesus, pleading that he cast the demon out. He first replied to her appeal with words that, on the surface, sound hard and harsh and out of character for Jesus. They must have been spoken to test her. She was a Canaanite or Mark says "a Syrophoenician woman." Jesus said to her, "It is not right to take the children's bread and throw it to the dogs." But with a determination that revealed her deep concern for her daughter, she replied, "Yes, Lord; yet even the dogs under the table eat the children's crumbs." No wonder Jesus said to her, "For this saying you may go your way; the demon has left your daughter." And thank you, Father, that when "she went home" she "found the child lying in bed, and the demon gone" (Mark 7:24-30)!

There is one group of children to which some special attention should be given. They were the *fatherless* or *orphans*. They, along with the widows and sojourners, have been called "the special protégés of God." Considerable emphasis is given to the proper treatment of them in the Law, the Prophets, and even in the Writings—the threefold division of the Hebrew Scriptures.

The Law provided that widows, orphans, and sojourners should share with the Levites the tithes that were brought in every third year (Deut. 14:28-29; 26:12-13). Furthermore, the people were not only to be just in their dealings with the fatherless and widows but also to be generous in their treatment of them. They were instructed to leave the gleanings in the field, in the olive orchard, and in their vineyards "for the sojourner, the fatherless, and the widow" (see Deut. 24:17-22).

Job emphasized some relevant truths in the two great chapters—29 and 31—where he defended himself. In his prosperous days that he reviewed in chapter 29, he said that he "delivered the poor . . . and the fatherless" (v. 12) and "caused the widow's heart to sing for joy" (v. 13). He was a father to the poor and needy (vv. 15-16). In chapter 31 he claimed, among other things, that he had not eaten his bread alone but had had the fatherless to eat with him (v. 17).

There are a number of references to the fatherless in the *Psalms*. The psalmist said that God "hast been the helper of the fatherless" (10:14) and would incline his ear "to do justice to the fatherless and the oppressed" (10:18). Furthermore,

> The Lord watches over the sojourners,
>   he upholds the widow and the fatherless
>   (146:9).

The *prophets*, as was true of Jesus years later, were particularly concerned about the underprivileged. This included orphans or the fatherless. Two or three examples must suffice. Isaiah, the prince of the prophets, after he had described the wretched condition among his people in the first chapter, concluded by telling them what they needed to do to be right with their God. It included more than mere faithfulness to the formalities of their religion, which seems to be a continuing problem in religious circles. He began the positive part of his message by saying, "Wash yourselves; make yourselves clean"; He continued by saying:

> Learn to do good;
>> seek justice,
>>> correct oppression.

Then notice what follows immediately:

> Defend the fatherless,
>> plead for the widow (Isa. 1:16-17, also see vv. 4-15).

Similarly, Jeremiah, speaking for God concerning his people, said:

> They know no bounds in deeds of wickedness;
>> they judge not with justice
>> the cause of the fatherless (Jer. 5:28).

Ezekiel, in pronouncing judgment on "the bloody city," said, "Father and mother are treated with contempt in you; the sojourner suffers extortion in your midst; the fatherless and the widow are wronged in you" (Ezek. 22:7).

Zechariah said, "Thus says the Lord of hosts, Render true judgments, show kindness and mercy each to his brother, do not oppress the widow, the fatherless, the sojourner, or the poor" (7:9-10). Finally, Malachi, speaking for the Lord, said that the Lord would draw near for judgment "against those who oppress the hireling in his wages, the widow and the orphan" (3:5).

Remember the familiar and often quoted verse from *James*, "Pure religion and undefiled before God and the Father is this, To visit the fatherless and widows in their affliction, and to keep himself unspotted from the world" (1:27, KJV). That is an admonition that many contemporary Christians, and even churches, need to hear.

Customs Related to Them

The biblical perspective and teachings concerning children would not be complete without some attention to some of the prevalent customs in biblical times.

We know that the baby was born in the home (caves or tents). *Midwives* evidently presided over most births. This seemed to have been true in spite of the fact that midwives are specifically mentioned only a few times. One of those occasions was when Rachel was in "hard labor" for the delivery of her second son. "The midwife said to her 'Fear not; for now you will have another son'" (Gen. 35:17). But Rachel died. What a tragedy for Jacob, who lost the wife he loved and for Benjamin who never knew the love and concern of his natural mother.

A midwife was also present when Tamar gave birth to twins (Gen. 38:28). An occasion when midwives were used of God to help to accomplish his purpose is recorded in the first chapter of Exodus. Pharaoh had become concerned about the increase of the Hebrews. He first tried placing added burdens on them. "But the more they were oppressed, the more they multiplied" (Ex. 1:12). "The king of Egypt said to the Hebrew midwives . . . 'When you serve as midwife to the Hebrew women . . . if it is a son, you shall kill him.' . . . But the midwives feared God, and did not do as the king of Egypt commanded them, but let the male children live" (Ex. 1:15-17). "So God dealt well with the midwives; and the people multiplied and grew very strong. And because the midwives feared God he gave them families" (Ex. 1:20-21). This is the immediate background of the birth of Moses. When a babe arrived, he or she was wrapped in *swaddling clothes*, as was the case with Jesus (Luke 2:7,12).

Several of the other customs prevalent in the Old Testament were followed by Joseph and Mary in the case of Jesus. For example, a reading of the second chapter of Luke will reveal that "at the end of eight days" Jesus was *circumcised* and was given the name "Jesus" (Luke 2:21).

The custom of *circumcision* was not only practiced by the Jews but also by other peoples of the East. For the Jews, however, circumcision had deep religious significance. It was a sign or symbol of the Abrahamic covenant. On the occasion when God promised Abraham that Sarah would bear him a son, he entered into covenant with Abraham. The opening words of that covenant were: "I will make my covenant between me and you" (Gen. 17:2; see vv. 4,7). God, at the conclusion of his covenant with Abraham, said, "This is my covenant, which you shall keep, between me and you and your descendants after you: Every male among you shall be circumcised. . . . He that is eight days old among you shall be circumcised; every male throughout your generations. . . . So shall my covenant be in your flesh an everlasting covenant" (vv. 10-13). And later when Isaac was born, Abraham circumcised him on the eighth day "as God had commanded him" (Gen. 21:4).

The practice of circumcision was considered so important that Joshua was commanded to circumcise the people of Israel. "And this is the reason why Joshua circumcised them: all the males of the people who came out of Egypt, all the men of war, had died on the way . . . . all the people that were born on the way . . . had not been circumcised" (Josh. 5:4-5).

Circumcision became a source of considerable conflict between Paul and some who opposed him. The Judaizers contended that Gentile converts needed to be circumcised. But the Christian movement represented a new covenant. The basis for entrance into the covenant was drastically different. Paul plainly said, "For in Christ Jesus neither circumcision nor uncircumcision is of any avail, but faith working through love" (Gal. 5:6). "For neither circumcision counts for anything, nor uncircumcision, but a new creation" (Gal. 6:15). And that new creation is through union with Christ which is by faith.

A type of circumcision is still needed, but it is not the circumcision of an eight-day-old lad. Rather, it is a circumcision of the heart. The new covenant is inner and spiritual rather than outer and physical. So it is with circumcision. Paul said that "true circumcision" is not "something external and physical" but "real circumcision is a matter of the heart, spiritual and not literal" (Rom. 2:28-29). This was and is a circumcision "made without hands" (Col. 2:11).[6]

Much of the preceding discussion of circumcision is not directly related to children. However, it may have considerable significance on the teaching and training of children. The new covenant, with its new and inner circumcision of the heart, helps to explain the fact that some major church groups, such as Baptists, do not baptize infants. They believe that entrance into the new covenant is by faith and that faith has to be exercised personally.

Another custom related to the birth of a child, which was followed by the mother of Jesus, was purification. "And when the time came for their {["her," KJV] purification according to the law of Moses, they brought him up to Jerusalem to present him to the Lord" (Luke 2:22). Most older manuscripts and most translations have "their" instead of "her" as in the King James (see NASB, NEB, NIV). The Mosaic law considered the mother unclean for forty days after the birth of a son (eighty days after the birth of a daughter). There is nothing about the father being unclean. Why he is included here is not clear.

It was "after their purification had been completed . . . they brought him [Jesus] up to Jerusalem to present him to the Lord" (Luke 2:22, NEB; see NASB and NIV). But why should Mary, the mother of our Lord, need to observe the days of purification? The best explanation is that "her act was simply one of devout obedience to the law under which she lived" (Ell.).

The purpose Joseph and Mary had when they went to Jerusalem was "to *present* him [Jesus] *to the Lord*"(author's italics). The law is then referred to: "(as it is written in the law of the Lord {Ex. 13:2,12}, 'Every male that opens the womb shall be called holy to the Lord')" (Luke 2:22-23).

By the parents making an offering, the firstborn son could be redeemed (Ex. 13:13). The offering was determined by the economic status of the family. "If she [the mother] cannot afford a lamb, then she shall take two turtledoves or two young pigeons" (Lev. 12:8). For Mary the offering was the latter. This was "another indication of the poverty of Joseph and his espoused wife" (Ell.).

When Jesus was *presented in the Temple*, the Holy Spirit had revealed to Simeon that he would "not see death before he had seen the Lord's Christ." He took Jesus up in his arms and blessed God and said,

> Lord, now lettest thou thy servant depart in peace,
> for mine eyes have seen thy salvation.

No wonder Joseph and Mary "marveled at what was said about him." They must have marveled even more when they heard Simeon add:

> Behold this child is set for the fall and rising
> of many in Israel.
> and for a sign that is spoken against.

He then added what Mary must have wondered about frequently in the years to come: "(and a sword will pierce through your own soul also)" (Luke 2:25-35). The aged Anna also recognized something unusual in this child and "gave thanks to God" (Luke 2:38).

There were some customs in biblical days regarding the caring for children that may be of considerable interest for the contemporary period. There has been in recent years some unusual emphasis on "natural" *childbirth* and on the mother *nursing* her baby. The psalmist beautifully said,

> But I have calmed and quieted my soul,
> like a child quieted at its mother's breast
>   (131:2).

The prophet Isaiah represented Zion or Israel and then gave God's response:

> "The Lord has forsaken me,
> my Lord has forgotten me."
> "Can a woman forget her sucking child,
>   that she should have no compassion on the son of
>   her womb?
> Even these may forget,
> yet I will not forget you" (49:14-15).

This section on customs related to children would not be complete without brief attention to the *weaning* of the child. This took place at a later age than in the contemporary period or even two or three generations ago, when it was done at a later time. Evidently, in biblical days, weaning is generally thought to have been two or three years of age.

The weaning of a child was considered such an important event that in some cases it was the occasion for a feast. Of Isaac it says, "And the child grew, and was weaned; and Abraham made a great feast on the day that Isaac was weaned" (Gen. 21:8).

Dedication of Them

The Old Testament law required the dedication to God of the *firstborn* of animals, the first fruits of the produce of the land, and also the firstborn male in the home. Roy Honeycutt, citing a considerable number of Scriptures, says, "There are legal passages within the Old Testament which call for the dedication of the first-born son at infancy (cf. Exod. 22:29b-30; 34:19-20; 13:1-2; 13:14-15; Deut. 15:19-20; Num. 18:15-18; 3:47)."[7]

It is assumed that the children of promise previously mentioned in this chapter, such as Isaac, were dedicated by their parents to the purpose and will of God. In a few cases, such dedication is specifically stated. For example, Manoah's wife was barren. An angel of the Lord appeared to her and revealed to her that she would conceive and bear a son. Then the angel gave her specific instructions concerning that son. He was to be a Nazirite[8] to God from birth; and he would "begin to deliver Israel from the hand of the Philistines" (Judg. 13:3-5). Then Manoah made a request that would be appropriate for every Christian father and mother, "O, Lord, I pray thee, let the man of God whom thou didst send come again to us, and teach us what we are to do with the boy that will be born" (Judg. 13:8).

The best known and possibly best loved story in the Old Testament of the dedication of a child to God was Hannah and Samuel. She had promised the Lord that if he would give her a son that she, in turn, would give him back "to the Lord all the days of

CHILDREN   103

his life," and then there is the added promise, "and no razor shall touch his head" (1 Sam. 1:11). This was one of the requirements of the Nazirite (Num. 6:5), so it is likely that Samuel was a Nazirite from birth.

What a beautiful story. Hannah's word to her husband, Elkanah, was, "As soon as the child is weaned, I will bring him, that he may appear in the presence of the Lord, and abide there for ever" (1 Sam. 1:22). When Hannah presented Samuel, she reminded Eli that her son was a gift from God. She then said, "Therefore I have lent ["dedicated," NASB] him to the Lord; as long as he lives, he is lent to the Lord" (1 Sam. 1:28). And the closing appropriate words of the chapter are, "And they worshiped the Lord there" (v. 28).

Hannah, Elkanah, and their special son, Samuel, must have had a happy reunion each year. On one of those yearly visits, Eli blessed them and said, "The Lord give you children by this woman for the loan which she lent to the Lord" (1 Sam. 2:20). The Bible does not say that Hannah made a special request for other children, but she did have three more sons and two daughters (v. 21). This is simply another demonstration that we cannot outgive God.

Hannah could not have known the full significance of what she was doing when she dedicated Samuel to the Lord and his service at the Temple. She probably never dreamed that Samuel would be the last of the judges and the first of the prophets. She did not dedicate him to greatness but to the Lord for his purpose and will. The same has been true and continues to be true of Christian parents. They cannot know fully what the Lord will do with a child of theirs who is given to him.

The Childhood of Jesus

We do not know a great deal about the childhood of Jesus. His birth and a few incidents of his early days, such as his presentation in the Temple and his circumcision, have already been mentioned.

We do know, from Luke's account, that an angel of the Lord appeared to some *shepherds* and announced to them the birth of Jesus. In response to the message of the angels, the shepherds said, "Let us go over to Bethlehem and see this thing that has happened, which the Lord has made known to us" (Luke 2:15). They then went to Bethlehem, found the baby Jesus, and revealed all that had been said to them about him. Is there any wonder "Mary kept all these things, pondering them in her heart" (Luke 2:19)? This and another statement about Mary when Jesus was twelve years of age clearly reveal that she did not comprehend fully the purposes of God for and the nature of this miraculous child of hers.

We also know that some *Wise Men* from the East came searching for the baby Jesus. They brought gifts to him (Matt. 2:1-12). *Herod* sought to locate Jesus to kill him. "An angel of the Lord appeared to Joseph in a dream and said, 'Rise, take the child and his mother, and flee to Egypt, and remain there till I tell you'" (Matt. 2:13). Later, after Herod's death, an angel again appeared to Joseph, saying, "Rise, take the child and his mother, and go to the land of Israel" (Matt. 2:20). They went back and dwelt in the city of Nazareth.

There is a single verse in Luke that may *summarize* several years of *the life of Jesus*. It says, "And the child grew and became strong, filled with wisdom; and the favor of God was upon him" (Luke 2:40).

The next thing we specifically know about Jesus was when he was *twelve years of age* and went with his parents to Jerusalem for the feast of the Passover. This incident, when he remained behind as they left the city, has already been mentioned. But there was a statement made about him that sets a pattern for children of all ages. Although he evidently sensed at that time that he had a unique relation to God, nevertheless "he went down with them . . . and was obedient to them" (Luke 2:51). Then notice again, "and his mother kept all these things in her heart." This chapter in Luke closes with the familiar summary statement, "And Jesus increased in wisdom and in stature, and in favor with God and man" (v. 52).

It is generally assumed that Jesus as a child and youth *worked with Joseph* at the carpenter's trade. At least he is referred to as the carpenter's son (Matt. 13:55). It is possible that some of the terms he used, such as "my yoke is easy" (Matt. 11:30), were derived from his work as a carpenter. We do not know how old Jesus was when Joseph died, but we assume that, following the Jewish custom, he as the oldest son in the family *took* over *the responsibilities of the headship of his home.* We know that he had brothers and sisters, but we do not know their ages.

Jesus and Children

The love of Jesus for children was quite evident during his earthly ministry. It is no wonder that "they were bringing children to him, that he might touch them; . . . And he took them in his arms and blessed them, laying his hands upon them" (Mark 10:13-16; see Matt. 19:13-15; Luke 18:15-17). It may be, as some interpreters suggest, that the blessing parents and others sought was a more or less ceremonial form of the laying on of hands which was practiced by the Jews, as in the case of Isaac's blessing of Jacob and Esau (Gen. 27) and Jacob's blessing of his sons on his deathbed (Gen. 49). It is doubtful, however, if the children would have been brought to Jesus unless parents and others sensed his love for them.

None of us can have the proper understanding of or appreciation for the Bible unless we have "a holy imagination." The capacity to visualize situations, to fill in between the lines, needs to be kept under proper control, but we can never fully grasp the message of the Bible in many places without such an imagination. Regardless of why the children were brought, can you visualize or imagine a father or a mother saying to a growing son or daughter, "Jesus was here one day, he took you in his arms, placed his hand on your head, and blessed you"? What a blessing Jesus was, not only to children he touched but also to men and women of all ages whom he touched, not so much by his hands but by the life he lived while he walked among them.

There may be some question about the proper interpretation of *"little ones"* in some places, but there can be no question about Jesus' love for the "little ones" whether little physically, socially, or spiritually. He had a special concern for the underprivileged, and "little ones" of all kinds. There can be no question about the proper interpretation of Matthew's account of a statement by Jesus which is also found in Mark and Luke, Matthew reported Jesus as saying, "Whoever receives one such child in my name receives me; but whoever causes one of these little ones who believe in me to sin, it would be better for him to have a great millstone fastened round his neck and to be drowned in the depth of the sea" (18:5-6; see Mark 9:42; Luke 17:2).[9]

Again, Jesus said, "See that you do not despise one of these little ones; for I tell you that in heaven their angels always behold the face of my Father who is in heaven" (Matt. 18:10). "The idea that each little one has a personal guardian angel who has immediate access to God provides a clear statement of the value of each person."[10]

After the parable of the lost sheep (18:12-13), Jesus added, "So it is not the will of my Father who is in heaven that one of these little ones should perish" (v. 14). Cobble suggests, "The reason for the awesome peril of causing one of the little ones to fall is that it places the responsible party in direct conflict with the will of God. The concern of God for their welfare is supreme evidence of the true value of the little ones, whether they be the children of men or the children of the Spirit."[11]

One evidence that Jesus loved and placed a *high value on children* is the fact that he noticed them at play and also used them to teach some of his greatest lessons. On one occasion, observing some children playing as if they were at a marriage or at a funeral, he said, "To what shall I compare this generation? It is like children sitting in the market places and calling to their playmates,

'We piped to you, and you did not dance;
we wailed, and you did not mourn'
(Matt. 11:16-17; see Luke 7:31-32).

In other words, the Jews who would not listen to him or to John the Baptist were compared to the children who would not participate in the play of the other children.

On several other occasions, Jesus *used children in his teaching ministry*. One of the great teachings of Jesus which was difficult for his disciples to understand, as it is also difficult for us to comprehend, was the basis of true greatness. It was evidently a topic of rather frequent discussion and some debate among his disciples (see Luke 9:46-48; 22:24-27). They even differed in their judgment as to which one of them was the greatest. Some of the twelve surely could not have thought of themselves as the greatest. It may be that they questioned whether the greatest was Peter, John, James, or possibly one of the other better-known disciples.

We do know that on one occasion John and James, with their mother, requested the honored seats in Christ's kingdom. He pointedly told them that greatness in the kingdom was based on service (Matt. 20:20-28; Mark 10:35-45, Luke 22:24-27).

According to Matthew, the disciples on one occasion "came to Jesus, saying, 'Who is the greatest in the kingdom of heaven?'" Notice carefully and try to visualize what Jesus did then. "And calling to him a child, he put him in the midst of them, and said, 'Truly, I say to you, unless you turn and become like children, you will never enter the kingdom of heaven.'" He then answered specifically their question, "Whoever humbles himself like this child, he is the greatest in the kingdom of heaven." He then added, "Whoever receives one such child in my name receives me" (Matt. 18:1-5). In reporting the same conversation or a similar one on another occasion, Mark said that Jesus "took a child, and put him in the midst of them; and taking him in his arms, he said to them, 'Whoever receives one such child in my name receives me; and whoever receives me, receives not me but him who sent me'" (Mark 9:36-37). Luke added, "He who is least among you all is the one who is great" (Luke 9:48).

We cannot know all that Jesus meant or implied by his comparison of childlikeness to greatness. It is at least possible that he meant that real greatness, from his and the Father's perspective, is characterized by unpretentiousness, by humility, by a consciousness of one's limitations.

No wonder children responded to Jesus and praised him. Let us close this section on "Jesus and Children" and the chapter by quoting at some length the record of a visit of his in the Temple, after his triumphal entry into the city.

And the blind and the lame came to him in the temple, and he healed them. But when the chief priests and the scribes saw the

wonderful things that he did, and the children crying out in the
temple, "Hosanna to the Son of David!" they were indignant; and
they said to him, "Do you hear what these are saying?" And Jesus
said to them, "Yes; have you never read,
            "Out of the mouth of babes and sucklings
                thou hast brought perfect praise"'?
And leaving them, he went out of the city to Bethany and lodged
there (Matt. 21:14-17).

Jesus might have said to the Pharisees what he said on another
occasion, "If these were silent, the very stones would cry out" (Luke
19:40). Notice the contrast between the children and the chief
priests and scribes.

Notes

1. Herbert Lockyer, *All the Children of the Bible* (Grand Rapids: Zondervan, 1970), p. 43.
2. See 2 Kings 4:8-37 for the beautiful story of Elisha and the "wealthy woman" of Shunem.
Her son was a "child of promise," although he was not attributed directly to the intervention of
God.
3. Lockyer, p. 44.
4. Ibid.
5. This statement about Jesus was strikingly similar to a statement about Samuel: "Now the
boy Samuel continued to grow both in stature and in favor with the Lord and with men" (1
Sam. 2:26).
6. A circumcision of the heart is even spoken of in the Old Testament (Deut. 10:16; 30:6; Jer.
9:25-26).
7. Roy Honeycutt in *Children and Conversion*, Clifford Ingle, ed. (Nashville: Broadman Press,
1970), pp. 20-21.
8. The law of the Nazirite is in Numbers 6:2-21. The vow of a Nazirite could be for a limited
time or for life. It is possible that John the Baptist was a Nazirite. At least, the word to
Zechariah was that "he shall drink no wine nor strong drink" (Luke 1:15), which was one of
the requirements for a Nazirite.
9. For other places where Jesus identified himself with the "little ones" see Matthew 10:42:
25:40,45.
10. William B. Cobble in Ingle, p. 48.
11. Ibid.

5

Single Adults

Single adults make up one of the most rapidly expanding groups in the United States. Found in any adult age category, they are the widowed, the divorced, and the never married. Yet, churches have only in recent years begun to give attention to a ministry among them. This relative inattention stems from several reasons. In the case of the widowed and divorced, there are often difficult ministry situations which develop. Also, the failure of churches to minister to single adults may be the result of culturally embedded half-truths such as: marriage is the only meaningful life-style; singleness is legitimate only as a transition experience before or between marriages; sex is as essential to normalcy as food, drink, exercise, and rest; the single must be so because of being unattractive, too bright, or handicapped.[1]

With singleness as an increasing reality and option, we should examine and evaluate the biblical perspective. Some overlap with other chapters will be inevitable.

The Bible deals, except for some brief statements by Jesus and Paul, implicitly rather than explicitly with single adults, particularly the never married. In the Bible, however, individuals are not judged primarily on the basis of their marital status. Instead, the emphasis is upon the quality of their relationships with God and their fellows. This perspective is grounded in the creation itself, particularly the word by the Creator, "Let us make man in our image" (Gen. 1:26). Men and women are equally created in the image of God, capable of thinking, making decisions, and communicating with one another. Thus, each child of God has the freedom and responsibility to decide whether marriage or singleness is the purpose and will of God for their lives. This means that custom and even family pressure to marry can be and should be secondary considerations.

There are many individuals in the Bible who were or almost certainly were single. Attention will be called to some of these. We will also seek to set forth the teachings of the Scriptures directly related to the three types of singles: widows, divorced, never married. There is so much material on widows in the Bible that there will be two sections devoted to the material: Widows in the Bible; Treatment of Widows.

Widows in the Bible

There are a considerable number of nameless widows who are mentioned in the Scriptures. Among these are the women of Midian (Num. 31:7-9) taken captive by the Israelites as spoils of war. These women, their children, and all their possessions were delivered to Moses and Eleazar. Moses was angry that these had been saved and ordered all the women who had been married and all male children killed (Num. 31:13-17).

A nameless *widow* had a special place in the record of Old Testament miracles. She is the one *at Zarephath* whom God prepared to sustain Elijah during the drought. When her son fell deathly ill, Elijah's supplication to God revived him (1 Kings 17:8-24). In a rather perplexing situation, David decided his ten concubines should live in widowhood. This was the result of Absalom's sin against his father with the concubines (2 Sam. 16:20-23). The Bible tells us David took care of them "but did not go in to them. So they were shut up until the day of their death, living as if in widowhood" (2 Sam. 20:3).

In a biographical description of Hiram, the builder of Solomon's house, reference is made to the fact that Hiram's mother, a member of the tribe of Naphtali, was a widow (1 Kings 7:14).

Second Kings 4:1-7 is the story dealing with the compassion of *Elijah* for *a nameless widow*. Her husband left a debt that was to be collected by her two sons going into slavery. Pleading with Elijah, she said, "Your servant my husband is dead; and you know that your servant feared the Lord." Using her only possession, a pot of oil as an occasion for a miracle, Elijah aided her so that she gained some financial independence.

Naomi, a rather prominent widow in the Old Testament, and her daughters-in-law Ruth and Orphah had all lost their husbands. Earlier Naomi had moved from Bethlehem to Moab. Her two sons, Mahlon and Chilion, married the Moabite women Ruth and Orpah. After ten years the sons also died. Naomi requested that her daughters-in-law remain in Moab while she returned to Bethlehem. Orphah honored that request and never appeared again in the biblical record. Ruth insisted that she remain with Naomi. Her words are a poetic, as well as a tough-minded, expression of devotion:

> Entreat me not to leave you or to return from following you; for where you go I will go, and where you lodge I will lodge; your people shall be my people, and your God my God; where you die I will die, and there will I be buried. May the Lord do so to me and more also if even death parts me from you (Ruth 1:16-17).

There is at least one striking case of a *widower* in the Old Testament. In the course of hearing from God the parable of the boiling pot, *Ezekiel* learned that his wife would die. The word of the Lord to him was, "Son of man, behold, I am about to take the delight of your eyes away from you at a stroke; yet you shall not mourn or weep nor shall your tears run down. Sigh, but not aloud; make no mourning for the dead. Bind on your turban, and put shoes on your feet; do not cover your lips, nor eat the bread of mourners" (Ezek. 24:16-17). In assuming his new state as a widower, Ezekiel used his own loss to interpret for the Jews that his loss was comparable to or was symbolic of the nation's loss of Jerusalem (vv. 18-27).

There are also several widows mentioned in the New Testament. Luke included in his account of the presentation of Jesus in the Temple (Luke 2:21-39) the prophetess Anna,[2] "of great age" or "very old" (NIV). She had "lived with her husband seven years from her virginity" or "after she first married" (NEB). She was known as one who did not depart from the Temple, who served God with fastings and prayers night and day.

Jesus, on three different occasions, taught some valuable lessons with a *widow* as the *central character*. Of the devotion of the poor widow who placed "two ["small," NASB; "tiny," NEB] copper coins" into the treasury (Mark 12:41-44; Luke 21:1-4), Jesus said, "Truly I tell you, this poor widow has put in more than all of them; . . . she out of her poverty put in all the living that she had" (Luke 21:4). The widow's evident trust in God for her own care and the gift of her money has provided motivation through the centuries for countless others to give to God's cause.

So far as we know, the first person Jesus raised from the dead was the son of the *widow of Nain* (Luke 7:11-17). Leaving Capernaum, Jesus went to Nain. Near the gate of the city he met a funeral procession. Luke captured the pathos of the moment when Jesus surveyed the situation of a widow who had lost her only son. Luke wrote, "When the Lord saw her, he had compassion on her and said to her, 'Do not weep.'" With that, Jesus touched the bier or coffin (NASB, NIV) and commanded the son to rise (v. 14). The effect upon the crowd of seeing the dead come back to life was one of fear mixed with adulation. Jesus' reputation as a great prophet spread.

Another widow was referred to by Jesus in one of his parables (Luke 18:1-5). She is usually known as the *"importunate"* widow. Her continual pestering of the judge, "who neither feared God nor regarded man," finally won from him the willingness to avenge the widow of her adversary. Such persistence, Jesus said, is needed in prayer.

Paul may have known many widows. It may be that some of those mentioned by him in his special greetings, such as in Romans 16, were widows. At least it is assumed that many of those listed were unmarried. As will be seen in the next section on the treatment of widows, Paul gave particular attention to a ministry to them and by them.

Treatment of Widows

Both the Old and New Testaments refer to widows as those who had suffered great losses. From the root *alam*—to be put to silence, struck dumb, or tongue-tied—the Hebrews developed the word *alman* which denoted a sense of bereavement or one who was discarded or forsaken. The same root, *alam,* gave rise to the frequently-used term *almahnah,* a widow.[3]

The New Testament writers used the term *chera* to denote widows. The root word gives the idea of a chasm, a vacancy, an impassible interval, or gulf.[4] The idea of deficiency, lacking a husband, thus served to describe rather vividly one who was a widow.

Building on this sense of loss, bereavement, and emptiness, the Bible gives considerable attention to widows. The relationship of both the Hebrews and those of the *early church* to their widows provides insight especially into the biblical perspective of true religion and a God-approved ministry. This perspective is applicable to the contemporary situation.

Widows appeared to be in an inferior position in the *Hebrew community*. For instance, instructions concerning the high priest said that he should only marry "a wife in her virginity" but "a widow, or one divorced, or a woman who has been defiled, or a harlot, these he shall not marry" (Lev. 21:13-14). The Book of Ruth paints a dark picture of the condition of widowhood (Ruth 1:20-21). Isaiah referred to "the reproach of your widowhood" (Isa. 54:4). Perhaps the widow's condition was symbolized but also worsened by the fact that she wore identifying garments (Gen. 38:14,19).

In relation to *Tamar,* the *first widow* specifically mentioned (Gen. 38:11), there is also a reference to levirate marriage. The latter was provided for in the law (Deut. 25:5-10). For childless widows, provision was made for the dead husband's brother, if there was one, to take the widow as a wife. Their firstborn son would be considered the child of her first husband. If a man refused to marry his brother's widow, he was publicly reprimanded and disgraced. Though this provision was made primarily to protect the family inheritance, as seen in the Book of Ruth, the security and welfare for the widow was also involved.

Other *rights of widows* included the privilege, in the case of childlessness, for a widow to return to her father's house. At least this was true if her father was a priest (Lev. 22:13). Also, a widow might wait for a levirate marriage. Clearly, she had the right of remarriage (Ruth 1:9-13; 1 Sam. 25:39-42; Ezek. 44:22). If she did not marry again or if levirate marriage was not possible, she had little recourse other than to adapt to her situation.

Exodus 22:22 sets the *tone of the Law,* the Prophets, and the Writings *regarding widows.* The verse says, "You shall not afflict any widow or orphan." The punishment for one who broke this law was death. "If you do afflict them, and they cry out to me, I will surely hear their cry; and my wrath will burn, and I will kill you with the sword, and your wives shall become widows and your children fatherless" (Ex. 22:23-24). The recurring emphasis is that God "executes justice for the fatherless and the widow, and loves the sojourner, giving him food and clothing" (Deut. 10:18). Widows were part of the covenant community and, therefore, candidates for the same mercy as extended to other groups (Deut. 14:29; 16:11-14). They were eligible for available food, especially that which could be gleaned after a harvest (Deut. 24:19-21). Also, a tithe of the third year's produce was for widows, orphans, Levites, and strangers (Deut. 26:12-13).

Justice for widows included the provision that their garments could not be taken in pledge, or as security against debts (Deut. 24:17). Administrators and judges were warned, "Cursed be he who perverts the justice due to the sojourner, the fatherless, and the widow" (Deut. 27:19).

Apparently, conditions for widows worsened as the years passed. It was necessary to repeat and stress earlier instructions concerning widows. The prophets pronounced some stern rebukes to those who behaved uncompassionately toward widows. The decline in the nation's moral condition was clearly seen in the way the weak and innocent were treated, including the widows.

Isaiah condemned the Hebrews for observing the form and ritual of the sacrificial system, while losing sight of justice and mercy:

> What to me is the multitude of your sacrifices?
> says the Lord;

. . . .

> Bring no more vain offerings;
> incense is an abomination to me.
>
> . . . .
>
> Wash yourselves; make yourselves clean;
>   remove the evil of your doings
>   from before my eyes;
> cease to do evil,
>   learn to do good;
> seek justice,
>   correct oppression;
> defend the fatherless,
>   plead for the widow (1:11,13,16-17).

Summing up the situation, Isaiah rebuked the leaders' treatment of widows, "Your princes are rebels . . . the widow's cause does not come to them" (v. 23). Again:

> Woe to those who decree iniquitous decrees,
>   and the writers who keep writing oppression,
> to turn aside the needy from justice
>   and to rob the poor of my people of their right,
> that widows may be their spoil,
>   and that they may make the fatherless their prey!
>   (10:1-2).

Jeremiah continued this theme as he proclaimed God's call for repentance by the Jews. "If you do not oppress the alien, the fatherless or the widow, or shed innocent blood in this place, and if you do not go after other gods to your own hurt, then I will let you dwell in this place, in the land that I gave of old to your fathers for ever" (Jer. 7:6-7; see 22:3).

Ezekiel, in Exile, reiterated Isaiah's charge against Israel's leaders and their oppression of widows, "Father and mother are treated with contempt in you; the sojourner suffers extortion in your midst; the fatherless and the widow are wronged in you" (22:7).

Zechariah, who came after the restoration, reminded the Israelites of the Word of God before the captivity, "Render true judgments, show kindness and mercy each to his brother, do not oppress the widow, the fatherless, the sojourner, or the poor"

(7:9-10). When the people of God failed to do these things, "great wrath came from the Lord of hosts" (v. 12). Malachi included a word of judgment "against those who oppress the hireling in his wages, the widow and the orphan" (3:5).

Running through the Prophets is the continuing emphasis on justice, mercy, and righteousness. A test of the acting out of these qualities included right treatment of widows.

Though held in somewhat lower esteem by the Hebrews, *the Writings* also contained "the same central emphasis on God and on His expectation that His people should be like him."[5]

A few examples from this division of the Old Testament will suffice to illustrate the same attitude toward and treatment of widows.

Job (31) made his case for personal integrity. There, in a long series of hypothetical sinful acts, Job said he was due the judgment of God if he had "caused the eyes of the widow to fail" (v. 16). The Psalms portray the attitude of God toward and his activities on the behalf of widows. He is a "protector of widows" (68:5) and one who "upholds the widow and the fatherless" (146:9). Proverbs portrays God as one who "tears down the house of the proud, but maintains the widow's boundaries" (15:25).

The attitudes and emphases found in the Old Testament are also apparent in the New Testament. As would be expected, Jesus reaffirmed the Old Testament view of God's concern for widows. He spoke specifically about the scribes' treatment or mistreatment of widows. In a list of charges against their religious practices, Jesus inserted a description of how low these men were. They "devour ["eat up," Williams; "grow fat on," Phillips] widows' houses" (Mark 12:40; Luke 20:47). In the tradition of the eighth-century prophets, Jesus related religious profession and true character. Significantly, he used the treatment of widows to press home his point.

Luke drew special attention to the Greek widows in the Jerusalem church (Acts 6:1). The Greeks or the "Hellenists" complained that their widows were being "neglected in the daily distribution." This led to the selection of the seven who were the forerunners of the deacons. There is another person mentioned in

Acts (9:36-42) who, by implication, was a widow. She was "a disciple named Tabitha, which means Dorcas [or Gazelle]. She was full of good works and acts of charity." This much beloved woman of Joppa died but was brought back to life by Peter. Many of her friends were also widows.

Paul gave specific directives concerning attitudes toward widows in the young Christian congregations.

In 1 Corinthians 7, where Paul discussed more fully than anywhere else certain relationships in the family, two or three verses refer specifically to widows. Verse 8 says that it would be good for them to remain single as Paul was. He did say that if they could not exercise self-control they should marry. Then he came back to the subject of widows in verses 39 and 40. Evidently a question had been asked in the letter from the Corinthians about the remarriage of widows. Paul first made a basic statement, "A wife is bound to her husband as long as he lives. If the husband dies, she is free to be married to whom she wishes." However, Paul added a qualifier, "only in the Lord" or one who "must belong to the Lord" (NIV) or "provided the marriage is within the Lord's fellowship" (NEB). He did say that he believed that each widow would be "happier if she remains as she is" to which he added, "And I think that I have the Spirit of God" (v. 40).

In 1 Timothy 5:3-16, Paul gave his young protégé counsel with regard to widows. There are some explicit instructions for dealing with what must have been a distinct group of widows. Paul referred to them as "real widows" or "widows indeed" (KJV) or "one who is alone in the world" (NEB).

Widows were not categorized as *"real widows"* if they had some means of support or a family to take care of them. It was considered honorable to God and less a burden to the congregation if children, grandchildren, or other relatives took care of their own relatives who were widows. Paul considered a nonprovider for a needy widow as one who had "disowned ["denied," NEB] the faith" and as "worse than an unbeliever" (v. 8).

Paul urged Timothy to enroll these real widows only after the application of some rather stringent criteria. They were eligible for church assistance when there was a real need. Also, they were to have been no less than sixty years of age and to have been the wife of one man. Some of the conditions laid down by Paul in 1 Timothy placed a heavy burden on younger widows who may have remarried and then were widowed again after sixty. Paul seemingly had two motives in mind, both of which expressed his concern for the church. For example, the church might have to assume a longtime financial burden if the younger widows were enrolled. Also, he suggested the possibility that younger widows might grow "wanton against Christ" and desire to marry. He suggested that such younger widows should "marry, bear children, rule their households, and give to the enemy no occasion to revile us" (v. 14).

Paul's concern for the widow's life and witness is reflected in his suggestion that Timothy consider those who have a reputation for doing "good deeds" (v. 10). In verses 5 and 6 Paul contrasted the widow who trusted in God and "continues in supplications and prayers night and day," over against the widow who was "self-indulgent" or "lives for pleasure" (NIV). Those in the latter category were not living up to the standards of the gospel. In actuality, they were "really dead though still alive" (Williams). They probably had not realized the impact of their bereavement nor sensed any closer relationship to God or spiritual enrichment because of their experience. Widowhood may be an occasion for spiritual collapse.

Furthermore, the real widow must have been hospitable to strangers, washed the saints' feet, "relieved the afflicted, and devoted herself to doing good in every way" (v. 10).

Though more could be said concerning Paul's insights concerning widows, attention will now be turned to James. As much as anything, the Epistle of James is known for the idea that one's faith is dead if it is not accompanied by works. James's position can be summed up as follows, "So faith by itself, if it has no works, is dead" (2:17). There is an earlier statement in the epistle which is foundational to his concept of the relation of faith and works, "Religion that is pure and undefiled before God and the Father is this: to visit orphans and widows in their affliction, and to keep oneself unstained from the world" (Jas. 1:27).

Rather than giving an all-inclusive definition of religion, James, like the Hebrew prophets, emphasized that mere external religiosity is unacceptable to God. "A religious worship that is pure and stainless in the sight of God the Father" (Williams) is that which gives special attention "to look after" (NIV) or goes "to the help of" (NEB) those who are least able to help themselves—orphans and widows. Curtis Vaughan says that this statement by James "comprehends all the duties of love. It suggests that Christians are to take a personal interest in and express loving concern for orphans and widows. We are to supply their material needs, comfort them in their sorrows, and give any other assistance they may require."[6] It should not be forgotten that this activity is in conjunction with living an otherwise unstained or "untarnished" (NEB) life.

Divorced

A later chapter (9) will be devoted to divorce and remarriage. In the present chapter, there will simply be presented a brief summary statement of the biblical teachings concerning divorce.

The *Old Testament Law* permitted a husband to put away or divorce his wife under certain conditions. The wife had no comparable right. She could become the wife of another man, but if she did she could never go back to the first husband (Deut. 24:1-4). There is also in the Old Testament clear evidence of God's disapproval of divorce. The priest or the high priest could not marry a divorced person (Lev. 21:7,14). The prophet Malachi plainly said that God hates putting away or divorce (2:16).

When *Jesus* was faced with the Old Testament law regarding divorce by the Pharisees, he went back of the law to the original purpose of God who was the Lawgiver. God's intention clearly was that one man and one woman should be joined together as husband and wife for life. Jesus personally said, "What therefore God has joined together, let not man put asunder" (Matt. 19:6). In other words, Jesus did not approve divorce; or, at best, he did not approve it except on the ground of adultery (Matt. 5:32; 19:9). The exception is not given in Mark's account of the same incident.

Paul did not approve of divorce on any grounds. He did not know anything about the exception clause we find in Matthew. He specifically suggested that if a wife left her husband or if a husband divorced his wife they were to remain unmarried.

Never Married

Jesus, in his conversation with the Pharisees concerning divorce and specifically in what he said to his disciples after that incident has considerable significance for any consideration of single adults, particularly the never married. As the result of what Jesus had said concerning divorce, the disciples said to him, "If such is the case of a man with his wife, it is not expedient to marry" (Matt. 19:10). Jesus replied, "Not all men can receive this saying, but only those to whom it is given" (Matt. 19:11). These words imply, if they do not actually say, that one cannot live the single life undisturbed sexually or even without a consciousness of the lack of human companionship without the bestowal of a special spiritual gift or charisma to do so. Then Jesus spoke of three kinds of eunuchs or those who live without marriage as the normal outlet for the expression of their sexual desires. He suggested that there were some who were born eunuchs or without the capacity for full or normal sexual relations. Others had been "made eunuchs by men." The third type of eunuchs, significant for the study of single adults, included those who had "made themselves eunuchs for the sake of the kingdom of heaven" (v. 12). This last group might be called "spiritual eunuchs." They are the ones who voluntarily give up "the use of their reproductive powers to serve better the kingdom."[7]

"To serve better the kingdom" suggests the God-approved motivation for a Christian to live the single life. A Christian should not choose to live single for ascetic reasons, to escape marital responsibilities, or with the opinion that singleness is superior to marriage. The never married should be convinced that singleness is the will and purpose of God for their lives. Without such a conviction of being within the will of God, they—in many and possibly most cases—will be frustrated in their motivations and in their capacity to remain victorious in the single life.

Jesus closed his statement to his disciples by saying, "He who is able to receive this, let him receive it" (v. 12). This clearly says, or at least strongly implies, that one who should be a celibate or a spiritual eunuch must have a special divine gift to live that kind of life.

Possibly there should be injected a relatively brief and somewhat parenthetical statement concerning *eunuchs in the Old Testament* before we call attention to Paul's statement somewhat comparable to the one by Jesus.

The eunuch was "usually [some would say always] a castrated male person."[8] This practice "was established in the Orient in early times in order to provide guards over harems of the oriental potentates and rulers."[9] However, a eunuch might be a high government official, as was the case of the Ethiopian eunuch whom Philip led to faith in the resurrected Christ (Acts 8:26-40).

The Old Testament law disapproved the castration of men and even implied the disapproval of the castration of animals. For example, regarding the latter, the only kind of sacrifice acceptable to *Yahweh* or the Lord was "a male without blemish, of the bulls or the sheep or the goats" (Lev. 22:19). One blemish specifically mentioned was "any animal which has its testicles bruised or crushed or torn or cut" (v. 24).

It is not surprising that in another place, the law states that any man "whose testicles are crushed or whose male member is cut off should not enter the assembly of the Lord" (Deut. 23:1). The allusion in this verse "is to the two surgical operations by which the condition of a eunuch was most commonly produced at that time" (ICC). Bodily mutilation of any kind for an animal or a man was "inconsistent with the character of Jehovah's people" (ICC). We should be grateful, however, that one of God's great prophets went beyond the law and held out a word of hope even for eunuchs.

> Let not the foreigner who has joined himself to the
>   Lord say,
>   "The Lord will surely separate me from his people";
> and let not the eunuch say,
>   "Behold, I am a dry tree."
> For thus says the Lord:

"To the eunuchs who keep my sabbaths,
    who choose the things that please me
    and hold fast my covenant.
I will give in my house and within my walls
    a monument and a name
    better than sons and daughters;
I will give them an everlasting name
    which shall not be cut off" (Isa. 56:3-5).

The preceding from Isaiah approaches the marvelous grace of God which is so central in the life and teachings of Jesus and the writings of Paul, John, and others in the New Testament.

There are some notable *examples of the never married* in both the Old and the New Testaments. Apparently *Miriam*, the sister of Moses and Aaron, was not married; at least she is never associated with a husband. She exemplified one who served in a leadership role (see the song of Miriam, Ex. 15:20-21) and yet when she, with Aaron her brother, attempted to usurp too much authority she suffered God's judgment (Num. 12:1-16). *Rahab*, a harlot, seems on the surface to be an unlikely person to be included in the Bible (Josh. 2:1-21; 6:22-25). However, she exhibited the kind of faith that is pleasing to God (Heb. 11:31; Jas. 2:25). Earlier *Abel* seemingly never married. It is true, however, that the early chronologies of the human race in Genesis 5 mention none who apparently were single. In fact, the chronology revealed a marked tendency toward observing God's imperative: "Be fruitful and multiply, and fill the earth" (Gen. 9:1).

Among the prophets of Israel little is known of the marital status of most of them, such as Amos, Obadiah, Nahum, and Joel. In contrast, *Jeremiah* used his singleness to illustrate spiritual messages. The word from God to Jeremiah was for him not to marry, not to have children nor attend funerals and weddings (Jer. 16:1-9). These things contributed to his loneliness; but for Jeremiah to have done otherwise would have been, to a degree, a contradiction of his prophecies of the impending destruction which would preclude normal social relationships. Laetsch suggests that this divine injunction to Jeremiah is consistent with his first call (Jer. 1:5-19). It is also consistent with God's promise to comfort, strengthen, and deliver the prophet.

Now the Lord expects His ambassador to trust the word of his Creator and Redeemer that all would be well with him. In such unflinching trust he is to shoulder the burdens and hardships incidental to his high calling, and not become disheartened because so little of the joy and happiness one might expect of so glorious an office would fall to his lot.[10]

Ezekiel, as has been suggested, lost his wife and was told by the Lord not to remarry.

Daniel, another prophet of the Exile period, was probably single. He evidently did not use his singleness as a type of prophetic symbolism as was true of Jeremiah. It is possible, of course, that because of his singleness he ministered with less intimidation and less fear of reprisal for his prophetic statements.

Several individuals are mentioned in the New Testament who evidently never married. This is definitely true of the *daughters of Philip* the evangelist (Acts 21:8-9). In relating the fact that Paul lodged in Caesarea with Philip "who was one of the seven," Luke commented, "And he had four unmarried daughters, who prophesied."

John the Baptist is depicted as having never married. He burst upon the New Testament scene preaching about the kingdom of heaven and the coming Messiah, as well as baptizing (Matt. 3:1-17; Mark 1:4-9; Luke 3:1-22; John 1:6,15-37). Only Luke gave the intriguing events surrounding John the Baptist's birth (Luke 1:5-25,39-80). All three of the Synoptic Gospels report the ghastly death of this forerunner of Christ (Matt. 14:1-12; Mark 6:14-29; Luke 9:7-9), but none of the Gospel writers made any reference which would indicate John's status to be other than a single person.

Jesus offers, in his *attitudes* and actions, some insight into the New Testament perspective concerning those who never marry. One example was his relationship with *Mary of Magdala* whom it is assumed was single, although she was associated with married women. Luke introduced her with "Joanna, the wife of Chuza, Herod's steward, and Susanna" and others (Luke 8:3). All of these women were remembered as having "been healed of evil spirits and infirmities." This was true of Mary "from whom seven demons had gone out" (v. 2). This "Mary, called Magdalene" is mentioned on one other occasion in relation to Jesus. That was at the tomb following his resurrection (Matt. 27:56,61; 28:1; Mark 15:40,47; 16:1-9; Luke 24:10; John 19:25; 20:1,11-18).

Almost forgotten in the studies about the *prodigal son* (Luke 15:11-32) is the fact that he was a single man. Though usually referred to as a parable, Jesus' narrative recited circumstances all too common to real life to be dismissed as having no basis in fact. Jesus, in one of his parables, compared the coming of the kingdom of God to "ten maidens {"virgins," KJV, NIV; "bridesmaids," Williams; "girls," NEB} who took their lamps and went to meet the bridegroom" (Matt. 25:1).

Paul, in 1 Corinthians 7, gave some insight into the place of celibacy in the early church. The entire chapter points up the fact that we are "hearing only one side of the telephone conversation." In other words, Paul was responding to questions sent to him by the Corinthian fellowship. We would know better how to interpret some of the things he said if we knew the questions which had been asked. Note that he wrote, "Now concerning the matters about which you wrote" (v. 1). In the chapter, he discussed a considerable variety of family problems. Some of these will be discussed in later chapters.

The very first statement Paul made is, "It is a good thing for a man to have nothing to do with women" (1 Cor. 7:1, NEB). Paul, however, was conscious of the non-Christian life-styles in Corinth. This may be the reason he said, "But because of the temptation to immorality, each man should have his own wife and each woman her own husband" (v. 2).

Some elements of 1 Corinthians 7 applied, in a particular way, to the Corinthians. Paul evidently thought that they should consider seriously the single life. He did give some instructions concerning the sexual relations of husbands and wives "by way of concession, not by command" (v. 6). The important point is for each never married or single to consider how their sexuality is to be expressed within their Christian calling.

It is clear that *Paul* was *unmarried* when he wrote 1 Corinthians (see 7:8). Some suggest that he was a widower, but most believe that he was never married. He seemingly was largely free from sexual passion, as he lived out his Christian calling. He wished that all could have that freedom. He realized, however, that the celibate life could be lived successfully only when one had the charisma (a gift of grace) to do so. He suggested that "each has his own special gift from God" (v. 7). This implies that some may have the special, divinely given grace to live the celibate life, while others may have the gift or grace to keep in proper balance their responsibilities to the family and to the work of Christ or the kingdom of God. This was a foundational thought upon which Paul built further as he suggested that the Corinthians consider the multidimensional nature of the Christian life and the church.

In verse 8 Paul reintroduced singleness. Interestingly, he used the phrase "to the unmarried and the widows." His use of two terms, on the surface, may be confusing. It seems clear, however, that by "unmarried" Paul referred to those who had never married. By the addition of "widows" and by what he said later in the chapter, he evidently did not mean to include the divorced.

Reiterating the idea of verse 7—"that all were as I myself am," he made allowance for the incontinent to marry, "It is better to marry than to be aflame with passion" (v. 9). It sounds like Paul put the reason or motivation for marriage on a rather creaturely level. J. W. MacGorman says, "The assumption suggests that if one marries, he will no longer have to contend with sexual temptation. But married people know that struggles with sexual temptation continue beyond the marriage altar." MacGorman does conclude, "Even so, Christian marriage is a powerful contributor to sexual morality" (LBBC). Paul showed a willingness to deal with the basic drives of humanity in the light of the gospel, something which many of us in the contemporary period fail to do.

In 1 Corinthians 7:17-24, Paul enunciated a basic principle two or three times. The verses specifically refer to circumcision and to slavery, but the basic principle also applies to the married and to those who are not married. The basic principle is: "Let every one lead the life which the Lord has assigned to him, and in which God has called him" (v. 17). Similarly, he says, "Every one should remain in the state in which he was called" (v. 20). The same idea is repeated again: "So, brethren, in whatever state each was called, there let him remain with God" (v. 24). Then he proceeded with a statement that is confusing in the original language and is variously translated. This is particularly true of verses 36-38.

The variations in the translations of these verses underscore the uncertainty concerning Paul's meaning. Some translations make the reference to a father and his unmarried daughter (KJV, NASB, Williams) while others suggest that it refers to a young man and his fiancee (RSV, NIV, Phillips, TEV). *The New English Bible* considers the reference to spiritual marriage—a celibate man and celibate woman living together without sexual relations. This is doubtful. It seems that Paul was too much of a realist to approve such an arrangement.

Paul's general position regarding marriage and the single life may be summed up by two statements in this chapter in 1 Corinthians: "Are you free from a wife? Do not seek marriage. But if you marry, you do not sin" (vv. 27-28); "He who marries his betrothed does well; and he who refrains from marriage will do better" (v. 38). Paul did believe that the married would be concerned about worldly things and would have divided minds, trying to please both their spouses and the Lord. What he wanted was their "undivided devotion to the Lord" (vv. 32-35).

Paul, in this chapter, did not attempt to make a case for ascetic celibacy. Rather, Paul was speaking of a vocational celibacy. In other words, he thought "in view of the present distress" (v. 26) and the demands of the kingdom that it was better, at least for him, to remain single.

Rather than considering such statements as absolutes with regard to Christian singles or couples, we should recognize that the basic thrust of what Paul said was for each—married and unmarried—to seek integrity and order in their relationships and, most importantly, for them to give "undivided devotion to the Lord" (v. 35). On one hand Paul realized his own advantage in dealing with the demands of his missionary work without involving a wife or family. Yet, to strike some balance, he called for each to seek his own calling, leaving room for the building of homes and families, some of whose hospitality Paul no doubt had enjoyed.

Conclusions

1. Neither marriage nor singleness is a superior state. Both are found in the Scriptures. Both are treated with honor when perceived as a part of one's calling by and relationship to God. Most people will marry. Yet, only in recent years has much attention been given to helping couples understand those important elements which make marriage strong. This means grappling with cultural values which oftentimes are alien to a maturing Christian relationship. Also, there is needed more help in preparing for marriage. Always, the will of God must be sought regarding the reasons one seeks marriage, concerning a possible choice of a mate, and the direction a marriage will take.

2. There are those who have been married and either through divorce or death are now single. Whatever the situation, the church can aid these individuals in dealing with the ensuing grief process which follows the break in a relationship. Aiding such singles to know how to deal with loneliness can be especially significant. Likewise, they can be helped to understand whether remarriage should be considered as an option at some later time.

3. For a growing number of people, marriage is neither an immediate nor ultimate choice in life. The motivations for considering singleness must be deliberated upon with the primary idea of seeking God's will. In view of Jesus' and Paul's teaching, celibacy seems to be a spiritual gift not bestowed upon many. One who has this gift may be able to center his or her life more than would otherwise be possible around the work of the kingdom of God. For some of these people, marriage could be a hindrance. It will depend on the nature of their work for the Lord. Such persons will need the understanding of others who do not live the single life. Also, those who do not marry out of devotion to the kingdom of God should seek to communicate positively the reasons for their decision.

Also, seeking maturity in one's relationship to God is just as important for the single who senses marriage as a part of God's direction for him. There are interim periods between singleness and marriage when, because of such circumstances as school, career, and many other factors, one must put some constraint upon sexual passions. Research shows that the drive for sexual relations, unlike that for food, can be sublimated.

Such interim times can be seen as opportunities to develop in relating positively to others as people rather than as objects to be exploited.

4. Many singles do not give proper attention to building up their inner resources. In a constant, almost frantic pace of life, many of them frequently discover themselves to be out of energy. Some of them have created for themselves an inner vacuum. Unwholesome by-products may be self-pity, preoccupation with oneself, loneliness, boredom, and resentment toward others.

Thus, the single years one has—before marriage or when one loses one's partner—can be most profitable when utilized as an opportunity to gain one's primary perspective and to discover fulfillment in God's power and person. There may be the temptation to seek what is needed exclusively by association with friends and family members. These can provide, however, only a portion of the depths which we need and for which we crave. The establishment of a pattern of discovering fellowship with God, by the widowed, the divorced, as well as by the never married, can be a great source of strength in times of temptations and pressures.

5. There is a need for redefining what we mean by the word *family*. The term should include more than the father-mother-children unit. Paul's attention to the treatment of fellow believers as family members (1 Tim. 5:1-8) should move us toward a more closely knit Christian fellowship that overrides biological barriers.

6. The church could help a great deal at several specific points regarding single adults. More education and biblical emphases are needed. Relatively few biblical studies exist concerning single adults. Singles need help in understanding celibacy and service in the kingdom. Both the Old and New Testaments stand as testimonials to the relationship of theology and ethics concerning

ministry to widows. This particular segment of a church's membership may be the most overlooked of all in its ministry. More attention needs to be given to how single adults—widowed, divorced, never married—can be ministered to and in turn can minister in and through the church to others in need.

Notes

1. Sarah Frances Anders, "Singleness as Family" in *Proceedings of the 1979 Christian Life Commission Seminar "Help for Families"* (Nashville: 1979), p. 30.
2. Feminine *prophetes* is used to describe one who was a female foreteller or an inspired woman.
3. See the "Hebrew and Chaldee Dictionary" found in James Strong, *Strong's Exhaustive Concordance* (Grand Rapids: Associated Publishers and Authors, Inc., n.d.), p. 95.
4. See the "Greek Dictionary," *Strong's Exhaustive Concordance,* p. 77.
5. T. B. Maston, *Biblical Ethics* (Waco, Texas: Word Books, 1967), p. 71.
6. Curtis Vaughan, *A Study Guide—James* (Grand Rapids: Zondervan Publishing House, 1969), p. 42.
7. *International Bible Dictionary,* 2:180.
8. Ibid., 179.
9. *Universal Jewish Encyclopedia,* 4:193.
10. Theodore Laetsch, *Bible Commentary: Jeremiah* (St. Louis: Concordia Publishing House, 1965), p. 156.

6

Older Adults

Who are older adults? It is difficult to determine exactly when one should be labeled *old*. There are several reasons for the difficulty. One is the relativity of old age. For example, a professional athlete is considered old when he reaches the age of thirty-five or forty. A minister may be old or at least considered beyond his prime when he is fifty or sixty. In contrast, many members of congress and the justices of the supreme court continue to serve in their seventies and even occasionally after they are eighty or more.

Gray and Moberg suggest that it is difficult to define "old age" because of the relative positions from which judgments are made. Children, youth, mature adults, and old people usually judge aging differently. "A third source of differences among definitions of old age is the tremendous variations in individual characteristics." Some are older at thirty than others are at sixty or seventy.[1]

It seems that the most feasible and possibly the only way to define "old age" is by chronological age. At least it is the most generally accepted. It is true, however, that there is such a great difference among older people that some distinction needs to be made within the "older adult" group such as "young old" and "old old."

Regardless of the definition, older adults in recent years have become an increasingly large and more vocal group in our churches and in the population in general. For example, in 1900 in the United States, there were approximately 3 million adults sixty-five years of age and older. That was 4.1 percent of the total population or about one out of twenty-five. A recent magazine article suggested that now there are 21.8 million or one out of ten of our population who are sixty-five or older. It is predicted that by 2000 they will be 30.1 million in number or one-eighth of our population.[2] There are not only more older people but also they are living longer.

Without spelling out the reasons for the marked increase of older people, this should be enough to underscore their increasing importance to our nation and to our churches. Our churches, their leaders, and all of us should ponder the fact that "in the United States there are about three times as many persons past their sixty-fifth birthday as college students."[3] What about the relative time and attention given to the two groups in most churches?

We have had in recent years in the United States a youth revolution or rebellion. More recently there has been and still is a rather vocal women's revolution. It is possible that we are in the beginning of an "old folks revolution." They are becoming so many in numbers, are maintaining their health and vigor longer, and are so much better organized than formerly that it seems inevitable that they will have a more effective voice in church and society.

In the light of the increasing significance of the older years, it is important for us to examine what the Bible says about age, aging, and older adults in general. As we have suggested previously, anything the Bible says on any subject is important; properly interpreted and evaluated, it will speak a helpful word to us as individuals and to our churches.

Age and Aging

How do most of us visualize aging? One author, possibly somewhat but not entirely facetiously, suggests that aging is "balding, graying, wrinkling, sagging, cane, spectacles, fragility, frailty, dependence, and ugliness too." The same author continues, "We all know some other things, too. Aging is something that happens to us with time. The process is inevitable. The culmination is death." He also says, "A person begins to age at the moment he is conceived."[4]

It is true that "from the broadest possible perspective, aging refers to the simple process of moving from the beginning to the end of life. But common sense . . . provides a more precise . . . working definition of aging. In common usage the word 'aging' refers primarily to perceivable evidence of physical and mental decline."⁵

It is not surprising that both the Old Testament and the New Testament reveal considerable interest in age and aging. For example, the Book of *Genesis* is very age conscious. This is strikingly evident in chapter 5 which is "the book of the generations of Adam." There are two aspects of aging to which attention is called in a special way: the age when a man fathered his first son or in the case of Adam, Seth—his third, and the age when the man died. Some scholars question the exactness of the ages listed. Also, "how such figures were interpreted at the time is something that one may only guess at today" (An.B.). There are stated for each man three striking and significant words: "and he died." Enoch was an exception. He "walked with God; and he was not, for God took him" (Gen. 5:24). Regardless of how long one may live, death is inevitable. Possibly it should be added that the length of life is not the most significant thing concerning any life. The life of Methuselah, who lived longer than anyone else, is summed up in three verses. Contrast his life with Moses, Abraham, Jacob, David, and a host of others.

Sometimes in the Old Testament, there is simply a general statement about age and/or aging. For example, Genesis 25:8 says, "These are the days of the years of Abraham's life, a hundred and seventy-five years. Abraham breathed his last and died in a good old age, and was gathered to his people." Earlier when Abraham trusted "his servant, the oldest of his house" (Gen. 24:2) to select a wife for Isaac, who himself was forty years old, the record says, "Now Abraham was old, well advanced in years" (Gen. 24:1).

Jacob referred to his own "gray" hair (Gen. 42:38; 44:29) and was referred to as "an old man" by Joseph (Gen. 43:27) and by his other sons (Gen. 44:20). There are rather frequent references elsewhere in the Old Testament to old men. For example, the Lord said to Joshua, "You are old and advanced in years, and there remains yet very much land to be possessed" (Josh. 13:1). In other words, in spite of Joshua's age, God still had a task for him. Eli is referred to as "very old" (1 Sam. 2:22), while Samuel continued until he "became old" (1 Sam. 8:1). "First Chronicles closes with the final 'change of command.' After forty years as king, David 'died in a good old age, full of days, riches and honor; and Solomon his son reigned in his stead' (29:28)."⁶

There is considerable material in the *Psalms* regarding aging. The main thrust, however, is on the brevity of life. A frequently quoted verse from the Psalms is 90:10:

> The years of our life are threescore and ten,
> or even by reason of strength fourscore;
> yet their span is but toil and trouble;
> they are soon gone, and we fly away.

The psalmist then made an appeal that is abidingly relevant:

> So teach us to number our days
> that we may get a heart of wisdom (v. 12).

Overshadowing the whole Book of *Ecclesiastes* "is the preoccupation with the brevity of life and its inevitable end in Sheol (5:18). Man lives in uncertainty . . . 'it pains like a shadow' (6:12). . . . He can even say that better is 'the way of death, than the day of birth' (7:1)."⁷

There are only two or three specific references to the aged in *the Prophets*. For example, Joel, in the beginning of his message to all the people, first addressed the "old men":

> Hear this, you aged men,
> give ear, all inhabitants of the land! (1:2).

Possibly the old or aged men were the ones who should have remembered most vividly the dealings of God with his people and their people in the past. They were to pass on what they knew to succeeding generations. This is a continuing opportunity and responsibility of older adults.

Zechariah foresaw the time when the Lord would return to or restore Jerusalem. One evidence of the restoration of the city was to be the fact that "old men and old women shall again sit in the streets of Jerusalem, each with staff in hand for very age" (8:4). This is a picture of the security within the city; that even the "old-old" would be safe there. Another evidence of that security would be a fact was that "the streets of the city shall be full of boys and girls playing in its streets" (v. 5).

There are only two or three specific references to age and aging in the *New Testament*. Luke said that both Zechariah and Elizabeth "were advanced in years" (Luke 1:7). Zechariah, in response to the angel's announcement that Elizabeth his wife was to bear him a son, said, "How shall I know this? For I am an old man, and my wife is advanced in years" (v. 18).

How grateful we should be for the Synoptic Gospels. Although, in the main, they record the same teachings of and incidents in the life of Jesus, each one gives some special insights from time to time. Luke, the doctor, gave us more about the birth and the early days of Jesus than any of the others. He alone told us about the presentation of the baby Jesus in the Temple. Simeon took him in his arms and blessed God that he had lived to see the Lord's Christ. We do not know the age of Simeon, but we assume he was rather old.

There is no question about the "prophetess, Anna" who was "of a great age, having lived with her husband seven years from her virginity, and as a widow till she was eighty-four. . . . Coming up at that very hour [when Simeon was speaking to Mary about Jesus] she gave thanks to God, and spoke of him to all who were looking for the redemption of Jerusalem" (Luke 2:36-38).

Jesus and Paul, except in the Pastoral Epistles, said little about age and aging. One possible reason for this lack of emphasis was the fact that in Judaism age was highly respected and hence there was little need to call attention to the aged. Also, they

> recognized human rights and responsibilities to be universally the gifts of God's love, and both saw good and evil in terms of inner qualities, not in terms of outward distinctives. . . . Had "agism" been a problem comparable to "racism" or "sexism," they probably would have addressed this problem more directly and emphatically.[8]

Paul did have quite a bit to say concerning older people in the Pastoral Epistles. For example, Paul wrote to Timothy, "Do not rebuke an older man but exhort him as you would a father . . . older women like mothers" (1 Tim. 5:1-2). Paul also gave some special instruction to Titus concerning older men and women, as well as younger men (Titus 2:2-6).

"Elders"

The term *elder* is quite prevalent in the Scriptures. It is found in approximately half of the books of both Testaments, beginning with Genesis (50:7) and closing with Revelation (19:4). In this section quotation marks are used with the word *"elder"* because it is difficult at times to determine whether it is used to refer primarily to age or to a position.[9] A rather casual examination of the biblical material will reveal that the word translated "old" or "elder" went through a developmental process. The term evidently first referred to the matter of age. For example, Genesis 18:11 says, "Now Abraham and Sarah were old, advanced in age" (see 24:1; 25:8). Likewise, Isaac, when he died, was "old and full of days" (Gen. 35:29). Joseph inquired of his brothers, "Is your father well, the old man of whom you spoke? Is he still alive?" (Gen. 43:27). The brothers also referred to Jacob as an old man (Gen. 44:20).[10]

In addition to the preceding, there are places where the contrast with the young clearly proves that the reference is to the old and not someone who holds an official position. For example, Moses said to Pharaoh, "We will go with our young and our old" (Ex. 10:9). Another rather striking example is the following:

> The glory of young men is their strength,
> but the beauty of old men is their gray hair
> (Prov. 20:29).

Isaiah referred to captives, "both the young and the old" (Isa. 20:4). Jeremiah spoke of the wrath of the Lord that will be poured out

> " . . . upon the children in the street,
> . . . .
> the old folk and the very aged" (Jer. 6:11).[11]

Stagg concludes that "seemingly, the role of 'elder' arose within the family and was extended to towns and the nation, as senior adults were turned to for administering family, civil, and religious justice and as they were called upon to serve in other capacities where age should be an advantage."[12] He further says, "The biblical term 'elder' . . . reflects a proper inclination to respect age as a likely source of wisdom" but adds a very wise precaution: "To equate age with wisdom or competence is another form of agism."[13] Nevertheless, the very fact that the same word was used for "old" and "elder" at least implies great respect for older or aged people.

A complete picture of the "elders" would necessitate an examination of biblical references where "elder" clearly refers to a government official of some type. Space will not permit a full discussion. There are frequent references to "elders of Israel" in the Pentateuch (see Ex. 12:21; Lev. 9:1; Num. 11:16,24-25,30; 16:25); in the historical books (Josh. 8:10*b*; 20:1-9; 24:31; Judg. 2:7-10; Ruth 4:2-11; 1 Sam. 8:4-5; Ezra 5:5,9; 6:7-14; 10:8-14); and in the writings of the prophets, particularly in Ezekiel (7:26; 8:11-13; 14:1-5; 20:1-4).

The preceding correctly implies that the term *elder* came to refer primarily to a member of an official group or ruling class with a lessening emphasis on age as such. It does seem, however, that "elders" were originally older persons. Stagg concludes that "older men were given prominent and powerful positions in the government of both Jewish and early Christian people. . . . Early Christians seem to have followed the Jewish pattern in coming to 'the elders' for wisdom and justice at the decision-making level."[14] It was natural and more or less inevitable that the early church would be patterned somewhat after Judaism, particularly in its organizational structure. The "elders" filled an important place in the leadership of the early church. The first specific reference to elders of the church is in Acts 11:30 when relief was sent "to the elders by the hand of Barnabas and Saul" for the needy in Jerusalem. Paul and Barnabas, on their first missionary journey, "appointed ["helped them select," Williams] elders . . . in every church" (Acts 14:23). Robertson says, "It is fairly certain that these elders were chosen to correspond in a general way with the elders in the Jewish synagogue after which the local church was largely copied as to organization and worship" (W.P.).

At least we know that the "elder" was a well-recognized official in New Testament churches (see Acts 11:30; 14:23; 15:4,6,22-23; 20:17; 21:18). In addition to the Book of Acts, there are a few references to "elders" in the New Testament Epistles (1 Tim. 4:14; 5:17,19; Jas. 5:14; 1 Pet. 5:1) and approximately a dozen references in Revelation (4:4,10; 5:5-6,8,11,14; 7:11,13; 11:16; 14:3; 19:4). Some verses in 1 Peter (5:1-5) are particularly interesting. He referred to himself as "a fellow elder" (see 2 John 1 and 3 John 1), set forth some duties for elders, and then added, "Likewise you that are younger" which plainly suggests that the "elders" were older adults. This may not have been universally true, but it seems to have been the usual practice.

The preceding and the additional fact that the same Hebrew word in the Old Testament is used when it clearly means "old" or on the other hand "elder" justifies and really necessitates this discussion of "elders." Our consideration of "The Bible and Older Adults" would have been incomplete without it.

Their Qualities

Why is the same word used in the Hebrew for "old" and for those who were designated as "elders"? What are some of the qualities or character traits that are usually associated with older adults that help to answer the preceding question?

There is no quality more frequently associated in the Bible with the aging process than *understanding and wisdom.*

> Wisdom is with the aged,
> and understanding in length of days (Job 12:12).

"Aging should favor one in both wisdom and spirit, but whether it does so or not depends upon the basic direction of life. If one is going the wrong way, the passing years simply worsen the condition."[15]

However, the direction of one's life may change. Stagg cites some biblical examples in other places in his book where this did happen. The change of direction may be for good, such as Jacob, the deceiver, the trickster, the supplanter, who became a "prince of God"; or the change can be bad, such as was true of Saul and Solomon. In the case of the latter, he showed more wisdom in his early years than in his later years. It is generally, but not universally true that we, in our later years, are usually an extension of what we were earlier. For example, that gruff old man or that sweet old lady, in most cases, had something of the same dispositions and spirits in their earlier years. In other words, the early years of life will usually, but not always, predict rather accurately the direction and quality of life in the later years.

The preceding means, among other things, that wisdom and other qualities usually associated with "older adults" are not automatic with the aging process. They cannot be assumed simply because of age. For example, the Book of Proverbs, which has more to say concerning wisdom than any book in the Bible, "sees age central which should serve wisdom, but such does not naturally, automatically, or invariably follow."[16]

Really, the Bible clearly reveals that God is the source of wisdom. Job, in the verse immediately following the one quoted previously (Job 12:12), said:

> With God are wisdom and might;
> he has counsel and understanding (12:13).

Job also said, "With him is strength and wisdom" (12:16). Nevertheless, God can and sometimes does take "away the discernment of the elders" (12:20). It was Elihu, the youngest of Job's four friends, who had waited for the older men to speak, who concluded:

> It is not the old that are wise,
> nor the aged that understand what is right
> (32:9).

He possibly should have inserted the word *necessarily* or *exclusively*: "It is not necessarily the old. . . . " Whether an old or a young person is really wise will be determined primarily by his relationship to God, the final and real source of wisdom. The psalmist said:

> Thy commandment makes me wiser than my enemies,
>
> . . . .
>
> Through thy precepts I get understanding
>
> (119:98,104).

Another quality that should characterize older people and should qualify them, to varying degrees, for leadership in church and community is *maturity*. That should be true, but it is not always the case. It is possible for one to mature in years without maturing morally and spiritually. Paul and the writer of Hebrews struggled with the immaturity of Christians to whom they sought to minister. Paul's word to the Corinthians was: "But I, brethren, could not address you as spiritual men, but as men of the flesh, as babes in Christ. I fed you with milk, not solid food; for you were not ready for it; and even yet you are not ready" (1 Cor. 3:1-2). But at least Paul thought of spiritual maturity as belonging to adults. There is a sense in which we all continue to be "babes," but we are "babes in Christ." The fact that we are "in Christ" should assure some growth and maturity. The more vital our relation to Christ, the more will be our growth and maturity in and for him.

That may sound paradoxical, but our Christian faith is full of paradoxes. For example, the more mature we become as children of God, we seem to become more conscious of our immaturity. Paul, writing to the Philippians from a Roman prison, said: "Not that I have already obtained this or am already perfect; but I press on to make it my own, because Christ Jesus has made me his own. . . . I press on toward the goal for the prize of the upward call of God in Christ Jesus." Then note what he said, "Let those of us who are mature be thus minded" (Phil. 3:12-15). If Paul would say that he had not yet reached the goal of his life in Christ, how much more is that true of you and me? Can we say with him, "I press on toward the goal for the prize of the upward call of God in Christ Jesus" (v. 14)? God's call for young and old is always an "upward call"—"come up higher, reach for full maturity in Christ."

Quite similar to Paul's statement to the Corinthians, the writer of the Book of Hebrews said:

> For though by this time you ought to be teachers, you need some one to teach you again the first principles of God's word. You need milk, not solid food; for every one who lives on milk is unskilled in the word of righteousness, for he is a child. But solid food is for the mature, for those who have their faculties trained by practice to distinguish good from evil (5:12-14).

These verses are followed with an exhortation that is appropriate, to varying degrees, to all of us: "Therefore let us leave the elementary doctrine of Christ and go on to maturity" (Heb. 6:1).

If we are rightly related to Christ, maturity, at least to some degree, will be inevitable. Naturally, there will be different degrees of maturity, depending largely on the vitality of our relationship to him. "Age should be on the side of maturity" but there is no necessary correlation between age and emotional, moral, and spiritual maturity.

Memory is another characteristic of older adults. It may be a blessing or a curse. It will be a curse if we live in and unjustifiably glorify the past. It can also be a curse if we brood too much over the mistakes and sins of the past. We need to ask God to forgive and to accept fully his forgiveness. Memory can be a blessing to all of us, but particularly to those of us who are older adults. This will definitely be true if we let past experiences with the Lord inform the present for us and let us help others be alert to the movement of God in their lives and in the church and world.

There is still another characteristic of the older people in the Bible that may have considerable significance for us today. Many of them carried on *active, productive lives* long after they would have been retired in our youth- and efficiency-oriented age. This was true of Abraham, Isaac, Jacob, Joshua, Caleb, Samuel, and many others.

The preceding was also true of Zechariah, father of John the Baptist. He was an old man, advanced in years but "he was serving as priest before God when his division was on duty" (Luke 1:8). Sad to say, many churches consider a man too old to consider as pastor if he is fifty or more. There are entirely too many older adults in our churches who are put on the shelf prematurely. Many of them are still vigorous and have more time than they have ever had to give to their Lord and their church. Also, many of them have the spiritual maturity to minister effectively to the deeper needs of people. They represent in many churches the greatest untapped resource for effective leadership and ministry.

The prophet Joel said, quoted by Peter on the day of Pentecost, that there would come a time when God would pour out his "Spirit on all flesh." As a result, young men would see visions and old men would dream dreams (Joel 2:28; Acts 2:17). In other words, old men and women who are in tune with the Spirit of God can still dream dreams. They should not and do not have to live in the past. They can look forward to the future filled with the presence and blessing of the Father.

Possibly a few additional statements should be made concerning the *danger of* generalizing or *stereotyping*. One should avoid generalizations concerning any age group. For example, the only thing that can be said about older adults that will be universally correct is that they are old. Wisdom may more frequently characterize older people. After all, the experiences of the years should make one wiser, to some degree. But all old people are not wise.

In the Bible, a wise and mature Abraham is balanced by a wise Joseph when he was still a young man. At least we know that Joseph was a young man of thirty "when he entered the service of Pharaoh king of Egypt" (Gen. 41:46). When he was called before Pharaoh to interpret the latter's dream, he was wise enough to say that he did not have the wisdom that was needed but that the interpretation belonged to God (Gen. 41:16,25). Strikingly similar, young Daniel, when called before the king to interpret the latter's dream, attributed his interpretation to God (Dan. 2:25-30,45). God is the true source of wisdom, whether found among young or old.

There is no one character trait or quality that is exclusively the possession of any age group. Stagg, using Old Testament terminology, makes the following excellent statement: "Young or old can march under the sign of 'Exodus,' moving over from bondage to the promised land. Young or old can remain bogged down in Egypt, unequal to the Exodus."[17]

Attitudes Toward Them

Attitudes toward and treatment of older adults, as is true of children and other age groups, depend a great deal on the prevailing values of the culture or society. For example, being old in a youth-oriented culture will tend to mean a rather low status for older people. The same will be true in a culture that magnifies productivity. "By contrast, in a society whose members exalt wisdom and believe that wisdom comes with age and experience, growing old can mean increasing status and prestige."[18] The latter, as already indicated, was the prevailing attitude in biblical days and, incidentally, still prevails in some areas of the world, particularly among the less industrialized peoples.

Another factor that helps to determine the attitude toward and particularly the treatment of older adults is the type of prevailing family life. For example, in biblical days, particularly in the Old Testament, the prevailing family pattern was patriarchal and the extended family. It was not unusual for a family to be so inclusive that it might properly be considered a clan. In the extended family, the older members were an integral part of the family. Being a patriarchal family the oldest male continued, with possibly rare exceptions, to be head of the family or clan.

But today the predominant pattern is the nuclear family. Such a family is composed of father, mother, and children until the latter mature. And increasingly, the mother, as well as the father, works outside the home, particularly after the children reach school age. In such a home, it is predominantly true that older members of the family, such as a needy or an incapacitated grandfather or grandmother, are not cared for in their children's home. They are, from the perspective of the well-being of older grandparents, too readily placed in a nursing home or in some other way cared for outside the homes of their children. Care of the aged is no longer considered by many children and mature adults in general to be the responsibility of the nuclear family.

Still another factor in the *changing attitudes* toward the aging members of the family has been a shift, in the USA and in Western civilization in general, from a rural- to an urban-oriented way of life. Crowded living conditions are conducive to the nuclear family. Also, in the urban areas, nursing homes and other ways of providing for aging and no longer productive parents are more readily available.

Regardless of the reason for the reduced attention to and respect for the older members of the family, some of us believe that this is unfortunate not only for the older adults but also for the family itself. Older grandparents and even aunts and uncles can make a distinct contribution to the family and particularly to the growing children. How much of a blessing a three- or four-generation family will be is determined not only by the adaptability and spirit of the older adult but also by the attitude toward and treatment of the elderly by the other members of the family.

In families of biblical days and in earlier days of our culture, birth and death were family experiences. It may be that we do not want to and possibly cannot move back to the experiences of a more primitive day. But it is also possible, with the predominance of the nuclear urban family which has largely moved us away from the three-generation family of a generation or two ago, that we have lost something that was very meaningful to families in the past. In the contemporary culture, both birth and death and even the aging process itself tend to be very impersonal. Most members of the family tend to be detached from the deeper and most meaningful experiences of life.

The Bible clearly advocated *respect for older people.* The first explicit command is in the great nineteenth chapter of Leviticus, "You shall rise up before the hoary head ["grayheaded," NASB], and honor the face of an old man ["give honour to the aged," NEB], and you shall fear your God: I am the Lord" (Lev. 19:32). The custom of standing in the presence of the aged may have been a cultural matter, but the respect that the standing implied was not and is not supposed to be cultural. Respect for aging is a divine command. The wise man stated this great truth negatively when he said, "Do not despise your mother when she is old" (Prov. 23:22).

In the Book of Job, there is evident a basic respect for age. Elihu, the youngest of Job's friends, waited until the older ones and Job had spoken (Job 32:4). "It is proper for youth to hear their elders, and it is proper for the present to hear the past."[19] Respect for or deference to age does not necessarily imply agreement with what one's elders say or even the life they live.

Respect for age, so prevalent in the Bible, is frequently associated with the relation of children to parents. This emphasis is particularly frequent in Proverbs and will be considered in the later chapter on "Parents and Children." There is at least one verse that refers in general to older people:

> A hoary head is a crown of glory;
> it is gained in a righteous life (Prov. 16:31).

This statement is like many others in the Wisdom Literature; it is generally but not always true. However, the exceptions do not nullify the general rule.

One sign of the decadence of any civilization is disrespect and mistreatment of older people. In painting a dark picture of the conditions that would be in Israel, the prophet Isaiah said, "the youth will be insolent to the elder" (3:5). But in another place Isaiah quoted God as saying something that should give older men and women assurance:

> Even to your old age I am He [He is the unchanging I am],
> and to gray hairs I will carry you (46:4).

While respect for older men and women is commanded or at least suggested, there is some evidence on the surface of a decreasing value given to older people (Lev. 27:1-8). These verses, however, apply to the redemption price for a vow and seemed to be humanitarian in motivation. The value evidently was based on their assumed productivity. There was some difference not only on the basis of age but also sex. The value "of a male from twenty years old up to sixty years old shall be fifty shekels of silver," a female of the same age, thirty shekels. Then a specific value is placed on a male and female five to twenty years of age, a month old to five years. "If the person is sixty years and upward, then your valuation for a male shall be fifteen shekels, and for a female ten shekels." That was the lowest valuation of any age group except the youngest. If one was so poor that he could not pay the valuation, then the priest made the decision "according to the ability of him who vowed" (Lev. 27:2-8). That sounds somewhat like our contemporary way of evaluation of older people, but it should be remembered that it was for the redemption of a vow or pledge.

Let us close this section on attitudes toward older people with the beautiful and gripping story of the concern and care of Joseph for his dying father. Read the helpful and inspiring story in Genesis 43—50. Let us simply point out some of the most striking and revealing statements or incidents. Before he revealed his identity to his brothers, Joseph "inquired about their welfare, and said, 'Is your father well, the old man of whom you spoke? Is he still alive?'" (Gen. 43:27). On a subsequent visit from his brothers, his first word after revealing his identity was, "Is my father still alive?" (45:3). He also told his brothers, "Make haste and bring my father down here" (45:13; also see 45:23-28; 46:4).

Sometime after Jacob and his other sons and their families had settled in Egypt, word came to Joseph that his aged father was ill. He took his two sons, Manasseh and Ephraim, and went to see Jacob. When Jacob was informed, "'Your son Joseph has come to you'; then Israel summoned his strength, and sat up in bed" (48:2). It does not give the age of Jacob or Israel but his eyes "were dim with age, so that he could not see" (48:10); which reminds us of Jacob's father Isaac, who, when he blessed Jacob and Esau "was old and his eyes were dim so that he could not see" (Gen. 27:1).

After blessing the sons of Joseph, pronouncing the greater blessing on the younger as his father had done for him, Jacob said to Joseph, "Behold, I am about to die, but God will be with you, and will bring you again to the land of your fathers" (48:21). Then he called together all his sons and "blessed them, blessing each with the blessing suitable to him" (49:28). Jacob gave them instructions concerning his burial. Evidently in the presence of the family, "he drew up his feet into the bed, and breathed his last, and was gathered to his people" (49:33).

"Then Joseph fell on his father's face, and wept over him, and kissed him" (50:1). Joseph and his brothers, with a "very great company," including "the elders of the land of Egypt" (50:7-9) followed Jacob's request and took him back to bury him with his "fathers."

While this rather long report of Joseph and Jacob may not be typical, it does underscore the fact that in the biblical days there was evidently on the part of some if not most children a sense of responsibility to *care for aging parents* who were in need.

The same perspective is evident in the New Testament. It is true that Jesus and Paul did not have much to say about the treatment of older people. The possible reason for the lack of such an emphasis was that it was not needed much in their day. The Jews in general had great respect for the elderly.

Jesus did on one occasion strongly reprimand the Pharisees for avoiding caring for father or mother by saying that what they had was "'Corban' (that is, given to God) . . . thus making void the word of God through your tradition" (Mark 7:9-13). The word or commandment of God to which he referred was "Honor your father and your mother" (Ex. 20:12).

The Pauline Epistles give some attention to the elderly. Among other things, Paul instructed Timothy not to rebuke "an older man but exhort him as you would a father" and to treat "older women like mothers" (1 Tim. 5:1-2). He also suggested that "if a widow has children or grandchildren, let them first learn their religious duty to their own family and make some return to their parents; for this is acceptable in the sight of God" (1 Tim. 5:4). Paul followed this with, "If any one does not provide for his relatives, and especially for his own family, he has disowned the faith and is worse than an unbeliever" (1 Tim. 5:8). The reference evidently in this verse was to widowed mothers or grandmothers, since verse 9 specifically refers to widows, as was true of verses 3-4.

An Example

The Bible teaches some of its greatest truths or lessons by the lives recorded on its pages. We could cite a number of cases or examples of older adults, whose lives could teach us some important lessons. This would be true of Moses, Joshua, Eli, Samuel, David, and others in the Old Testament. Then we could also mention Paul and John who were busy communicating with some of their friends and Christian brothers when they were at the age that many men and women retire in the contemporary period.

Let us concentrate, however, on the life of *Caleb*. He is not as well known as many other biblical characters but his life has a special message for older adults. He was one of the twelve sent out by Moses to spy out the Promised Land. In contrast to the other ten who advised against going up to possess the land, Caleb and Joshua measured the giants against the strength of the Lord and advised the people to go up and possess the land. In other words, ten of the spies saw great giants and a little God. Caleb and Joshua saw a great God and little giants. The people refused to follow the advice of Joshua and Caleb. You remember what happened. The people of Israel wandered for forty years, a year for each day the spies were in the Promised Land. During that time, all the men over twenty years of age died (Num. 14:22-24).

After they had entered the Promised Land, Caleb, then eighty-five years of age, presented his case to Joshua (Josh. 14:6-12). An examination of the life of Caleb will reveal several great truths that are particularly applicable to older adults.

First, we see *no* evidence of *jealousy* on the part of Caleb. Joshua was Moses' right-hand man. Joshua succeeded Moses. During the conquest of the land, evidently Caleb served under Joshua, who later divided the land. Caleb could have said, as many would have, "I went with Joshua as one of the spies. I gave the same report he gave. I was just as courageous as he was. Why do I always fill a secondary place?"

One of the most difficult adjustments for many older adults is their decreasing significance as leaders in business, community, and even in their churches. It is difficult for all and seems almost impossible for some not to be jealous of younger people who are taking over leadership positions and roles that they formerly filled. One of the surest indications of maturity in general and spiritual maturity in particular is one's ability to adjust to the inevitabilities of life. Certainly the aging process and the decreasing place of leadership are two of those inevitabilities.

Another great truth we see in Caleb's life is the fact that, at eighty-five, *his life* was *an extension of what he was* at forty. He did not suddenly become the courageous old man who said, "Give me the hill country where the giants are." Someone has said of Caleb, "Forty-five years was a long time for faith to live on a promise." But his faith had doubtlessly been strengthened through those years as he had observed God at work in and for his people.

What is our attitude now toward the aging process, with the ultimate decline in health and the aches and pains that will come to most of us as we mature? Our attitude now will largely determine what our attitude will be when we come to the years of retirement and declining health.

There is another lesson to be learned from the life of Caleb. It may be of particular importance for our churches. *Caleb's request* was not for one of the rich valleys. He might have said to Joshua, "I was with you as a spy, I have supported you through all these years. Now, I am an old man. I think I deserve the best." No, his request was for the "hill country" or the mountains (14:12). Also, the *Anakim* or the giants, the sons of Anah, lived there. What a request from an old man! And don't forget, he knew what he was asking for.

Many older adults have many more productive years to give church and community. They may not be able to say, as Caleb did, "I am this day eighty-five years old. I am still as strong to this day as I was in the day that Moses sent me" to spy out the land (Josh. 14:10-11). Whether they can say that or not, they should not prematurely retire from all activities in community and church.

Caleb was not ready to be laid on the shelf. He did not live in the past but in the future. Many older people are incapacitated by ill health and are unable to participate actively in the life and work of church and community. But there are many "Calebs" in our churches, still strong and vigorous and frequently with more time for the work of the church and the Lord than they have ever had. Entirely too frequently these "Calebs" are pushed aside. One of the most untapped resources for effective ministry in many churches are the older adults. Our churches can maintain a good ministry for older adults, such as friendship clubs, Bible study, arts, and crafts. Many churches now have these. But even more important, our churches should seek to utilize the energy and time of older adults to minister in and through the church to many in every community who need that ministry.

Do you feel that we should be grateful for Caleb and the fact that our Bible gives us some striking insights into his life? He was not a Moses or even a Joshua, but Caleb was closer akin to most of us than either of them or many others of God's better-known men and women. Thank you, Lord, for Caleb!

Their Crises

It will help all of us if we recognize that *crises* of some type and some degree of seriousness *are the common lot of all* people: no matter what age, race, or sex. When problems or crises come, we "have joined the human family." The crises may vary in nature and seriousness, but they come. How we react to them often will determine what God can do for us and for others through the crises. Remember that one of the best tests of our moral and spiritual maturity is what we let the inevitabilities of life do to us. It will help, whatever the nature of our problem or crisis, for us to remind ourselves of what Paul said, "I know how to be abased, and I know how to abound" (Phil. 4:12). Particularly helpful for many of us would be his word to the Philippians: "My God will supply every need of yours according to his riches in glory in Christ Jesus" (Phil. 4:19).

Some of the problems that plague many contemporary older adults were *unknown in biblical days*. For example, there was no such thing as retirement at sixty-five, seventy, or any other age. Also, in the rural, more or less nomadic, extended family, there was not the neglect of older members of the family which happens entirely too frequently in the contemporary world.

There are, however, some problems or crises among contemporary older adults that were prevalent to some degree in biblical days. Just the fact that the problems existed back then may be a source of some encouragement to older people now.

One such problem, which may create an acute crisis for some older adults, is *disappointment in their children.* This disappointment is not unique to the present day. Some of the great characters of the Bible had similar disappointments. Adam and Eve had a son (Cain) who killed his brother (Abel). The sons of Eli and Samuel did not follow in the footsteps of their fathers. "The sons of Eli were worthless men; they had no regard for the Lord" (1 Sam. 2:12). Eli remonstrated with them, "But they would not listen to the voice of their father" (1 Sam. 2:25). The elders of Israel said to Samuel, "Behold, you are old and your sons do not walk in your ways; now appoint for us a king to govern us like all the nations" (1 Sam. 8:5; see v. 3).

Then think of the tragedies that came to David because of his family. One of his sons (Amnon) raped Tamar, his half sister (2 Sam. 13:1-14). Another of David's sons (Absalom, the brother of Tamar) had Amnon killed (2 Sam. 13:23-29). Also, Absalom sought to take the kingdom away from his father (2 Samuel 15—18). David himself said, "Behold, my own son seeks my life" (2 Sam. 16:11). In spite of his instructions to the commander, "Deal gently . . . with the young man Absalom" (2 Sam. 18:5), the latter was killed. When David got the news, he wept. The Bible records his pathetic cry, "O my son Absalom, my son, my son Absalom! Would that I had died instead of you, O Absalom, my son, my son!" (2 Sam. 18:33). Whatever problems older adults may have regarding their children, few if any of them have had anything as serious as David.

Another problem that may create a real crisis for some older people is *declining health and vitality.* This may be personal or it may be declining health of a loved one, particularly a husband or a wife. It may be acute or chronic. It may involve decreasing sensitivity of one or more of the senses, particularly a progressive loss of hearing, sight,[20] and memory. There may even be times when we will feel like repeating the words of the psalmist:

> Do not cast me off in the time of old age;
>   forsake me not when my strength is spent
>   (71:9).

There may also arise a rather acute crisis because of personal or family emotional problems. One thing that will help all of us retain our health and vigor, mentally as well as physically, is to keep active. At least, we should remember that "rust sets in when movement stops."

Most of the help from the Bible concerning health will be indirect instead of direct. From our days as children and youth, we should remember that our body is "a temple of the Holy Spirit" (1 Cor. 6:19). It should be presented to the Lord as "a living sacrifice, holy and acceptable to God" (Rom. 12:1). These verses should be enough to convince us that we should avoid health-destroying habits, such as drinking, drugs, smoking, and overeating. Also, we should cultivate good health habits which may determine, to a considerable degree, our length of days and the vitality of those days. Those good health habits include eating sensibly, resting sufficiently, exercising appropriately, and working relaxed. Such habits are of increasing importance as one gets older. While older adults should take necessary medication prescribed by their doctors, they should resist the temptation to become hypochondriacs, "pilloholics," or individuals who constantly talk about their ailments.

Death of a loved one or contemplation of one's own death may create a serious crisis for some older adults, even for some who have been active Christians for years. All of us, particularly older adults, should prepare intellectually, emotionally, and spiritually for death. The better prepared, the less chance for a serious crisis when death approaches or comes. Really, the acceptance of death tends to transform death.

We all know, at least theoretically, that Christians should not fear death. There may be and generally are some lingering uncertainty and anxiety. For too many "death remains a fearful and cruel monster."[21] Paul said, "The last enemy to be destroyed is death" (1 Cor. 15:26). But the same Paul, in the same chapter, asked a couple of questions and gave a triumphant answer to his questions (vv. 55-56). The psalmist said:

> Even though I walk through the valley of the
>   shadow of death,
>   I fear no evil;
> For thou art with me;
>   thy rod and thy staff,
>   they comfort me (23:4).

While the reference here is not directly to death, it can and should be comforting to us. Possibly a more accurate translation of verse 4 would be, "Even though I walk through a valley as dark as death" (NEB).

Isaiah said, "He will swallow up death for ever, and the Lord God will wipe away tears" (25:8; see Rev. 7:17; 21:4).

There can be no question about the meaning of the statement of Jesus to the mourning Martha, "Whoever lives and believes in me shall never die" (John 11:26). Paul Tournier, world-renowned psychiatrist, concludes his book on growing old with this statement: "My home is in heaven, and the more I have advanced in age, the more has earthly life seemed to me like an apprenticeship in the love and knowledge of God."[22]

Elizabeth Kübler-Ross, from her work with dying patients, concluded that intensely religious people accept death more easily than others. This is true, however, only "if they are authentic and have internalized their faith." It is not so much what one believes theoretically but how deeply and genuinely he believes.[23]

Thus, the fuller and more meaningful life is for a child of God in the here-and-now, the calmer he will be able to accept death and to look forward to a meaningful life after death.

There may come a time when we will welcome death as a friend for ourselves, a friend, or a loved one. "I could no longer pray for her to live" was the word of a husband about a wife who had suffered terribly with cancer for weeks. The same can be true in severe cases of arthritis, a disease which plagues many people, particularly older people. It may be wise for all of us to remember that death is like a swinging door. Such a door provides a way in, as well as a way out. We may not know much about what awaits us on the other side, but we do know Who waits for us. He will be there and if he is there, that will be enough. We can rest in and on that assurance. Furthermore, we should remember what Paul Tournier said, "I am not alone as I face death. I am with Jesus who faced it himself."[24] The apostle Paul said, "Christ will be honored in my body, whether by life or death. For me to live is Christ, and to die is gain" (Phil. 1:20-21). Both options were attractive, and Paul was willing to accept either at the proper time.

In the last book of the Bible, we read that when the new heaven and the new earth arrive the sea will be no more (Rev. 21:1); seas separate. Also, God "will wipe away every tear from their eyes" (v. 4). The occasion for tears, death, and pain will be no more. A. T. Robertson suggests that this symbolism, as is true generally in Revelation, should not be pressed too literally, "but a stern and glorious reality exists behind it all." (W.P.)

There are other conditions or occasions that create crises for some older adults. Some cause crises in those of other age groups. However, the crises are usually more serious for older persons.

Among the things that frequently contribute to potential crisis situations are the following: loneliness; feeling neglected; disappointment in achievements; sense of guilt for past mistakes and present level of living; dissatisfaction with ability to contribute significantly to church and work of the Lord; disapproval of church's priorities—longing for "the good old days"; doubts concerning prayer, the promises of God, and the vitality of their relation to the Lord; a feeling of isolation from God—uncertainties about his concern and care for them.

Whatever may be the problem, imaginary or real, the great promises in the Bible can be sources of reassuring grace and strength. As we mature in the Lord, we will discover that there are many words in his Word, particularly the matchless promises, that will give us the peace that passes understanding in the midst of the storms of life.

Some favorite promises are: "Underneath are the everlasting arms" (Deut. 33:27); several in the Psalms (23; 37:7; 55:22; 74:16-17); "Fear not, for I am with you" (Isa. 41:10); and Micah 7:8:

> When I fall, I shall rise;
> When I sit in darkness,
> the Lord will be a light to me.

A few of many favorites in the New Testament are the following: "Come to me, all who labor and are heavy laden" (Matt. 11:28-30); "Peace I leave with you; my peace I give to you" (John 14:27); "We know that in everything God works for good" (Rom. 8:28); "My grace is sufficient for you" (2 Cor. 12:9); and "My God will supply every need of yours" (Phil. 4:19).

Whatever the burdens, the problems, the crises, all of us as children of God, whatever our age, should never forget that nothing shall or can "separate us from the love of Christ" (Rom. 8:35). All of us should rest in the words of the old hymn we used to sing:

> Be not dismay'd whate'er betide,
> God will take care of you.
> . . . .
> Thro' ev'ry day, o'er all the way;
> He will take care of you.

Also, how grateful we should be, young or old, that

> Just when I need him most;
> Jesus is near to comfort and cheer.

Notes

1. See Robert M. Gray and David O. Moberg, *The Church and the Older Person*, rev. ed. (Grand Rapids: Eerdmans, 1977), p. 17.

2. Charles S. Harris, research coordinator, *Fact Book on Aging: A Profile of America's Older Population* (Washington: The National Council on the Aging, Inc., 1978), p. 6.

3. Gray and Moberg, p. 16.

4. Segerberg Osborn, Jr., *The Immortality Factor* (New York: E.P. Dutton & Co., Inc., 1974), p. 128.

5. Seward Hiltner, ed., *Toward a Theology of Aging* (New York: Human Sciences Press, 1975), p. 154.

6. Frank Stagg, *The Bible Speaks on Aging* (Nashville: Broadman Press, 1981), p. 67. Throughout this chapter we will be heavily indebted to this book by Stagg. It is the only book discovered that deals in a systematic way with aging in the Bible.

7. Ibid., p. 89.

8. Ibid., p. 154.

9. It is interesting and may be somewhat significant that the same Hebrew word is the main one that is translated "old" and "elder."

10. For a few additional references where the word that is later used for the "elders of Israel" is translated "old," see Leviticus 19:32; Deuteronomy 28:50; Judges 19:16,17,20,22; 1 Samuel 2:31-32; Job 42:17; Proverbs 17:6; Joel 2:28.

11. For additional references where "young" and "old" are used together, see Jeremiah 31:31; Lamentations 2:21; Ezekiel 9:6.

12. Stagg, p. 24.

13. Ibid., p. 25.

14. Ibid., p. 135.

15. Ibid., p. 69.

16. Ibid., p. 86.

17. Ibid., p. 176.

18. Wilbur H. Watson and Robert J. Maxwell, eds., *Human Aging and Dying: A Study in Sociocultural Gerontology* (New York: St. Martin's Press, 1977), p. 12.

19. Stagg, p. 77.

20. For some older people who had lost or were in the process of losing their sight, see Genesis 27:1 (Isaac); Genesis 48:10 (Jacob); 1 Samuel 3:2 (Eli); 1 Kings 14:4 (Ahijah).

21. Paul Tournier, *Learn to Grow Old* (New York: Harper & Row, 1976), p. 222.

22. Ibid., p. 227.

23. Elizabeth Kübler-Ross, *Questions and Answers on Death and Dying* (New York: Macmillan, 1974), pp. 161-162.

24. Tournier, p. 239.

PART III
FAMILY RELATIONSHIPS

In recent years, some rather drastic changes have taken place in the family. This has been particularly true in the industrialized nations of the world, such as the United States and in Western Europe. These changes will not be examined in any detail in the chapters of part 3. Rather, the emphasis will be on what the Bible says regarding relationships in the family: Husbands and Wives, Sex and Sexual Relations, Divorce and Remarriage, and Parents and Children.

More attention will be given to the interpretation of pertinent Scriptures than has been true of previous chapters. You may want to review the section on "Its Interpretation" in chapter 1.

Approach the study of these chapters with a searching mind and a prayerful spirit. May our Heavenly Father through the Divine Spirit, who inspired the writers of the Scriptures, give the insight that all of us need. Only through his guidance will we be able to interpret correctly and to apply wisely and consistently what the Scriptures would say to us about some of the perplexing situations that many of us face personally, or with some member of our family, or as a counselor with others. May we seek to handle "rightly ["correctly," NIV] the word of truth" (2 Tim. 2:15).

7

Husbands and Wives

According to one saying, as the home goes, so goes everything else—including civilization itself. It can likewise be said, with rare exceptions, that as the husband and wife go, so will go the home: the relation of parents and children, children to one another, and all the members of the family to the church, the community, and the world.

The relationship of husband and wife was highly respected and honored in the Scriptures. One evidence of this was the use of their relation as a symbol of God's relation to his people. This is particularly prevalent in the Prophets which will be spelled out more in detail in a later section of this chapter.

In the New Testament, Jesus is compared to the bridegroom (Mark 2:19-20; John 3:29; see Matt. 25:1-13). Paul beautifully said of and to the Corinthians, "I betrothed you to Christ to present you as a pure bride to her one husband" (2 Cor. 11:2). The Revelation speaks of "the marriage of the Lamb" (Rev. 19:7). In the next to the last chapter of the Bible, John "saw the holy city, new Jerusalem, coming down out of heaven from God, prepared as a bride adorned for her husband" (Rev. 21:2). Then he spoke of "the Bride, the wife of the Lamb" (Rev. 21:9).

This should be enough to underscore the importance and sacredness of the relation of husbands and wives. Incidentally, some of their relationships have been touched on previously. Also, some will be discussed in subsequent chapters.

Choice of Companion

The choice of one's life companion is comparable in importance to the decision concerning one's life work. The only decision of greater importance is the one regarding our relation to Christ, "What shall I do with Jesus who is called Christ?" (Matt. 27:22).

The Bible gives some direct and more indirect help concerning the choice of a husband or a wife. In Old Testament days, as was true in the ancient world in general and still is in some parts of the world, young men and women had little voice in the decision. Marriages were arranged by the families involved and particularly by the father of the young man.

We know, however, that in some cases considerable care was exercised in the choice of a wife. One outstanding example in the Old Testament, the choice of a wife for *Isaac,* will have to suffice. This whole story (Gen. 24) may sound strange in some of the customs revealed, but it is a beautiful story with some abidingly relevant insights. The steward, who was trusted by Abraham with the task of finding a wife for Isaac, asked the Lord to give him a sign (v. 14). Contemporary Christian young people may not ask the Lord for a sign, but it is a decision they should pray about. Furthermore, parents should make it a matter of prayer, although wisely they cannot and should not have a major voice in the decision.

The Record says that Rebekah "was very fair to look upon, a virgin, whom no man had known" (v. 16). What a blessing it would be if all Christian young people and even young people in general could enter marriage as virgins. And the young man should not only look for a bride who is a virgin; he should recognize that he has as much responsibility as she to keep himself for the "one and only."

Also, Rebekah was a helpful person. She not only gave the steward a drink but also volunteered to draw water for the camels (v. 19). What a venturesome soul! When faced with the decision whether she would leave her home and go to be the wife of a man she had never met, her answer was, "I will go" (v. 58). This was a leap of faith.

Entrance into any marriage involves an element of risk. The risk can be reduced to the minimum by seeking the guidance of the Lord. Rebekah doubtlessly responded as she did because she sensed that the whole matter was a phase of the Lord's will for her life. And imagine what the results might have been if she had not responded as she did!

There is relatively little in the New Testament that will help directly in the choice of a companion for life. However, two references in Paul's Epistles emphasize one particular thing that is quite important.

One of those references is in 1 Corinthians 7, where Paul discussed several matters regarding marriage and the family. He said that a widow "is free to marry to whom she wishes, only in the Lord" (1 Cor. 7:39). "Every marriage ought to be 'in the Lord'" (W.P.).

In his other epistle to the Corinthians, Paul said, "Do not be mismated with unbelievers" (2 Cor. 6:14). The "prohibition is enforced by five rapid argumentative questions, which show *how* incongruous such yoking would be" (Cam.B.): "What partnership . . .? What fellowship . . .? What accord . . .? What . . . in common . . .? What agreement . . .?" (vv. 14-16). This seems to have been a general exhortation but it would have included marriage. It is even possible that "the most obvious application of such a prohibition would be to intermarriage with the heathen, which was continually forbidden to the chosen people . . . and this is probably the thought here" (Exp.Gr.).

Special emphasis was given in the books of the Law and certain historical books, particularly in Ezra and Nehemiah, regarding the marriage of the children of Israel with surrounding peoples who worshiped other gods. Thus, both the Old Testament and Paul would counsel young people to marry one who worships the same God they worship.

In other words, if a Christian young person wants a Christian home, he or she should choose as a companion one who is a Christian. And since there are many who profess to be Christians who are only nominally so, it should be added that if a young man or woman wants a real Christian home, he or she should choose a real Christian as a companion for life. The more serious one is about his or her Christian faith, the more important is such a choice.

Ordinarily people would be wise to choose as a marriage partner one who belongs to the same denomination. If a person does "fall in love" with someone of another faith, the two should work through this matter before marriage. Unfortunately, in many divided homes, the children frequently grow up with no abiding commitment to any Christian faith. You may know, as I do, some outstanding exceptions to the preceding but they are exceptions and not the rule. Paul was wise for his day and our day when he said, only let it be "in the Lord" (1 Cor. 7:39) and "Be ye not unequally yoked together with unbelievers" (2 Cor. 6:14, KJV).

Contrasting Perspectives

In the Scriptures and in society in general, there are contrasting and frequently conflicting perspectives concerning the relation of husbands and wives. For example, there is a rather marked contrast between the predominant perspective in the Old Testament and in the New Testament. But there are also considerable contrasts *within* the *Old Testament* itself. This is certainly true of the ideal set forth in the first two chapters of Genesis and some subsequent trends recorded in the Old Testament. God's original and his continuing purpose for marriage was and is one man and one woman joined together as husband and wife for life. Polygamy, concubinage, and other subsequent developments represented departures from God's purpose for the home.

Also, in the days of the prophets, there was a pronounced contrast between their position in general on most moral issues, including relationships in the home, and the perspective and practices of the rulers and prominent members of society. It does not seem, however, as suggested in a previous chapter, that the masses of the people had departed from God's original plan for husbands and wives. At least, this was true regarding one man and one woman as husband and wife.

There are places in the Old Testament where there are relatively sharp contrasts within a particular book. This is most clearly evident in the Book of Proverbs. The contrast is restricted largely to the appraisal of a wife. There are some verses unfavorable to the wife, while others paint an entirely different picture. In a particularly graphic passage, the writer said:

> A continual dripping on a rainy day
>   and a contentious woman ["quarrelsome wife," NIV] are alike;

> to restrain her is to restrain the wind
> or to grasp oil in his right hand
>
> (27:15-16; see 19:13; 21:9,19).

In contrast:

> He who finds a wife finds a good thing,
> and obtains favor from the Lord (18:22).

Again, the wise man said:

> House and wealth are inherited from fathers,
> but a prudent wife is from the Lord (19:14).

Then there is that wonderful portrayal of a wife in Proverbs 31. A question is asked, "A good ["capable," NEB] wife who can find?" When found, "she is far more precious than jewels" (v. 10).

There are some contrasting perspectives in *the New Testament*. This was clearly true of Jesus and some of the Pharisees, regarding the interpretation of Deuteronomy 24:1-4—the law regarding divorce. Jesus typically went back of the law to the original intent of the Lawgiver.

There are evident, at least on the surface, some contrasting perspectives in Paul's Epistles. For example, he said that in Christ "there is neither Jew nor Greek, there is neither slave nor free, there is neither male nor female" (Gal. 3:28). They were and are all one in Christ Jesus. And yet in the Ephesian letter he counseled wives to be submissive to their husbands (Eph. 5:23-24) and slaves to be obedient to their masters (Eph. 6:5).

Elsewhere Paul said that Christian men and women were called to freedom—a radical ideal—but they were not to use that "freedom as an opportunity for the flesh, but through love be servants of one another" (Gal. 5:13). It seems that Paul was fearful that some of the new converts, particularly wives and slaves, would go too far too fast in exercising the new freedom they had in Christ. This explains his conservative application of the radical ideal.

The problem that Paul had of maintaining a proper balance between the Christian ideal and the very real situation in the society in which the Christians of his day lived is a problem faced in every age. This is particularly true of pastors and counselors as they seek to help those who are caught in the problems and tensions that are faced by Christians. The proper balancing of the ideal and the real is nowhere more important than in family relationships, particularly of husbands and wives. The ideal should always be preached and taught. When actual situations are faced, however, pastors and teachers and others may find it necessary to adjust to the situation but without losing the challenge of the ideal. This will continually create the tension that is necessary if there is to be movement toward the ideal. In other words, pastors and others must start where people are but never let them lose sight of the ideal. This means, among other things, that the concept of tension is abidingly relevant.

The real situation in regard to the relationship of a husband and wife stands under the judgment of the ideal. This is true of such varied areas as sexual relations, relation to relatives, discipline of children, handling of finances, social and recreational life, relation to the church and the cause of Christ, and many others.

Incidentally, contrasting perspectives concerning the relation of husbands and wives carry over into the contemporary period. This is not only true in society in general but also in Christian circles and even among interpreters of the Scriptures. An example of this is the present discussion and continuing controversy regarding the "Chain of Command" or "Hierarchy of Command" theory that is advocated by many preachers and some theologians. While the theory is grounded primarily on 1 Corinthians 11:3-10, sometimes it is supported by references to other Scriptures such as 1 Timothy 2:8-15. As suggested in the chapter on women, most who advocate the "chain of command" theory fail to give proper consideration to 1 Corinthians 11:11-12. Also, it was suggested that if one considers 1 Corinthians 11:3 in a literal sense and applies it fully to our day, why does he not accept as literal and as applicable to our day what Paul said concerning the dress and customs concerning women?

Paul Jewett, in an introductory "Abstract to the Argument," says that he rejects "a hierarchical model of the man/woman relationships in favor of a model of partnership. . . . man and woman are properly related when they accept each other as equals whose differences are mutually complementary in all spheres of life and human endeavour."[1] Jewett's book from time to time specifically argues against the hierarchical view of marriage or the "chain of command" as some prefer to label it.[2]

Nature and Roles

There are at least two great truths revealed in the first two chapters of Genesis concerning the nature of men and women, and hence of husbands and wives. These truths, examined previously, have major significance for the relation of husbands and wives in their roles in the home and in society in general.

One important insight is the fact that the first man and woman were *created in the image of God*. This has significance not only for family relationships but for human relations in general. It means that men and women, husbands and wives, stand in the presence of God as equals. This equality is deepened and made more meaningful when they are brought into union with Christ. In him there is neither male nor female (Gal. 3:28). The fact that they are created in the image of God and recreated as one in Christ means that all people, Christian or non-Christian, male or female, and those of all ages, classes, and races should be treated with respect. They are children of God by creation and potentially by recreation. This means that people should never be used or manipulated. They should be respected as a "thou" and never treated as an "it."

The first chapters of Genesis also reveal that the first man and woman were not only created in the image of God but they were also created *male and female*. They are alike in worth and dignity, but they are unlike in some very significant ways. They were created to supplement or complement one another. This means that by nature they were fitted to perform some unique functions and hence to play some distinctive roles. A single example is the fact that the woman alone can bear and nurse children. Also, "male and female are designed physically and emotionally to complement each other in establishing a new completeness in life."[3]

Some of the distinctiveness of men and women and the different roles they play are products of the culture. Parents, teachers, and others begin at an early age to emphasize masculine qualities in the life of boys and feminine qualities in girls. The distinctive qualities, however, of men and women are not entirely or even largely products of the culture. The most important distinctives, which make us male or female, were written into the nature of men and women by the Creator himself. God said, "It is not good that the man should be alone; I will make him a helper fit ["suitable," NASB] for him" (Gen. 2:18). Some of the problems more or less prevalent in many contemporary homes and in society may evolve from the fact that men and women have become too competitive with one another. The competitiveness stems, to some degree, from the fact that too many men and women consider the historic, distinctive roles of a woman and particularly of a wife and mother innately inferior to the role of the man or husband. Whether the preceding statement is correct or not, there are in process in the United States and in Western civilization some major changes in the family that deeply affect the roles of husbands and wives. Some of these changes are inevitable. For example, there is not the same need as formerly for the husband and father to protect the family. And while there is still some pressure on the husband and father to provide for the material needs of the family, that pressure is considerably less than formerly. Also, the wife and mother, and women in general, are not as dependent on men economically as formerly.

Largely as a result of the preceding, husbands and wives who formerly had more or less fixed and well-understood roles find themselves in the *contemporary period* with *fluid roles*. Also, the family as such is in the process of changing from the extended family to the nuclear family. Still another contemporary trend that affects both husbands and wives, but particularly the latter, is the tendency to have fewer children but to have them during a shorter span of time.

The preceding, along with a number of other factors, such as the women's liberation movement, have contributed to an increasing number of women, including many wives and mothers, finding much of their sense of fulfillment outside the home. They do this by becoming a part of the work force in factory, store, and shop or a profession such as medicine, law, social work, and so forth. Some who do not enter the business or professional world use their increased time and energy for self-development projects and/or church and community activities.

There is a question that is quite important for our study of the Bible and the family, which may also be quite significant for the well-being of the home. That question is: *Are the roles of husbands and wives as seen in the Scriptures God-ordained for all time*, or were they for a particular type of culture at a particular time in history? The answer to that question is not easy. It is possible that there may be some permanent as well as some passing aspects of the biblical perspective concerning the relationship of husband and wife and of the home in general.

There are two extremes that need to be guarded against. Some people tend to be too literalistic in interpreting the Scriptures. They accept at face value and would apply fully to the contemporary situation some of the most minute teachings of the Scriptures. This has been and is true in regard to some things Paul said concerning men and women. Such interpreters do not accept the possibility that some things, especially in Paul's Epistles but to some degree elsewhere in the Scriptures, were and are historically or culturally conditioned and cannot be applied fully to the present situation. If a writer (such as Paul who wrote most of his Epistles to particular churches in a particular situation facing particular problems) met the needs of the people to whom he wrote, he had to discuss some unique or distinctive problems of that day. This seems to have been true regarding some things Paul said concerning the dress of women. It is at least possible that the same could be said regarding some things Paul said concerning the conduct of women in the home and the church.

The other reaction in the contemporary period that is equally dangerous is to read back into the Scriptures contemporary problems or at least the prevailing perspective concerning those problems. In other words, there is a tendency by some to let the present situation be too prominent a factor in interpreting the teachings of the Bible. In no area is this tendency more prevalent than in the relationship of husbands and wives. Too frequently a speaker or a writer starts with a preconceived idea of what he or she thinks the Scriptures should teach and then reads back into the Scriptures his or her own ideas. This usually results in a one-sidedness or a misinterpretation of the Scriptures.

The preceding may be done in the name of hermeneutics, which is the art or science of correct interpretation. The proper use of the principles of interpretation or hermeneutics can be an invaluable servant but if misused those principles may become an intolerable master. There are few areas where there is more confusion and debate concerning and/or resistance to the teachings of the Bible than regarding the relationship of husbands and wives.

This confusion stems, at least to some degree, from a rather prevalent viewpoint that the traditional role of the woman as wife and mother is of secondary importance. Too many people have lost sight of the fact that God does not judge as people judge. This is just as true of the roles of men and women, husbands and wives, as it is of other functions or roles. It may be that from God's viewpoint, the role of wife and mother is superior to any other role for a woman and may be more important than the typical role of the man and husband. There is enough possibility that this is correct that we should never belittle this traditional female role. This is one great truth that some but not all leaders of the modern women's liberation movement need to learn.

Howell summarizes the relation of husbands and wives as follows, "In the one-flesh union of marriage, by analogy, the oneness which is possible is a dynamic unity of persons in which equality of personhood exists yet functional subordination to one another also exists for the fulfillment of tasks related to family life."[4] "The fulfillment of tasks related to family life" necessitates some differences in the roles husbands and wives fulfill. Let us repeat, however, that differential in roles does not mean primary and secondary or superior and inferior roles.

Equality and Submission[5]

Before we discuss the biblical teachings concerning equality and submission of husbands and wives, it may help if we summarize the *New Testament teachings regarding* the *freedom* the child of God has through his union with Christ. These teachings are important for a proper interpretation and evaluation of the teachings concerning equality and submission in the husband and wife relationship. Jesus said on one occasion, "If the Son makes you free, you will be free indeed" (John 8:36; see v. 32). He was referring primarily to freedom from the enslavement of sin, "Every one who commits sin is a slave to sin" (v. 34, see Rom. 6:20-22).

Paul said, "For freedom Christ has set us free" and then exhorted the Galatians, "stand fast therefore, and do not submit again to a yoke of slavery" (Gal. 5:1). The yoke he referred to was the yoke of the law, particularly of circumcision (v. 2), which some were insisting was necessary for the Gentile converts.

It was Peter who said, "Live as free men, yet without using your freedom as a pretext for evil; but live as servants [*douloi*—"bondslaves," NASB; "slaves," NEB] of God" (1 Pet. 2:16).

Real freedom for the child of God comes through union with and enslavement to Christ. Really, the more completely we are slaves of his, the deeper and more meaning will be the freedom that we have in him. Even in human relations, such as the home, the fullest freedom comes through mutual submission and unselfish devotion and service to and for one another.

The concept of freedom and equality so clearly expressed in the New Testament was in rather sharp contrast to the spirit of the ancient world. In New Testament days, the newly discovered freedom by recent converts created some problems in some of the churches and in society in general. This seemed to have been true particularly in Corinth and especially among women and slaves. They were not accustomed to the equality that freedom in Christ provided. Many evidently did not know how to use it or adjust to it. They reacted somewhat similarly to adolescent youths who are moving from childhood to adulthood. Such individuals, adolescent or otherwise, frequently try out their freedom to see how free they really are. It takes time for them to arrive at full maturity.

This was a problem that Paul, Peter, and other New Testament writers faced. We cannot properly interpret what they said concerning submission or subordination apart from an understanding of the situation they faced. Their advice to the recent converts may have been, "You are free in Christ, but do not forget that it is 'in Christ' and should be exercised in such a way as to glorify him and to strengthen his cause in the world. This may mean in some areas of your life you will need to restrain yourself and not use or demand for the present all the freedom you have in him. And after all, you, he, and we know that you are free in him and that human distinctions based on sex or condition of life make no difference to him. That is the main thing, everything else is secondary."

With a somewhat different perspective from the preceding, Feucht says, "The New Testament sees no contradiction between freedom in Christ and subordination in many rules and places in society. . . . It is sin that has turned authority into tyranny and liberty into license."[6] There still remains, however, the problem of whether the "no contradiction" was and is applicable to every age and culture.

The contemporary discussion and, at times, controversy concerning the relationship of husbands and wives and the place of women in the contemporary world centers, to a considerable degree, on the interpretation of some of the things in *Paul's Epistles*. In the Old Testament in general, rights belonged to men and husbands and responsibilities to women and wives. The New Testament position, including Paul's Epistles, goes beyond the Old Testament perspective. What Paul wrote regarding the relation of women to men in general is found largely in 1 Corinthians (11:2-16; 14:33-36), in 1 Timothy (2:8-13), and in Titus (2:4-5). In these Scriptures, there is some limited application to husbands and wives. These Scriptures were examined, at least to some degree, in chapter 3 on women.

Possibly the most helpful passage in the Bible on the relation of husbands and wives, and particularly on the concept of equality and submission, is Ephesians 5:21-33 (see Col. 3:18-19). One commentator says that these verses from Ephesians give "the loftiest conception" of the relation of husband and wife "that has ever come from human pen, and one that which no higher can be imagined" (Exp.Gr.) The passage opens with the general statement, "Be subject[7] to one another out of reverence for Christ" (Eph. 5:21).

One commentator has said, "The spirit of mutual subjection is cardinal to the whole Christian conception of social relations. . . . In substance it rests upon the example and precept of Christ, who 'did not count equality with God a thing to be grasped, but emptied himself, taking the form of a servant' (Phil. 2:6-7; cf. Matt. 20:25-28)" (Int. B.).

After Paul stated the general principle of submission and subordination, he applied it to three specific relationships: wives to husbands (5:22-33), children to parents (6:1-4), and slaves to masters (6:5-9). In every case, the point of reference was Christ: "out of reverence for Christ" (5:21), "as to the Lord" (5:22), "in the Lord" (6:1), "as to the Christ" (6:5). *Peter*, in a passage similar to Ephesians 5:21 *ff.*, wrote, "Be subject for the Lord's sake to every human institution" (1 Pet. 2:13). "Every human institution" is then spelled out, somewhat comparable to Paul: citizens to rulers, servants to masters, wives to husbands. There is also a comparable motive or point of reference, "Be subject for the Lord's sake" or for the sake of the Lord's cause or work. The most basic statement in the verses from 1 Peter is "you are joint heirs of the grace of life" (1 Pet. 3:7). This is Peter's Galatians 3:28.

There are at least two *kinds of subjection:* as inferior to a superior or an equal to an equal. It is clear from the biblical teachings in general that the subjection spoken of by Paul and Peter was an equal to an equal. Paul not only said in Galatians 3:28, which Paul Jewett refers to as "The Magna Charta of Humanity,"[8] but also elsewhere (1 Cor. 12:13; Col. 3:11) that in Christ the usual human distinctions are of no consequence.

Also, the submission of one person to another could be involuntary or voluntary. It is clear in the passage in Ephesians 5 that whatever submission was enjoined on wives was voluntary. Paul did not say, "Husbands see that your wives are submissive," but rather, "Wives, be subject to your husbands" (v. 22) and "as to the Lord." The Lord is always the ultimate point of reference for the child of God in every relationship and in every decision. In the New Testament, "the ultimate basis and meaning of life rests in our relationship to God through Jesus Christ, and . . . nothing in all creation, not even God's gift of home and family, replaces in importance that relationship."[9] The wife and her Christian husband are both in the Lord and stand as equals in his presence. But even in the relation of equals, there are differences in responsibilities and functions. Otherwise there will usually be chaos if not anarchy.

Paul placed as heavy, if not a heavier, responsibility on husbands than he did on wives. At least the instructions to husbands are as demanding and as difficult to fulfill. "Husbands, love your wives, as Christ loved the church." How much did Christ love the church? He "gave himself up for her" (v. 25). "Even so husbands should love their wives as their own bodies" (v. 28). The church is Christ's body—he loved it enough to give his life. Husband and wife are one flesh or one body. "He who loves his wife loves himself" (v. 28).

The challenge to husbands is deepened when we realize that the word for "love" here is that distinctly New Testament word *agape*. C. S. Lewis called it "a gift love" in contrast to *eros* (not in the New Testament)—"a need love." By its nature *agape* is a love that gives itself unselfishly to the object loved. It is the word of John 3:16 and John 15:13, "Greater love [*agape*] has no man than this, that a man lay down his life for his friends." It is the kind of love that can be equated with God: "God is love [*agape*]" (1 John 4:8,16).

Few wives would object to being even in absolute subjection to their husbands if their husbands loved them as Christ loved the church. Such a husband would not only never demand but also he would never expect his wife to do anything that was not best for her and honoring to her Lord. "As Christ loved" should be the standard for every Christian husband in every relation with his wife, including the most intimate relations. For many and possibly most husbands, this whole concept will necessitate a self-control or denial of self that at least would approximate submission or subordination.

Paul, in this passage in Ephesians, suggested that the relation of a Christian husband and wife should be on such a high and holy plane that it would be an approximate symbol for the relation of Christ to his church. Although these verses were addressed to

Christian husbands and wives, they set forth the ideal toward which every marriage, Christian and non-Christian, should seek to move. God's basic purposes, as well as his ideal for the home, are written into the nature of men and women whom he has created. And we should never forget that God's purposes, as well as his basic laws, are for our good and best for the world.

After a careful analysis of the major New Testament passages related to the general concept of submission, Gordon Dutile[10] draws some conclusions. The most pertinent ones for our purpose and from our perspective are as follows: (1) It is voluntary. "The New Testament never speaks of one person making another submissive." (2) Submission within marriage is to be mutual; it "is to be given and received in love." (3) It does not infer or mean inferiority in worth or position. (4) As important if not more important than any other of his conclusions is the fact that "submission in marriage does not negate the priesthood of the believer. A marriage partner is never to disobey God under the guise of submission."[11]

The concept or principle of mutual dependence and/or submission as stated in Ephesians 2:21, which is applicable to the relation of men and women in general, is applied in a particular way to husbands and wives. It is true that Paul and Peter gave more emphasis to the submission of the wife, but this emphasis doubtlessly resulted, at least to some degree, from some of the problems they faced in the churches to which they ministered.

The New Testament, particularly the Pauline Epistles, makes it quite clear that there is an element of *mutuality* not only in the relation of husbands and wives but also in the relation of Christians to one another in general. The idea of mutual deference or submission represented something new in the culture of that day and was an advance over anything found in the Old Testament. This "spirit of mutual subjection is cardinal to the whole Christian conception of social relations," including the family (Int. B.). The thing that gives the subjection of Christian husbands and wives to one another its real depth and meaning is the fact that they "are united with each other even as they are united with Christ. This is the heart of the sacred and spiritual relationship between a Christian husband and wife."[12] In other words, the basis for the mutuality of husbands and wives in every relationship of their lives is grounded on or evolves from the fact that they are one in Christ.

One area of mutuality, spelled out specifically by Paul, was their sexual relations. He did this in his first letter to the Corinthians, where he began answering some specific questions or dealing with some particular problems that they had asked about. This passage (1 Cor. 7:1-4) will be discussed more fully in a later chapter on "Sex and Sexual Relations." Attention to the passage here will be restricted to its element of mutuality. Notice particularly the use of the word "likewise" in verses 3 and 4, "The husband should give to his wife her conjugal rights, and *likewise* ["equally," NEB] the wife to her husband. For the wife does not rule over her own body, but the husband does; *likewise* ["equally," NEB] the husband does not rule over his own body, but the wife does" (author's italics), or "the husband cannot claim his body as his own, it is his wife's?" (NEB). The mutuality of their relationship is also evident in the first words of the next verse, "Do not refuse one another except perhaps by agreement for a season." Notice that it is "by agreement." These verses represented a considerable advance over the theory and practice of Paul's day. It is even possible that it represents a perspective that is beyond the practice in many contemporary homes, even so-called Christian homes.

There is a comparable emphasis on mutuality later in the same chapter when Paul dealt with the matter of separation or divorce of a husband and wife who were believers (1 Cor. 7:10-11) and also where one was a believer and the other an unbeliever (1 Cor. 7:12-16). These verses will be considered in the chapter on divorce. For Paul, the right of divorce, if it be a right, was not restricted to the husband as it was in the Old Testament (Deut. 24:1-4).

The "likewise" perspective is also evident in 1 Peter 3:1-7. These verses are introduced with the statement, "Likewise you wives, be submissive to your husbands." This "likewise" refers back to what he had said about subjection or submission "to the emperor as supreme" (2:13) and the submission of slaves to their masters. But this "likewise" applied to wives is followed by one applied to husbands, "Likewise you husbands, live considerately with your wives . . . since you are joint heirs of the grace of life" (3:7). "Joint heirs" puts husbands and wives on the same level.

The admonition by Peter to husbands is followed by an admonition that clearly implies mutuality. Peter wrote, "Finally, all of you [which would include husbands as well as wives], have unity of spirit, sympathy, love of the brethren, a tender heart and a humble mind" (v. 8). As suggested previously, humility is closely akin to the mutuality that should characterize the relation of husbands and wives. All of us, and particularly women and wives, should be deeply grateful for Paul's and Peter's "likewise" or "equally"!

There is also a mutuality of love of a husband and wife for one another. A concordance will reveal many references to the love of a husband for his wife. For a few of many possible examples, see Genesis 24:67 (Isaac for Rebekah), Genesis 29:20,30 (Jacob for Rachel), Exodus 21:5 (slave for his wife), 1 Samuel 1:5 (Elkanah for Hannah), 1 Kings 11:1 (Solomon and many foreign women), Ecclesiastes 9:9 ("Enjoy life with the wife whom you love"). There is at least one specific reference to the love of a wife to or for her husband to be (Michal for David—1 Sam. 18:20). The Song of Solomon is a love poem or song, with an interplay of expressions of love by both male and female lovers. A footnote in *The New English Bible* says concerning The Song of Solomon, "*The Hebrew text implies, by its pronouns, different speakers, but does not indicate them.*" The New American Standard Bible suggests the speakers. The nearest thing to the Song of Solomon elsewhere in the Old Testament is Psalm 45.[13]

The main specific emphasis in the Pauline Epistles concerning the relation of wives to their husbands was respect (Eph. 5:33). It is doubtful, however, if a wife could or would respect a husband she did not love. Neither could nor would she love a husband she did not respect. Paul did instruct Titus to "bid" the older women to "train the young women to love their husbands and children" (2:4), "to be loving wives and mothers" (NEB), or "to be affectionate wives and mothers" (Williams).

Surely, it is correct to say that love of the wife for her husband was assumed in both Old Testament and New Testament. In the culture of that day, the husband generally was the predominant member of the family. The emphasis needed was on the love of the husband for his wife. This may help to explain the limited emphasis on the wife's love for her husband.

Covenant and Commitment

There are few if any greater needs for many contemporary families than a deepened sense of commitment to one another of husbands and wives. One thing that will tend to deepen such a sense of commitment is a conviction that they entered into covenant with one another when they exchanged their wedding vows. In turn, this conviction with its accompanying sense of commitment will be deepened if a husband and wife recognize that they have also entered into covenant with their Heavenly Father who has written the home into their natures. The preceding means, among other things, that covenant and commitment belong in one package.

The covenant concept with its accompanying commitment is very prevalent in the Old Testament.[14] Really, the covenant and the ideas derived from and related to it are among the most basic and distinctive elements in both Testaments.

One thing that underscores the high regard for the husband and wife relationship in general and their covenant with and commitment to one another is the fact that their relationship is frequently used to describe God's relation to his people. Isaiah represented God as saying:

As the bridegroom rejoices over the bride,
    so shall your God rejoice over you (62:5).

Ezekiel said of the bride, "I [God] plighted my troth to you and entered into a covenant with you, says the Lord God, and you became mine" (16:8). Hosea, in a chapter full of family terminology, said that there would come a time when the Lord will say, "And in that day . . . you will call me, 'My husband.' . . . And I will make for you a covenant. . . . I will betroth you to me for ever" (2:16-19).

Similarly, Israel is referred to as God's wife:

> For your Maker is your husband,
> the Lord of hosts is his name (Isa. 54:5).

Grelot said, "With the prophets the comparison of the alliance between Jehovah and Israel with a marriage introduces into the subject a new element of great theological importance."[15]

The prophets, however, had to struggle with a people who had been unfaithful to the covenant they had entered into with their God. This unfaithfulness was quite evident before the Exile and was the reason for the deportation from the land that God had promised to them and their fathers. Even those who had been permitted to return from the Exile to their homeland had broken covenant with God. Many of them, including some of their leaders, had taken foreign women as wives for themselves and for their sons. This was so prevalent that Nehemiah said that half of their children "could not speak the language of Judah" (Neh. 13:24). When Ezra faced them with their guilt their response was, "Let us make a covenant with our God" (Ezra 10:3).

A prophet of the restoration, crying out against the taking of foreign wives, said, "The Lord was witness to the covenant between you and the wife of your youth, to whom you have been faithless, though she is your companion and your wife by covenant" (Mal. 2:14).[16] "There seems to have been no religious service accompanying marriage under the O.T.; but even without being formally invoked, God observed how the marriage was kept" (Cam.B.) or not kept.

Walter Wegner, in a summary way, makes the following statement regarding the Old Testament, "As God's covenant love for his people became the keynote of prophetic teaching, family goals were raised through the higher ranking of wife and mother and through greater expressions of love, faithfulness, and forgiving grace *(chesed)*. This covenant concept also focused new attention on personal relations between spouses. . . . The love drama enacted by God toward Israel was to be the marriage-family pattern."[17]

This "love drama" was revealed, at least to a limited degree, in the relation of some *husbands* and *wives in* the *Old Testament*. The men might have had more than one wife, as was true of Jacob and Elkanah, and yet there was a special commitment to the one who was loved in a special way. Furthermore, there was a real commitment of husband to wife, as seen in the lives of Abraham and Isaac. And, after all, following the record of the creation of the woman as a helpmate or companion to the man, Scripture says, "Therefore a man leaves his father and his mother and cleaves to his wife, and they become one flesh" (Gen. 2:24). That involved, then and still involves, commitment.

What Wegner says regarding the Old Testament is deepened somewhat in the New Testament. In the latter, the church as the people of God is recognized as the new Israel. Christ's covenant with his church is a new covenant not made with hands but written on the heart.

The covenant and the accompanying idea of commitment represent the *central unifying concept of the Christian life*. This covenant is based on and derived from God's covenant with his people. It is lived out in and through the church, a covenant community. This covenant community, as is true of all covenants, has a two-way movement. For example, a member of a church has entered into covenant with that church and its members. In turn, the church and its members are in a covenant relation with the individual member. And it should be remembered that a covenant always involves a commitment.

The above is not only true of the church and its members but it is also true of any human institution and agency: the state and its citizens, employers and employees, coach and players, the family and its members. This is certainly true of the relation of husband and wife. Their marriage vows represent a covenant that involves a commitment to one another. A Christian couple also entered into covenant with God and should commit their new home to him as a channel for him to use to advance his cause and kingdom. It is recognized that this is not actually true of every so-called Christian couple, but it should be—that is the ideal.

Let us close this section on covenant and commitment and this chapter by quoting some sentences from Elizabeth Achtemeier. She says that Christ

> has committed himself totally to us, to be with us in life and death. It is that kind of commitment upon which Christian marriage is to be founded. It is love that gives itself away. . . . with that loving commitment to be with and to work for the good of the other, we are to commit ourselves in our marriage.[18]

It is encouraging to remember, to quote Achtemeier again, that "it is the mystery of love in marriage that commitment leads to freedom—freedom to move out from a sure base of security and acceptance, freedom to plumb all my creativity, freedom to be my authentic self much more than if I did not have such security."[19] In other words, a Christian couple, in their covenant with and commitment to one another, can discover or rediscover the true meaning of the words of Jesus, "Whoever would save his life will lose it, and whoever loses his life for my sake will find it" (Matt. 16:25).

Notes

1. Paul K. Jewett, *Man as Male and Female: A Study in Sexual Relationships from a Theological Point of View* (Grand Rapids: Eerdmans, 1975), p. 14.

2. See particularly ibid., pp. 50-61, on "An Examination of the New Testament Texts" used as a basis for the hierarchical view and pp. 61-86, where "The Hierarchical View . . . (is) Elaborated and Defended." In the latter section, Jewett examines and evaluates the perspective of Thomas Aquinas, Luther, and Calvin and gives a particularly thorough analysis and evaluation of Barth's position. Still later (pp. 129-149), there is a section entitled "The Rejection of the Hierarchical View of the Man/Woman Relationship in Favor of One of Partnership." Here Jewett states his own position.

3. John C. Howell, *Equality and Submission in Marriage* (Nashville: Broadman Press, 1979), p. 35.

4. Ibid., p. 42.

5. For two books that deal somewhat differently with the idea of equality and submission in marriage, see ibid. and Herbert J. Miles and Fern Harrington Miles, *Husband-and-Wife Equality* (Old Tappan, N.J.: Fleming H. Revell Co., 1978).

6. Oscar E. Feucht, ed., *Family Relationships in the Church* (St. Louis: Concordia Publishing House, 1970), pp. 220-221.

7. The idea of submission or subordination (*hupotasso*) is a rather distinctly Pauline concept. It is an "old military figure to line up under" (W.P.) and is "in contrast with pagan self-seeking and self-assertion" (Exp. Gr.). The word is found twenty-four times in Paul's Epistles and only sixteen times in the remainder of the New Testament: three in Luke, a traveling companion of Paul; seven in 1 Peter, many of its ideas are strikingly similar to Paul; five times in Hebrews, thought by many to have been written by Paul; and one time in James.

8. Jewett, p. 142.

9. Elizabeth Achtemeir, *The Committed Marriage* (Philadelphia: Westminster Press, 1976), p. 30.

10. Gordon Dutile, "A Concept of Submission in the Husband-Wife Relationship in Selected New Testament Passages," a Ph.D. dissertation, Southwestern Baptist Theological Seminary, 1980. Two other dissertations on closely-related subjects are: John Christian Howell, "A Christian Approach to Contemporary Sexual Problems" and Ebbie C. Smith, "The One-Flesh Concept of Marriage: A Biblical Study," both done at Southwestern Baptist Theological Seminary.

11. Dutile, pp. 213-219.

12. Oscar E. Feucht, ed., *Family Relationships in the Church* (St. Louis: Concordia Publishing House, 1970), p. 63.

13. Tobit in the Apocrypha is a beautiful love story, with some very high ideals.

14. The Hebrew word for covenant *(berith)* is found approximately 280 times in the Old Testament. The Greek word *diatheke*, usually translated "covenant," is found only 33 times in the New Testament. While there may be some significance to the number of times a particular word is used, the true importance of the covenant or idea cannot be exclusively decided on that basis.

15. Pierre Grelot, *Man & Wife in Scripture* (New York: Herder & Herder, 1964), p. 40.

16. The word *covenant* is found seven times in this one chapter.

17. Feucht, p. 47.

18. Achtemeier, p. 39.

19. Ibid., p. 44.

8

Sex and Sexual Relations

Revolutionary changes have occurred in recent years in the area of sex and sexual relations. One author charges that "society's perverted attitudes regarding sex are destroying the sanctity of the marriage relationship and promulgating false ideals of fulfillment in man-woman relationships." The author concludes: "It is time for the church to bring wholeness into this area of brokenness on the contemporary scene."[1]

One way Christians and churches can face up to the revolutionary changes in the area of sex and recover the wholeness that has so largely been lost is to examine the Bible and see what it says concerning sex and sexual relations. An honest searching of the Scriptures with an open mind will reveal that they speak quite frankly about sex. One will also discover that the perspective of the Bible regarding sex differs considerably from the viewpoint of many contemporary Christians.

Also, a study of the Bible will reveal that there are some problems in the area of sex and sexual relations in the contemporary period that were unknown in biblical days and hence are not dealt with in a specific way in the Scriptures. This is true of such matters as contraception, sterilization, abortion, artificial insemination, surrogate mothers, and the whole area of genetic engineering.

Basic Concepts

Several basic biblical concepts directly or indirectly related to sex are of major significance.

Sex is a good gift of God. At the close of each creative day, God pronounced that what he had made was good. After he had completed his creative work, climaxed by the creation of male and female, he surveyed all that he had created, and "behold, it was very good" (Gen. 1:31). God's creative work was good because each part of that creation fulfilled the purposes of God and functioned properly in relation to other phases of his creation.

That which was pronounced "very good" included the creation of male and female. In other words, it included sex and potential sexual relations. David Mace says that the fact that sex is a good gift of God is "the first, and the most fundamental fact which the Bible teaches us about sex."[2]

Unfortunately, many Christians through the centuries have considered sex as inherently evil. This idea, which is still more or less prevalent, did not stem from the Jewish background of our Christian faith. Rather, it came into the stream of the Christian movement in the early Christian centuries through the impact of some forms of Greek philosophy. In some Greek thought, a sharp distinction was between the material (considered evil) and the immaterial (which was considered basically good). The body was material, sex belonged to the body; hence it was considered evil.

Another factor that has contributed considerably to the idea of sex as evil has been a misunderstanding of some things Paul said in 1 Corinthians concerning the celibate life and regarding the conflict of the flesh and the Spirit (Rom. 7:14 to 8:4; Gal. 5:16-21). It seems clear that, in most places where Paul referred to the "flesh" (*sarx*), he did not equate it with the body. Rather, he was referring primarily to a fleshly, carnal nature that was in conflict with humans' spiritual nature. One place where this conflict is clearly stated is when he specifically spoke of a conflict between the fleshly nature and the Holy Spirit. Among other things, Paul said, "Walk by the Spirit, and do not gratify the desires of the flesh. For the desires of the flesh are against the Spirit, and the desires of the Spirit are against the flesh" (Gal. 5:16-17). Later he spoke of "the works of the flesh" (vv. 19-21) and the fruit of the Spirit (vv. 22-23).

Let it be repeated: the biblical perspective is that sex is a good gift from God. Sexual desire is no more evil within itself than the desire for food and drink. "Sexuality which is the work of God, will always be something good if the conditions of its use are in harmony with the intentions of the Creator."[3] But like the other basic desires of life, sex can be expressed in wrong, hurtful, and self-defeating ways. This means that sex may be a curse or a blessing. Like human freedom, the sexual urge may be and frequently is responsible for humans' highest achievements but also for their greatest sins. Many of the world's darkest deeds and most serious crimes are related, directly or indirectly, to sex. It has been observed that "the nobler anything is the more noisome are its abuses."

The Scriptures clearly suggest that the only full expression of sex approved by the Creator is the physical union of husband and wife. And possibly it should be added that even within marriage, sexual union will be degrading if there is lacking a proper respect for the total personality of the mate.

Man and woman are created in the image of God. This concept has been discussed in previous chapters. The fact that both male and female were created in the image of God and the companion fact that they were created to answer to or complement one another has major importance for their relations in general and particularly as husbands and wives.

The preceding means, among other things, that a person should never be used as a mere means of sexual satisfaction without regard to the effect on that person. This is just as true of husbands and wives as it is of extramarital or premarital sex relations.

One flesh. There is a sense in which man and woman are one in creation. They have been appropriately compared to two islands that may appear to be completely separated but which are in reality outcroppings of the same mountain range. They were originally one and will be one again if that which separates them is removed. It is sin that separates them from God and from one another.

The concept of one flesh is most clearly and deeply associated with the sexual union of husband and wife. The biblical perspective is that when a man and woman have sexual intercourse they become, in a unique way, one flesh. This "one-flesh" idea is first implied if not actually stated clearly in Genesis 2:24, "Therefore a man leaves his father and his mother and cleaves to his wife, and they become one flesh." The idea of one flesh lies at the center of the biblical perspective concerning sex. Jesus quoted Genesis 2:24 in his conversation with the Pharisees concerning divorce (Matt. 19:5; Mark 10:7-8). Paul referred to it when he wrote about the proper use of the body (1 Cor. 6:16) and about the relation of husbands and wives (Eph. 5:31).

Some of the translations leave off the word *flesh* in the New Testament references. The word *sarx* is there, and it possibly should have been translated as is done in most translations (KJV, NEB, NASB, and others). One possible justifiable reason for leaving off "flesh" is the fact that for the Jews the concept of "flesh" was indicative of the total person. Their's was a wholistic view of humanity. In other words, sexual union was not and is not exclusively a fleshly union. It is the union of two persons.

The union of two persons may occur even when there is no affection for one another. Paul said that a man's relations with a prostitute made them one flesh (1 Cor. 6:16). Two become one, however, on the highest level and in the most meaningful sense only when sexual intercourse is the loving relationship of a husband and wife who are committed to one another and enter into the union freely and deliberately. It may sound paradoxical but, in such a union of husband and wife, their distinctive identities are not only retained but also heightened while at the same time they become one in a unique way.

There are at least two purposes, from the biblical perspective, for the union of husband and wife that makes them one flesh. Those purposes are the procreation of children (Gen. 1:28) and the other, which is not stated as pointedly, is meaningful communication with one another or the mutual enjoyment of the experience. The latter may be implied from the fact that one word used for sexual intercourse meant "know." For example, "Now Adam knew Eve his wife, and she conceived and bore Cain" (Gen. 4:1; see 4:17,25; Judg. 19:25; 1 Sam. 1:19). This use of "know" carried over to the days of the New Testament. Joseph, in obedience to the word of God, took Mary as his wife, "but knew her not until she had borne a son; and he called his name Jesus" (Matt. 1:25). What a beautiful idea: a husband and wife know each other in the fullest way and deepest level of their beings when they enter into sexual intercourse with one another in God-approved ways and spirit.

The body belongs to the Lord. In a sense, the bodies of all people belong to God. This is true in a special sense for the bodies of the redeemed children of God.

Without any attempt at a detailed interpretation, let us examine 1 Corinthians 6:13 *ff.* Here Paul plainly said that the body *(soma)* is "not meant for immorality" or "lust" (NEB) "but for the Lord, and the Lord for the body." Then he asked, "Do you not know that your bodies are members of Christ?" or "are limbs and organs of Christ?" (NEB) (v. 15). He then asked an additional and pointed question, "Shall I therefore take the members of Christ and make them members of ["unite them with," NIV] a prostitute?" He exclaimed, "Never!" then added: "Do you not know[4] that he who joins himself to a prostitute becomes one body with her?" and quoted Genesis 2:24.

Paul, in verse 19, asked, "Do you not know that your body is a temple ["shrine," NEB] of the Holy Spirit?" (see John 2:19-21). The Temple in Old Testament days stood as a reminder of the presence of God in the midst of his people. It was a holy place. The Christian's body should be so dedicated to the will and purposes of God that it would symbolize the presence of God in the midst of his people.

The Spirit who dwells in the body of the Christian would like to have a clean, wholesome dwelling place. Also, the body is the vehicle the Spirit uses to reach out to others. He achieves his work and purpose through the bodies of responding children of God. When one defiles his or her body, the temple of the Spirit is defiled. To take the body that belongs to the Lord and join it to a prostitute, or anyone other than wife or husband, is "high treason."

Paul concluded his argument against immorality by reminding the Corinthian Christians that they had been bought with a price. We, as was true of them, are not our own. That eliminates the argument rather frequently heard, "My body is my own. It isn't anyone's business what I do with it." It is God's business. In a sense this is true of all people, but it is especially true for those who are Christians.

Paul's exhortation was, "So glorify God in your body" (v. 20). "Glorify" does not refer exclusively to the spoken word. It includes also the glory the Christian can and should bring to the One who has redeemed him by the life he lives. The immediate reference is to chastity, but it is all-inclusive. The body of the child of God, including husbands and wives in their most intimate relationships, should be presented "as a living sacrifice, holy and acceptable to God, which is your spiritual worship" (Rom. 12:1).

Celibacy and virginity. The idea of living the celibate life or as "eunuchs for the sake of the kingdom of heaven" (Matt. 19:12) has been discussed in the chapter on single adults. This section on basic concepts regarding sex and sexual relations would not be complete, however, without at least a brief statement regarding celibacy.

God wrote the home deep into the natures of the man and woman he created. However, it is clear that God does not will that all men and women marry and have families. Celibacy is recognized as an honorable and God-appointed alternative to marriage for some. It does seem from what Jesus and Paul said that one who should live the celibate life will have the divinely given grace to do so (see Matt. 19:12 and 1 Cor. 7:7). This need for special divine grace to live that kind of life should eliminate any basis for pride or a sense of superiority by the celibate or those who consider celibacy superior to marriage.

Paul, in writing to Timothy, his son in the ministry, predicted that there would come a time when some would "forbid marriage and enjoin abstinence from foods which God created to be received with thanksgiving by those who believe and know the truth." He then added, "For everything created by God is good" (1 Tim. 4:3-4). This would include marriage and the sex relations involved in marriage.

Sex Within Marriage

There are not many specific references in the Scriptures to sexual relations of husbands and wives. It seemed that the writers of the Scriptures assumed that the God-given sexual urge would find adequate if not always healthy expression in the normal relations of husbands and wives.

Two biblical passages, one from each Testament, will suffice for our study. The Old Testament passage is from the Book of Proverbs (5:15-21). These verses contain some counsel needed by many husbands and wives. The first two verses (15-16) are figurative and are interpreted in verses 18-20. The opening verse is:

> Drink water from your own cistern,
> flowing water from your own well.

Then follows a question:

> Should your springs be scattered abroad,
> streams of water in the streets?

Verse 18 is as follows:

> Let your fountain be blessed,
> and rejoice in the wife of your youth.

"Fountain" in this verse is parallel to "water" in verse 16 and "the wife of your youth" was the fountain that should supply the husband's need. "Well" is a symbolic expression for a supply of water. "The figure appears to be a general one—let thy own wife be thy source of enjoyment, as refreshing as water to a thirsty man" (ICC). A well is a source of refreshment in relation to one's house or home. In contrast, springs and streams are away from the home. One should find satisfaction in his own fountain, the wife of his youth. The latter relates to the fact that early marriage was the custom among the Jews.

Notice that the wife in this passage was not portrayed as a bearer of children but as a giver of pleasure. In some rather striking erotic terms, the wife is pictured as the one in whom the husband should find satisfaction for his bodily needs and sexual desires. Verse 21 gives a general reason for any man, including a husband, to be careful of what he does. It is a statement that would be wise for women as well as men of every age to take seriously:

> For a man's ways are before the eyes of the Lord,
> and he watches all his paths.

This is just as true of the bedroom in the home as anywhere else.

The New Testament passage is from Paul's first letter to the Corinthians. Beginning with the seventh chapter, he began answering some questions the church or at least a group in the church had asked in a communication to him. He first said, "It is well for a man not to touch a woman," possibly defending celibacy for those with the gift to live that kind of life. He continued by saying, "But because of the temptation to immorality, each man should have his own wife and each woman her own husband" (1 Cor. 7:2). Then, in very specific language, Paul spoke of sexual relations of husband and wife. His words are just as relevant today as when he first wrote them.

Paul plainly said, "The husband should give to his wife her conjugal rights ["what is due to her," NEB], and likewise the wife to her husband" (v. 3). The reference is clearly to sexual union. In other words, the sexual union of husband and wife is not a favor to be granted, but it is a right or a debt to be paid. Notice the mutuality of the obligation. Here, as elsewhere in the New Testament, the emphasis is not on the procreation of children but on companionship, a sharing of the self with one another.

Paul said that "the wife does not rule over ["cannot claim," NEB] her own body, . . . likewise ["equally," NEB] the husband does not rule over his own body." Separate ownership had ceased. They belong to one another. The sexual is lifted from the purely physical level to the moral. The mutuality of the relationship implies that there can and should be freedom on the part of husband or wife to initiate the desire for sexual relations and that such relations should be mutually satisfying. The emphasis is on mutual respect for one another and a desire to care for the physical needs of the other.

Paul, in a very specific way, recognized the place and significance of sexual intercourse in the relations of husband and wife. This is one of the areas where they need to have "regard for one another." He suggested, "Do not refuse one another except perhaps by agreement for a season, that you may devote yourselves to prayer; but then come together again" (v. 5). It is possible that some of the Corinthians, in their mistaken zeal, were refusing to have sexual relations with husband or wife. Paul did recognize that there might be occasions when normal sexual relations might not be compatible with a complete giving of oneself in prayer, but he did not say or imply that sex was unclean or sinful. Even sexual relations, important as they are, should not be permitted to interfere with spiritual duties.

But notice that the decision to forego relations for the sake of prayer was to be "by agreement for a season," and even this statement was preceded with the word "perhaps." The counsel of abstinence for the sake of prayer is followed with the advice that they "come together again, lest Satan tempt you through lack of self-control."

In these verses from the pen of Paul, the conditions for abstention from sexual union of husband and wife are clearly stated: (1) it must be by mutual agreement; (2) it must be for a spiritual purpose; (3) it must be temporary.

Paul was not married when he wrote 1 Corinthians. Whether he had ever been married, we do not know for sure; but the safest implication is that he was never married. Do you not agree, however, that he gave some remarkably sane advice to the Corinthians regarding marriage in general and sexual relations of husbands and wives in particular? And will you not also agree that his advice is just as applicable to us today as it was to the Corinthians?

Sex Outside of Marriage

The sexual union of husband and wife is the only full expression of the sexual urge approved in the Scriptures. Sexual sins were considered an offense against God and his purposes for the relation of men and women and in the Old Testament were strongly condemned and severely punished. It is true that, in conformity to the culture of that time, there were few restraints on men in the area of sex. In contrast, generally speaking, the wife did not have "any ground for complaint, . . . as long as he [her husband] did not deprive her of her necessary maintenance and her right to marital intercourse."[5]

Prostitution.[6] In Old Testament days, there were two types or kinds of prostitutes: common or secular and cultic or sacred. The former offered their bodies for hire to men. The cultic prostitute, who could be male or female, was affiliated with heathen temples. The function of the cultic prostitutes, particularly the male ones, are not spelled out specifically.

There are some references in the Old Testament to common or secular prostitutes without any evidence of condemnation. For example, it is simply recorded that Samson "went to Gaza . . . saw a harlot, and he went in to her" (Judg. 16:1). The most striking example is the familiar story of Rahab (Josh. 2:1-24; see Heb. 11:31; Jas. 2:21-26).

There is, however, evidence in the Old Testament of the disapproval of prostitution (Lev. 21:7,9,14). The sons of Jacob killed Hamor and his son Shechem because the latter had had relations with their sister and had treated her "as a harlot" (Gen. 34:31). The children of Israel were not to permit their daughters to become harlots (Lev. 19:29). Possibly some notice should be given to Tamar, a young widow who tricked her father-in-law into having relations with her. He had failed to keep his promise to give her Shelah, her younger brother-in-law, as her husband. Judah's first reaction when he was told that she was pregnant was to have her put to death (Gen. 38:11-24). But he did not (vv. 25-27).

The strongest condemnation of prostitution was of the cultic prostitutes, particularly the males. This condemnation is spelled out in the law (Deut. 23:17-18) and also in the Old Testament in general (1 Kings 14:24; 15:12; 22:46). It possibly should be mentioned that Jephthah, one of the judges, the son of a harlot, was rejected by his half-brothers but blessed by the Lord (Judg. 11:1-3). God is not as much concerned about where one has come from as where one is going and how a person can be used to fulfill the purposes of God. There are frequent warnings in Proverbs against the wiles of the harlot or prostitute (for example, 5:3-6; 6:23-26; 7:4-27).

The term *prostitution* or *harlotry* was also used figuratively or metaphorically. "Played the harlot" was a favorite term for the unfaithfulness of Israel (Judg. 2:17; 8:27,33; Jer. 3:1-2,6; Hos. 4:12). One of the darkest pictures ever painted of Israel is in Ezekiel 16. This prophet of the Exile referred at least six times (vv.

15,16-17,26,28—2 times) in this one chapter to Israel playing the harlot. There are numerous other references to her harlotry and unfaithfulness, frequently referred to as "adultery" (Jer. 5:7; 7:9; 23:14; 29:23; Ezek. 23:37,43), to the One who had entered into covenant with her, "I plighted my troth to you and entered into a covenant with you, says the Lord God, and you became mine" (Ezek. 16:8). Then at the close of this chapter, the Lord through Ezekiel reminded the children of Israel that they had broken the covenant but added, "Yet I will remember my covenant with you . . . I will establish with you an everlasting covenant" (vv. 59-60). Not only Israel but also we as individual children of God should be deeply grateful for the forgiving spirit of the gracious God and our Heavenly Father!

Adultery. One of the Ten Commandments, or "the Ten Words" (Deut. 4:13; 10:4, NEB) or "the words of the covenant" (Ex. 34:28), was, "You shall not commit adultery" (Ex. 20:14; see Deut. 5:18). This, along with the others of the Ten Commandments, had no penalty attached. This fact was due to the nature of the Commandments. They were apodictic or briefly stated unconditional laws in contrast to casuistic laws. The latter are frequently introduced with an "if" and with a specific punishment prescribed (see Ex. 21—23).

In the Old Testament the punishment for adultery, as for other sexual offenses, was specific and severe. For example, if a man had sexual relations with another man's wife, both were to be put to death (Lev. 20:10; Deut. 22:22). The same punishment was prescribed for relations with a betrothed virgin if the relations took place in the city (Deut. 22:23-24). In contrast, only the man was to be put to death if he had relations with a betrothed virgin in the open country (Deut. 22:25-27). The young woman was given the benefit of the doubt. It was assumed that she may have cried for help and no one could hear. In the case of relations with an unbetrothed virgin, the man was to give to her father fifty shekels of silver, had to take her as his wife, and could not put her away (Deut. 22:28-29; see Ex. 22:14-17). The laws against adultery in the Old Testament were based primarily on the property rights of the husband.

Later, as the nation of Israel declined, prophets arose as

spokesmen for God. They cried out against the sins of their people, including the sin of adultery. The following is an example from one of the great eighth-century prophets:

> Hear the word of the Lord, O people of Israel;
> for the Lord has a controversy with the inhabitants of the land.
> . . . .
> there is swearing, lying, killing, stealing, and committing adultery
> (Hos. 4:1-2).

In the dark days immediately preceding the Exile, Jeremiah painted a dark picture of God's concern for his people:

> O that my head were waters,
>   and my eyes a fountain of tears,
> that I might weep day and night
>   for the slain of the daughter of my people!
> O that I had in the desert
>   a wayfarers' lodging place,
> that I might leave my people
>   and go away from them!
> For they are all adulterers,
>   a company of treacherous men (Jer. 9:1-2).

The nation had played the harlot by deserting God and worshiping foreign Gods.

Homosexuality. Possibly it should be said in the beginning that "a major difficulty underlying any discussion of the phenomenon of homosexual experience is that of definition. . . . Is it a state of mind or a form of behavior?"[7] The biblical references to homosexuality are to homosexual behavior or "genital homosexuality" and not to homosexual "orientation." The latter did not seem to have been recognized in biblical days.

We hope that Kirk is correct when he says that people are "asking for a biblical word, a word from the Lord, rather than the changing opinions of men. They want both firmness and compassion, which reflect the character of our Lord when confronting moral laxity and broken people."[8]

There is not a great deal in the Scriptures concerning homosexuality, but there is enough to indicate that it was prevalent at times. It is generally agreed that the men of Sodom desired to have sex relations with the guests (men) in the house of Lot. Their request, or rather demand, was, "Bring them out to us, that we may know them" or "have intercourse with them" (NEB) (Gen. 19:5; see Judg. 19:22). The word translated "know," as is frequently true of English words, had many meanings and was used at times to indicate sexual intercourse (Gen. 4:1 *et al*).[9] The wickedness of Sodom became proverbial (see Isa. 3:9; Lam. 4:6; 2 Pet. 2:6-10; Jude 7). Also, *Sodomite* became a synonym for *homosexual*.

Specific Scriptures could be cited to support this conclusion. For example, "You shall not lie with a male as with a woman; it is an abomination" (Lev. 18:22). A little later in the Levitical law the death penalty was assessed for that abomination (Lev. 20:13).

The law against homosexual behavior was a specific, although negative, restatement of a fundamental divine principle regarding sexual relationships: sexual intercourse belongs within a monogamous heterosexual union of husband and wife. It is that principle "which is the basis for the view that all homosexual behavior falls outside the will of God for human sexuality."[10] Paul referred specifically to homosexuality in at least three of his epistles: Romans, 1 Corinthians, and 1 Timothy. Let us look at them in reverse order. In writing to Timothy, Paul suggested that the law was "not laid down for the just but for the lawless and disobedient." Then he listed some of those lawless ones, including "immoral persons, sodomites ["homosexuals," NASB], . . . and whatever else is contrary to sound doctrine" (1 Tim. 1:9-10).

Paul, in writing to the Corinthians, named some who would not inherit the kingdom of God. Homosexuals are in the list (1 Cor. 6:9-10). Here Paul did not say and the Bible in general does not say that any of those named cannot be saved and in that way enter the kingdom or reign of God. This is evident in what he said in verse 11, "And such were some of you. But you were washed, you were sanctified, you were justified in the name of the Lord Jesus Christ and in the Spirit of our God."

Paul did not stop, and we should never stop, at the point of judgment. We should always move to the area of at least the possibility of forgiven sin.. Also, many Christians do not make a distinction between one who simply has a homosexual orientation and a practicing or "genital" homosexual. After all, the former can avoid involvement in homosexual practices just as a heterosexual-oriented person can avoid adultery. Paul's consideration of homosexuality was restricted to actual homosexual involvement.

Kirk suggests that some verses in the first chapter of Romans contain "the most devastating passage in the Bible for practicing homosexuals."[11] Because of the depravity of man, Paul said that God "gave them up in the lusts of their hearts to impurity, to the dishonoring of their bodies among themselves" (Rom. 1:24). He then spelled out more specifically how God had given them up. The unnatural sins of the people, including homosexuality, were allowed or permitted by God as the natural consequences and as punishment for their idolatry and denial of him. "God gave them up to dishonorable ["shameful," NEB] passions" (v. 26). God gave them up in the sense that he "handed them over to the power of sin," or he "merely left them to their own self-determination and self-destruction," which is "part of the price of man's moral freedom" (W.P.).

Paul mentioned homosexuality in particular. He said, "Their women exchanged natural relations ["intercourse," NEB] for unnatural, and the men likewise gave up natural relations with women and were consumed with passion for one another, men committing shameless acts with men" (vv. 26-27). Notice that Paul considered the relation of men and women as natural and homosexuality as contrary to nature. He then concluded that they will receive "the due penalty for their error" or will "suffer in their persons the inevitable penalty for doing what is improper" (Williams). Robertson suggests that the debt will be paid in full: "Nature will attend to that in their own bodies and souls" (W.P.).

In the Old Testament and in Paul's Epistles, "the message is consistently the same: God created Man as male and female. Our sexuality is to be fulfilled in faithful heterosexual relationships within marriage. God does not alter His message to fit the culture.

. . . He calls his people to live in contrast to the culture."[12] And we might add that he expects his people to change the culture.

There is both "bad news" and "good news" for the homosexual in the Scriptures. The bad news is that homosexuality is contrary to the purpose and law of God; from the Christian perspective, it cannot be an approved life-style and is self-destructive and destructive of family life. The good news is that God is love and his love seeks to reach out to all kinds of people. He loves the homosexual, as well as all other sinners—saved and unsaved. However, his love does not gloss over sin, whatever its nature. He takes sin more seriously than we do. The encouraging word, however, first spoken by John the Baptist, is, "Behold, the Lamb of God, who takes away the sin of the world" (John 1:29). In other words, there is hope for the homosexual in this life and in the life to come.

Possibly an additional statement should be made: church members should beware of developing self-righteous, pharisaical attitudes toward the homosexual or any other particular type of sinner. After all, the most scathing denunciations by Jesus were reserved for self-righteous sinners.

Our God, who is *agape* (1 John 4:8,16), wants to reach out through us to touch the "untouchables" of our society. It is doubtful if any feel more like untouchables or outcasts than most homosexuals. But our love, as is true of his love, must not gloss over the sinfulness of homosexuality. We would be unfair to the homosexual if we did that and could not be effectively redemptive in our ministry to him or her.

Paul's list of vices. Several places in the Pauline Epistles give lists of vices that should be avoided. In some cases, these are joined with comparable lists of virtues. This harmonizes with Paul's balancing of the negative and positive aspects of his gospel. Examples of this balancing are Galatians 5: "the works of the flesh" and the "fruit of the Spirit" (vv. 17-23); and Colossians 3: "Put to death therefore" and "Put on" (vv. 5-17; see Eph. 4:22-32). In each of these lists of vices, "immorality" is listed first (see other lists: 1 Cor. 5:11; 6:9; Eph. 5:3). The prevalence of references to sexual vice in Paul's lists doubtlessly stemmed from the prevalence of sexual sins of all kinds in the pagan world of that day. In no area did early Christianity challenge the moral standards of the ancient world more than in the area of sex.

In the opening chapter of Romans (1:28-32), Paul painted an extremely dark picture of the moral conditions of that time. He seems to have heaped together all the hateful things he could think of. Those listed seemed to fall into two general classes: those of impurity—carnal, sexual vices—which defile the body and those that are primarily antisocial in nature—envy, murder, disobedience to parents, and so forth. It is in the midst of the listing of vices that Paul said that God "gave them up to dishonorable passion"— homosexual relations by both women and men. And they received "in their own persons the due penalty for their error" (Rom. 1:26-27).

The lustful look. When introducing his comparisons of the law and his teachings, Jesus clearly stated that he had not come "to abolish the law and the prophets [the two most authoritative portions of the Jewish Scriptures] . . . but to fulfill ["complete," NEB] them" (Matt. 5:17). How did he fulfill them? At least one way he fulfilled them was by going beyond them, by giving expression to their inner meaning. The ultimate goal of the law even as it is revealed in the Old Testament was that it might be inner, written on the hearts of the people (see Jer. 31:31-33).

The "I" in the statement by Jesus regarding adultery (Matt. 5:27-28), as elsewhere in the whole series of comparisons, is emphatic: "But *I* say to you that every one who looks at a woman lustfully has already committed adultery with her in his heart" (Matt. 5:28, author's italics).

The word translated "lustfully" is frequently translated "desire" (see Matt. 13:17, KJV; Luke 22:15). Also, the English word *lust* originally meant "desire of any kind, good or bad." It came to refer, however, primarily to evil desires. Today it refers almost exclusively to the wrong kind of sexual desire.

What did Jesus mean? He did not mean a fleeting glance or a momentary desire. He was talking about the continued gaze which deliberately stimulates the desire. In other words, the look is not casual but persistent; it is not involuntary and momentary, but voluntary and cherished.

When Jesus extended adultery to the lustful look, he did not say that it was as evil as the actual physical adultery. The overt act directly involves and injures at least one other person. While the lustful look may not be as hurtful, it is nevertheless sinful just as the overt act is sinful. In other words, Jesus made sin inner, as well as outer, and inner before it was outer.

Why is lust sinful? It is wrong or sinful because another person, created in the image of God, is thought of as an object, an "it" rather than a "thou"—a person. Those who think of others as objects tend to treat them as objects to be used and not as persons to be respected. Here, as is true of other comparisons in Matthew 5, there is clearly revealed what someone has called "Christ's doctrine of the extra"—going beyond that which is expected. In other words, he plainly and pointedly went beyond the law by placing the emphasis on the inner rather than the outer (see Matt. 15:17-20; Mark 7:20-23).

"In his heart" in Matthew 5:28 did not refer exclusively, in the days of Jesus, to the emotional part of people. It indicated the intellect, the affections, the will, the total inner life. For Jesus, adultery was in the heart and the eye before it became an outer physical act.

General Exhortations

Near the close of the last chapter of Hebrews, the writer said, "Bear with my word of exhortation" (Heb. 13:22). Earlier in the chapter, in the midst of some pointed exhortations, he had said, "Let marriage be held in honor among all, and let the marriage bed be undefiled; for God will judge the immoral and adulterous" (v. 4).

Paul, in writing to the Thessalonians, gave an exhortation needed in that day, and needed today, by many Christians as well as non-Christians. He said, "This is the will of God, your sanctification" or "that you should be holy" (NEB) (1 Thess. 4:3). The basic idea of holiness in the Bible is separation: negative—separation from the world and the things that contaminate; and positive—separation unto God and his purpose or will (see Lev. 20:26). The God we worship is holy; he expects his children to be like him (Lev. 19:2; 1 Pet. 1:15-16).

In these verses (1 Thess. 4:3-8), Paul spelled out the general concept of sanctification or holiness in relation to one particular area of life. He used three clauses, each introduced with "that." The clauses are: (1) "that you abstain from unchastity ["avoid sexual immorality," NIV]" (v. 3); (2) "that each one of you know how to take a wife for himself in holiness and honor" (v. 4); and (3) "that no man transgress and wrong his brother in this matter" (v. 6). Now, let us look at each of these exhortations a little more carefully.

The exhortation to abstain from immorality evidently referred to any kind of illicit or God-disapproved sexual expression by the married or the unmarried. This was in marked contrast to pagan religions of that day that did not require sexual purity of their adherents.

The second specific exhortation or at least an application of the general exhortation concerning sanctification is that one should take a wife in holiness and honor. The word translated "wife" is literally "vessel" and is so translated in the King James Version. *The New English Bible* and the *New International Version* say "body."

Verse 6 is a continuation of the specific exhortation found in verse 4. Paul said that Christians should not take a wife "in the passion of lust like heathen who do not know God" (v. 5). Children of God of every era and age should not be controlled by their passions but should keep their passions under proper control.

The third and last of the clauses mentioned previously is "that no man transgress, and wrong ["defraud," NASB] his brother in this matter" (v. 6). How can one transgress, defraud, cheat, or "wrong his brother in this matter"? One could and can defraud or wrong a brother by committing adultery with his wife, taking his brother's wife away from him, or even by robbing the brother's wife-to-be of her virginity. Paul warned the Thessalonians and would warn contemporary Christians that "the Lord is an avenger in all these things" (v. 6). He did not spell out how the Lord avenges, but he did repeat that God has called us to "holiness" (v. 7).

Paul then concluded with a "therefore"—one of his favorite words (see Rom. 12:1; Eph. 4:1,25; 5:1), "'Therefore whoever disregards this, disregards not man but God, who gives the Holy Spirit to you" (v. 8). Here Paul was saying, in effect, "These are not my instructions, they come from God." Will you not agree that many people in our contemporary world, including some Christians, both married and unmarried, need to hear the word of God from Mount Sinai, "You shall not commit adultery" (Ex. 20:14)? Also, they and we need to hear that "God's plan is to make you holy, and that means a clean cut with sexual immorality. . . . The calling of God is not to impurity but to the most thorough purity, and anyone who makes light of the matter is not making light of a man's ruling but of God's command" (1 Thess. 4:3-8, Phillips).

Paul closed this exhortation for sexual purity by reminding the Thessalonians that God had given his Holy Spirit to them. In other words, the body is the temple of the Holy Spirit (see 1 Cor. 6:15). To abuse one's body in sinful, sensual pleasures is to sin against the indwelling Spirit.

Conclusion: Jesus and the Sinner

In concluding this chapter, it may be encouraging to examine the attitude of Jesus toward and his relations to sinful men and women. He was a friend of publicans or tax collectors and sinners (Luke 7:34). The Pharisees and scribes said of Jesus, "This man receives sinners and eats with them" (Luke 15:2). This was the background for the parable of the prodigal son or compassionate father. The prodigal had "squandered his property in loose living" (v. 13). The older brother plainly said to the father, he "has devoured your living with harlots" (v. 30). In spite of what the younger son had done, the father was waiting for him, affectionately received him, and provided a special celebration because of his return.

Then there was the striking case when Simon, the Pharisee, invited Jesus to have a meal with him (Luke 7:36-50). During the meal, "a woman of the city, who was a sinner . . . standing behind him at his feet, weeping, she began to wet his feet with her tears, and wiped them with the hair of her head, and kissed his feet, and anointed them with the ointment" (v. 38). When the Pharisee saw what was happening, he said, "If this man were a prophet, he would have known . . . what sort of woman this is . . . for she is a sinner" (v. 39).

Jesus then rebuked Simon, describing what the woman had done for him, and said, "Her sins, which are many, are forgiven" (v. 47). Then he turned to the woman and said, "Your sins are forgiven" (v. 48). She may have been a prostitute or one who was "living an immoral life" (NASB), but Jesus accepted her gift and worship, as on another occasion he accepted a similar expression of appreciation and worship from Mary of Bethany (John 12:3 *ff.*).

The other incident to which we want to call attention was the woman taken in the act of adultery (John 8:1-11). There are some questions about this incident: Did it actually happen? If so, where does it belong in the Gospels?[13] In spite of its uncertainty, there are few things in the Gospels that reveal more clearly the spirit of Jesus and his attitude toward sinning men and women.

Assuming that this was an actual experience, there are some interesting questions that could be asked. Where was the man who had been involved in the adultery? Why didn't they bring him? After all, the law assessed the same penalty on him as it did against the woman. What did Jesus mean when he said, "Let him who is without sin among you be the first to throw a stone at her"? Did he refer to sin in general or to the same sin for which they were condemning her? On two occasions, he wrote on the ground or in the sand: What did he write? How did the woman feel when she stood alone in the presence of Jesus?

We cannot know for sure the answers to the preceding questions, but we do know what Jesus said to her. After the men had left, Jesus "looked up and said to her, 'Woman, where are they? Has no one condemned you?' She said, 'No one, Lord.'" Then those wonderful words of Jesus, "Neither do I condemn you." Let us never forget, however, his concluding words, "Go, and do not sin again" (John 8:10-11).

As in the case of the woman in the house of Simon, the

Pharisee, Jesus did not gloss over sin. He could do and did something that most of us find it difficult to do: he could separate the sinner and her sin—loving the sinner without approving her sin. He had the marvelous capacity of meeting people where they were and pointing them in the direction in which they ought to go. He has done that for those of us who have met him along the way. In turn, he would like to use us to reach out to touch others who have sinned and some short of the glory of God. Only the forgiven sinner can effectively reach other sinners and draw them in love to the One who can say to them, as he has said on more than one occasion to us, "Neither do I condemn you; go, and do not sin again."

There are other illustrations that could have been given of the attitude of Jesus toward sinners. The ones to which reference has been made were selected because in each case some type of sexual sin was involved. At least this should be enough to encourage anyone who has been or is involved in any type of sexual sin: prostitution, adultery, homosexuality, and so forth. They can know that Jesus will forgive and accept them, just as he will and does other sinners. And let us never forget that Jesus made sin primarily inner. If we will let that truth grip us, it will save us from any spirit of self-righteousness. "There is none righteous, no, not one" (Rom. 3:10, KJV). This is not only true of the unsaved but of children of God as well.

Notes

1. Lois Clemens, *Women Liberated* (Scottdale, Pa.: Herald Press, 1971), p. 62.
2. David Mace, *The Christian Response to the Sexual Revolution*, p. 15.
3. Pierre Grelot, *Man & Wife in Scripture* (New York: Herder & Herder, 1964), p. 36.
4. The words "Do you not know?" are found six times in this one chapter (1 Cor. 6:2,3,9,15,16,19), four times elsewhere in the epistle (3:16; 5:6; 9:13,24), for a total of ten times. The question is found only twice elsewhere in the Pauline Epistles (Rom. 6:16; 11:2). It may be that the Corinthians had used those words frequently in their letter to Paul.
5. E. Neufeld, *Ancient Hebrew Marriage Laws* (New York: Longman, Green and Co., 1944), p. 163.

6. Space will not permit a thorough discussion of the prevalence and treatment of prostitution in the Scriptures. This will also be true of some other topics under this general heading of "Sex Outside of Marriage." Additional information can be secured in a rather compact form by consulting a good Bible dictionary or encyclopedia.

7. Judd Marmor, *Homosexual Behavior: A Modern Reappraisal* (New York: Basic Books, 1980), p. 3. Many books have been written, in recent years, on homosexuality with several of them approaching it from the Christian perspective. Two of the best are D. J. Atkinson, *Homosexual in the Christian Fellowship* (Grand Rapids: Eerdmans, 1951), and Jerry Kirk, *The Homosexual Crisis in the Mainline Church* (Nashville: Thomas Nelson, 1978). Another volume by multiple authors with four of its twenty-two chapters on homosexuality is Ruth Tiffany Barnhouse and Urban T. Holmes III, *Male and Female: Christian Approaches to Sexuality* (New York: Seabury Press, 1976). Two particularly helpful, perceptive chapters are: "A Theological Approach to Homosexuality" by Norman Pittenger and "Some Words of Caution" by William Muehl.

8. Kirk, 49.

9. D. Shervin Bailey, in *Homosexuality and the Western Christian Tradition* (London: Longmans, 1955), argued that "know" in Genesis 19:5 and Judges 19:22 does not refer to homosexuality. Although disagreeing with Bailey, Atkinson considers the book "by far the most significant Christian book of recent years on this subject (homosexuality)."

10. Atkinson, p. 86.

11. Kirk, p. 58.

12. Ibid., p. 61

13. The translations vary considerably in the way they treat the incident: the Revised Standard Version prints it in smaller type at the foot of the page with some notations. The *New American Standard Bible* has a notation at the side: "John 7:53-8:11 is not found in most of the old mss." The *New International Version* prints the verses but has the heading, "The earliest and most reliable manuscripts do not have John 7:53-8:11." *The New English Bible* prints the verses at the end of John's Gospel with some notations.

9

Divorce and Remarriage

There is no surer barometer of the health or sickness of a nation or a civilization than its predominant family pattern. If this statement is only relatively correct, it should give us serious concern about the United States and Western civilization in general. One point of concern should be the high divorce rate in recent years. The recording of divorces by the Census Bureau began in 1890, when there were 33,461 divorces in the United States. The number reached 100,000 in 1914, with an increase to 200,000 fourteen years later. The number then fluctuated for several years. Since 1959 there has been a sharp increase with 1,000,000 or more for the past several years.

Many people are hurt in most divorces, but none more than the children who may be involved. Much of their hurt is deep. Its ultimate effects on them are unpredictable. The tragedy is deepened for them because, in practically every case, they are the innocent victims of something over which they have no control.

This should be enough to emphasize the importance of a study of the biblical teachings on divorce and remarriage. After some introductory statements, it seems logical in this chapter, as in one or two previous chapters, to divide our discussion into the teachings of the Old Testament followed by sections on Jesus and Paul. There will be a concluding section on "The Divorced." This will be an attempt to relate the teachings of the Bible to the contemporary situation. In the closing section, attention will be given more to the spirit revealed in the Scriptures, particularly by Jesus, than to specific teachings.

Introductory Statements

These statements could just as properly be considered "concluding statements," but it is hoped that keeping some of them in mind will help you in evaluating what will be discussed in succeeding sections. It must be admitted that some of the conclusions are more or less tentative. You are encouraged to think through to what you consider to be a soundly Christian position.

1. There is no systematic discussion of divorce in the Scriptures. No clear "doctrine of divorce" is set forth. That means that, from the biblical perspective, there are some unanswered questions regarding divorce.

2. It should never be forgotten, however, that God's original purpose for the home was and still is one man and one woman joined together as husband and wife for life.

3. Since divorce falls short of God's purpose, it involves sin. (One of the words translated "sin" means "miss the mark.") However, the sin of divorce is not unforgivable and should not be treated as such by Christians and/or the Christian church.

4. The fullest statements in the New Testament regarding divorce are in response to questions. In the case of 1 Corinthians 7, we do not even know the questions.

5. The preceding means that one should not be dogmatic about what Jesus and/or Paul would say concerning complex situations faced by some husbands and wives in the contemporary world.

6. Some of the Scriptures used in this chapter are among the most difficult in the Bible to interpret. All we can do is give our perspective and trust you to think and pray through to a personally satisfying position.

7. There are times when "divorce may be the only way out. But when this happens it is always a concession to man's weakness."[1] Whether a divorce and/or remarriage is justified must be a personal matter or decision. It is hoped, however, that the individual or individuals involved will seek to know and follow what they interpret to be the will of God. Also, they should give serious consideration to the effect their decision will have on all persons directly or indirectly involved. And as Christians they should

remember the possible effects of a divorce and/or remarriage on their church and the cause of Christ. They should at least be sure that their divorce is unhurried and thought through carefully.

The Old Testament

The importance of what is said in the Old Testament concerning divorce is amplified by the fact that most of what Jesus said concerning divorce was in response to a question about the interpretation of the Old Testament law regarding divorce. The law, as was true of the Old Testament in general, sought to give guidance to people where they were. At times this meant an adjustment of God's perfect, unconditional, or intentional will to the realities of life. This adjustment was clearly evident regarding divorce. Jesus said that Moses permitted them to put away their wives because of the hardness of their hearts or because their "minds were closed" (Matt. 19:8, NEB).

The first clear statement about divorce in the Old Testament is Deuteronomy 24:1-4. These verses are usually referred to as the Old Testament "law of divorce." But in a strict sense, Deuteronomy 24:1-4 was not a law. "The right of divorces is assumed, as established by custom . . . but definite . . . formalities are prescribed, and restrictions are imposed, tending to prevent its being lightly or rashly exercised" (ICC). Neufeld similarly concludes "that divorce was known in Israel from the earliest days. The . . . passage from Deuteronomy merely formulated as a definite law what had previously existed as a very old custom."[2]

What the verses in Deuteronomy did was to regulate divorce. In doing so, it gave the wife a degree of protection that she had not formerly had. It is true that only the husband could initiate a divorce. But there were requirements placed on the husband that provided some protection for the wife.

He had to give her a bill or certificate of divorcement which was evidently a legal document. This was placed in her hand, suggesting that it possibly was served upon her. Then he sent her away or dismissed her, the usual Hebrew word for divorce (Deut. 22:19,29; Isa. 50:1; Mal. 2:16). It seems that the whole procedure was a more or less formal legal act. The certificate of divorce was the woman's protection. She could use it as evidence that she was no longer married. Another man was free to take her as his wife.

The main purpose or thrust of Deuteronomy 24:1-4 is found in verse 4. The Cambridge Bible sums up the purpose of the law as follows: this "law tends to make divorce a much more serious affair than it was usually conceived to be in Israel, and so to check the too-frequent practice of it by diminishing the possibilities of re-marriage which tempted men to divorce their wives with a light heart."

There are two or three words or phrases that create some problems of interpretation. One is "some indecency," "uncleanness" (KJV), or "something shameful" (NEB)." It has been variously interpreted as "some improper or indecent behaviour" (ICC) or "some immodest exposure or failure in proper womanly reserve" (Cam.B.). Von Rad suggests that the meaning of the term must have been clear in the time of Deuteronomy, "otherwise the matter would certainly have been defined more exactly" (OTL). It could not have referred to adultery, as suggested by Shammai and his followers, since adultery was punishable by death (Lev. 20:10).

Another word that causes some concern is "defiled" or "unclean" (NEB). The word may refer to defilement by means of intercourse with the second husband. The same term is applied elsewhere to adultery (Lev. 18:20; Num. 5:13-14,20). The primary meaning could be that she was defiled for the first husband. But also the reference could be to defilement in general.

How could this defilement "bring guilt ["sin," NASB] upon the land"? The land and the people were considered as one. It was polluted by its inhabitants. There was such a close identity of the individual with the group that the sin of one person affected the whole group, such as the nation (see Lev. 18:19-28).

There were two conditions in the law under which a man could not divorce his wife: (1) if he falsely accused her of not being a virgin when he took her as his wife (Deut. 22:13-21); (2) if he had raped a virgin who was not yet betrothed and hence had to marry her (Deut. 22:28-29).

What we find in the Old Testament regarding divorce, as is

true concerning some other matters such as war, is a balancing of the ideal and the real. The ideal concerning the relation of husband and wife is a lifetime union. Deuteronomy 24:1-4 represented an adjustment of the ideal to the realities of life at that time. There are a number of places, in addition to Genesis 2:24, where the ideal is set forth or at least implied. An evidence of God's disapproval of divorce is the fact that priests and high priests were not permitted to marry one who had been divorced (Lev. 21:7,14; see Ezek. 44:22). One reason for this prohibition was the fact that "the priest is holy to his God" (Lev. 21:7). This implies, from God's perspective, that there was something unholy about divorce.

The prophet Malachi plainly said, "For I hate divorce, says the Lord the God of Israel" (2:16). The context reveals that the reference was in a particular way to the fact that many of the children of Israel had put away wives of their "youth." And the prophet said, "The Lord was witness to the covenant between you and the wife of your youth" (v. 14).

Small concludes that the Mosaic permission of divorce was not ideal but remedial. He further says, "This in itself is an exhibition of God's caring grace, and that the lesser of two evils must sometimes prevail. In a fallen world inevitably there will be conflict of values where at times a tragic moral choice must be made."[3]

Preachers, teachers, and counselors should keep in proper balance the ideal and the adjustment of the ideal to the realities of life, where frequently the choice is in the gray area rather than between black and white. The ideal should be preached and taught, but people must be ministered to where they are. This may and will mean constant tension to all concerned, but there is no progress in our relation to the Lord without tension.

Jesus

There are some differences in Matthew's and Mark's accounts of the response of Jesus to the Pharisees. This is also true of Matthew's record of the teachings of Jesus regarding divorce (Matt. 19:3-12) and Paul's instructions to the Corinthians (1 Cor. 7:10-11) where he claimed the authority of the Lord. These variations have contributed to different perspectives concerning the teachings of the New Testament regarding divorce. Some have concluded that, from the New Testament viewpoint, there is not justifiable grounds for divorce. Those taking that position have followed, in the main, the teachings of Paul; and when referring to Jesus, they have used Mark 10:2-12 rather than Matthew 19. They explain away Matthew's exception clause (5:32; 19:9) by suggesting that it is an interpolation, or at best it does not give the right of remarriage to the so-called innocent party.

There are many Christians in the contemporary period who not only would justify, on scriptural grounds, the divorce and remarriage of the "innocent" party in the case of adultery but also on the basis of desertion (the so-called Pauline privilege, 1 Cor. 7:15-16). Some take an even more liberal position, justifying divorce and remarriage on most any grounds.

What did Jesus and Paul really teach concerning divorce and remarriage? In this section on Jesus, we will be concerned primarily with what he actually said. In a later section, we will seek to apply not only what he actually said about divorce but also his attitude and relation to people in general that may help in the proper application of his teachings.

There are only four specific references in the Gospels to the teachings of Jesus regarding divorce (Matt. 5:31-32; 19:3-12; Mark 10:2-12; Luke 16:18). The first is one of the striking comparisons Jesus made of his teachings and the Old Testament law (Matt. 5:21-48). Each follows, in general, the same formula: "You have heard that it was said. . . . But I say to you."

Jesus clearly went beyond the Old Testament law regarding divorce. He evidently referred to Deuteronomy 24:1 and then added, "But I say to you that every one who divorces his wife, except on the grounds of unchastity, makes her an adulteress; and whoever marries a divorced woman commits adultery" (Matt. 5:32).

What did Jesus mean when he said "makes her an adulteress"? It could be that it would be assumed that she would remarry, which would make her an adulteress. In the culture of that day it was practically impossible for a woman to support herself. We shall postpone until later the discussion of the exception clause which "has given rise to much controversy that will probably last until the world's end" (Exp. Gr.).

Now, let us consider Matthew 19. What Jesus said concerning divorce, also recorded in Mark, was a part of a conversation with the Pharisees. The record in Matthew contains two clauses not found in Mark's record—the exception clause and the remarriage clause. Also, verses 10-12 of Matthew 19 include a statement of the disciples and the reply of Jesus.

Evidently, the Pharisees were attempting to trap Jesus. The question was, "Is it lawful[4] to divorce one's wife for any cause"? More than likely the background for the question on this occasion was the fact that there were two prominent schools of thought concerning the correct interpretation of "indecency" or "nakedness of a thing" in Deuteronomy 24:1. The followers of Shammai, a famous rabbi, emphasizing the idea of "nakedness," said the reference was to adultery. The followers of another famous rabbi, Hillel, emphasizing "a thing" and "finds no favor in his eyes," would permit divorce on the most trivial grounds. The Pharisees doubtlessly hoped to get Jesus into conflict with the followers of Shammai or Hillel. It is possible, however, that they were testing his wisdom by proposing to him one of their puzzles. They may have hoped to discredit him and the superior wisdom that he was supposed to have.

Jesus, in his reply, went back of the law to the original intent of the Lawgiver. He appealed from Deuteronomy to Genesis, "the latter represents the Divine purpose, the former a temporary concession" (Cam.B.) In the beginning God created them male and female. Also, Jesus quoted Genesis 2:24 and stressed the oneness or unity of husband and wife. He then stated the basic principle, "What therefore God has joined together, let no man put asunder" or "man must not separate" (v. 6, NEB).

The union of husband and wife is physical, but it is more than physical. George Buttrick says that "they form a unity of self more marvelous than the separate unity of either man or woman . . . to keep the unity is to find life's true fulfillment" (Int.B.) Another way to underscore this same concept of unity is to say that the sexual act unites them, makes them one the same as the junction of two streams makes one river, the union of hydrogen and oxygen in certain proportions make one substance, water. . . . Their duality no longer exists; it has been replaced by this structural unity. Before there had been two beings structurally fitted for each other; now their union makes this new structural unity (ICC).

Barclay says that "Jesus was laying down the principle that all divorce is wrong" and then concludes, "We must note that it is not a *law;* it is a *principle,* which is a very different thing." Somewhat similarly, another commentary says, "Christ did not come to be a new legislator making laws for social life. He came to set up a high ethical ideal, and leave that to work on men's minds" (Exp.Gr.). It should be remembered, however, that the principles of Jesus were in harmony with and expressive of the basic laws of God. Basic laws, in contrast to written laws, are written into the nature of men and women and of the world that God created and in which he works out his will.

If the Pharisees had not asked Jesus another question, it seems the conversation would have closed with verse 6, which would have meant no divorce. But they asked, "Why then did Moses command one to give a certificate of divorce, and to put her away?" The reply of Jesus, which has real significance for the proper interpretation of the Old Testament in general, was, "For your hardness of heart ["your minds were closed," NEB], Moses allowed ["permitted," NASB] you to divorce your wives, but from the beginning it was not so" (v. 8). This permission fell below the original intention of God. To use a helpful distinction that is sometimes made, what we find in Deuteronomy 24 does not represent the perfect or intentional will of God but his permissive, circumstantial, or conditional will.

Jesus concluded the conversation with the Pharisees with the statement, "And I say to you: whoever divorces his wife, except for unchastity, and marries another, commits adultery" (v. 9). In other words, "the Mosaic Law was an accommodation" (An.B.). What about the so-called innocent party? Does he or she have the right to remarriage? (Incidentally, the word *so-called* is used because there is seldom, if ever, a totally "innocent" party in a divorce.) Robertson suggests that "Jesus by implication, as in 5:32, does allow the remarriage of the innocent party, but not the guilty" (W.P.) Many scholars disagree.

Now, let us consider a little more fully the "exception clause" found in Matthew 5:32 and 19:9, but not in Mark, Luke, or Paul. Particularly perplexing is the fact that Mark, reporting the same conversation of Jesus with the Pharisees, did not include the "exception clause." And incidentally, most New Testament scholars believe that Mark was written before Matthew.

In addition to the fact that some scholars consider the "exception clause" an interpolation, there are other possibilities that are sometimes suggested. (1) Jesus actually said, "except for unchastity"; Mark did not include it, assuming that everyone would consider adultery a justifiable ground for divorce. The Pharisees and the Jews in general would not believe that anyone would fail to justify divorce on that basis. (2) Jesus did not actually use the words "except for unchastity," but Matthew knew or at least believed that Jesus would approve divorce on that ground. (3) Some scholars contend that Matthew added the exception clause to tone down what Jesus had said. That made what he said more in harmony with the practice of the day.

It must be admitted that the "exception clause" creates some real problems of interpretation. One problem is that it seems to be contrary to the general tenor of the teachings of Jesus. He generally set forth the perfect ideal of the Father. Divorce, even on the basis of unchastity, is an adjustment of the ideal to the realities of the situation. It should be known, however, that there seems to be no textual or manuscript support for deleting the exception clause in either 5:32 or 19:9.

There are two statements recorded only in Mark of considerable significance that Jesus made to the disciples "in the house," (Mark 10:10) following the conversation with the Pharisees. (1) "Whoever divorces his wife and marries another, commits adultery against her" (Mark 10:11). In other words, adultery is a sin *against* someone as well as *with* someone. (2) "And if she divorces her husband and marries another, she commits adultery." In other words, the wife, so far as divorce is concerned, was put on a par with the husband. This would be in harmony with the whole spirit and approach of Jesus, who, as was true of the Father, was and is no respecter of persons.

Matthew recorded a conversation of Jesus with his disciples, quite different from Mark's account.[5] "The disciples said to him, 'If such is the case of a man with his wife, it is not expedient to marry'" (19:10). The disciples were evidently saying, "If a man cannot put away his wife except for unchastity, it is better not to marry." Their statement suggests that the less strict view of Hillel was more popular not only among the Jews in general but also among the disciples of Jesus.

The reply of Jesus in verses 11-12, which have been discussed previously in chapter 5 on "Single Adults," contains two important principles: (1) remaining unmarried can be a proper choice for Christians; (2) remaining unmarried has its distinctive demands as is true of marriage.

Paul

Paul did not say much in his Epistles about divorce. The only place where Paul directly discussed divorce was in 1 Corinthians 7:10-16. It appears relatively clear that chapter 7 was in response to several questions that were asked in the letter that he had received from the church or at least a group in the church at Corinth. Some of the things Paul wrote in this chapter are among the most difficult to interpret of any of his writings.

He gave some instruction concerning divorce where a husband and wife were both Christians. This is followed by some words concerning a mixed marriage—one a Christian, the other not. For the first he claimed the authority of the Lord, doubtlessly referring to a written record or more likely to an oral tradition of what Jesus had said. The general opinion of New Testament scholars is that 1 Corinthians was written before any of the Gospels. Regarding the husband and wife in a mixed marriage, Paul had no record, written or oral, of a direct word of the Lord. Jesus did not have to deal with that issue. "This is a new problem, the result of work among the Gentiles, and did not arise in the time of Jesus" (W.P.).

To Christian couples Paul, citing the authority of the Lord, gave the "charge," "ruling" (NEB), "instruction" (NASB), "command" (NIV) "that the wife should not separate from her husband" (v. 10). We would not expect it, but here Paul referred first to a woman being separated from her husband. It is possible that he was replying to a question or some questions by women at Corinth. This may have been a result, at least to some degree, of the fact that "Christianity had powerfully stirred the feminine mind at Corinth (see xi.5-6, xiv.34)" (Exp.Gr.). Then in a parenthetical statement, Paul said if she separates or departs, in violation of the clear teachings of Jesus, she is to remain single or be reconciled to her husband. He makes no allowance for the remarriage of the so-called innocent party. He evidently knew nothing about the exception clause as found in Matthew.

Paul's instructions concerning the divorce of Christian husbands and wives imply that a wife could take the initiative. This represented a considerable advance over the Old Testament. Although this may have resulted from the current practice in the Greek world, we do note in this epistle an element of mutuality of the responsibilities and privileges of husband and wife. An example, previously mentioned, was their sexual relations (1 Cor. 7:2-7).

The Corinthian congregation may have asked Paul about a particular case. Also, there may have been a tendency on the part of some to separate or divorce on the basis of ascetic motives. It is even possible that some at Corinth were contending that the single life was to be preferred to married life because Paul was not married. Whatever may have been the motive, Paul clearly said that a Christian couple should not separate or divorce.

Then in verses 12-16 Paul addressed "the rest" or all others. We know by what follows that by "the rest" he was referring to those involved in a mixed marriage. One of them had been converted after marriage; now what should they do? We know, of course, that Paul would not approve a Christian marrying a non-Christian (2 Cor. 6:14b). "Paul would not sanction Christians marrying nonbelievers any more than Ezra (10:10) would permit Jews to marry Gentile women, but he did not call for the dissolution of such marriages"

(Int.B.). He suggested two major things: one assumed, the other plainly stated. (1) He assumed that a Christian husband or wife would not take the initiative in seeking a separation or divorce from a nonbeliever. Notice again, Paul's inclusion of both husband and wife in his instructions: "If any brother. . . . If any woman." This again is the mutuality of responsibility of husbands and wives, which is evident not only in 1 Corinthians 7 but also in the great passage in Ephesians (5:21-33) and elsewhere. (2) If an unbelieving or non-Christian husband or wife took the initiative and wanted or desired a separation or divorce, Paul said, "Let it be so" and added, "in such a case the brother or sister is not bound"—notice again the inclusion of "sister."

There is an additional difficult question relative to these verses: did the one whose husband or wife had taken the initiative and departed have the right or privilege of remarriage? This is the so-called Pauline privilege. Some, like Luther, would say yes. But "it is wiser to admit that we do not know what his counsel would have been" (Int.B.).

Possibly Paul's statement about the Christian not taking the initiative resulted from the fact that some Corinthian Christians thought that union with an unbeliever would defile them. They may have reasoned, "Will not the saint . . . be defiled, and the 'limbs of Christ' . . . be desecrated by intercourse with a heathen?" (Exp.G.). Paul's viewpoint was that the unbelieving husband or wife was sanctified, consecrated, or made holy by his or her association with the believing mate. It is clear from what Paul said later and elsewhere that the reference is not to salvation or moral character. Paul seemingly meant that the "sanctification of the one includes the other so far as their wedlock is concerned" (Exp.G.). Or, similarly, "clearly he only means that the marriage relation is sanctified so there is no need for divorce" (W.P.).

In other words, one is not contaminated or made unclean by having sexual union with an unbelieving husband or wife. If such a union defiled the Christian husband or wife, then the children born of such a union would be unholy, unclean, or possibly even illegitimate. Paul pointedly said that this was not true. Let us repeat, this whole section refers to a couple where one becomes a Christian after marriage.

Paul did say, as suggested earlier, that if an unbelieving mate takes the initiative and wants a separation or a divorce, the believer should not refuse. He said, "In such case the brother or sister is not bound," "is not under bondage in such cases" (KJV), or "is under no compulsion" (NEB). "Is not bound" literally means "is not enslaved." *Doulou* is the verb form of *doulos* (slave). The willful desertion of an unbelieving mate sets the other free. One reason the believer should permit the dissatisfied unbelieving mate to depart is that "God has called us to peace" (v. 15). Is the believing husband or wife free to remarry? Paul did not say. There are sharply different viewpoints. Martin Luther argued that the believer was free to marry again. The Interpreter's Bible suggests that the fact that Paul did not forbid it seems like allowance. Ellisen, while suggesting that Paul would permit remarriage, does say, "Remarriage is admittedly always wrong while the possibility of reconciliation to the former partner remains."[6] Others contend that, based on Paul's general position, it is safer to assume that he did not and would not permit remarriage. An example: the "inference that the divorced should remain unmarried is the safer position" (Exp.G.).

Verse 16 is another difficult passage to interpret: "Wife, how do you know whether you will save your husband? Husband, how do you know?" What did Paul mean? Was he giving an argument for or against accepting the separation or divorce? Robertson says the syntax allows either interpretation. The verse has been labeled a "curiously ambiguous" statement that may be used as a reason for or against the believer permitting or accepting the separation (Exp.Gr.).

If this verse is connected with what immediately precedes, then Paul was saying, in effect: "Why should you insist on maintaining the union with your unbelieving mate? If your motive is to win him or her to Christ, how can you be sure that that will be true?" One commentator's conclusion is: "The Apostle declares that the remote contingency of the unbeliever's conversion is too vague a matter for which to risk the peace which is so essential an element in the Christian life" (Ell.).

On the other hand, if verse 16 looks back to verses 12 and 13, as some suggest, then Paul was asking the question, in effect, "How do you know that you will not win that unbelieving mate to the Lord if you insist on continuing to live with him or her?" *The New English Bible* gives the verse this emphasis, "Think of it, as a wife you may be your husband's salvation; as a husband you may be your wife's salvation" (1 Cor. 7:16).

On the surface, the first of these interpretations seems the more logical one. But, although the most logical or natural interpretation is usually best, it is not always the correct interpretation. A good case can be made for the second interpretation. This is certainly true if we give proper consideration to Paul's general attitude and spirit regarding marriage and divorce.

The Divorced

As we begin the consideration of the divorced, it may be helpful to recognize that divorce, as is true of some other contemporary problems, is frequently discussed too exclusively either from the perspective of theology and a strict interpretation of the Scriptures or from the viewpoint of human hurt. One who too exclusively emphasizes the latter will tend to tone down what is found in the Scriptures. In this section, we will attempt to keep a balanced emphasis, taking the teachings of the Bible seriously while also being sympathetic to the hurts of men, women, and frequently children who are involved in any divorce.

It might be helpful for you to review the "Introductory Statements" at the beginning of this chapter. When we review these statements and the biblical material in general on divorce, will you not agree that few if any of us are wise enough to know what our Heavenly Father would approve in many contemporary situations where divorce and remarriage is being considered?

An important factor in properly interpreting the teachings of Jesus and Paul regarding divorce is whether they were speaking legalistically. This is particularly important for our understanding of Jesus. In other words, when he said, "But I say to you that every one who divorces his wife" (Matt. 5:32; 19:9) was he enunciating a new law?

T. W. Manson, a great British New Testament scholar, says some general things concerning Jesus as a teacher that are applicable, to some degree, to this study of divorce. Manson says:

> It is a mistake to regard the ethical teaching of Jesus as a "New Law" in the sense of a reformed and unified exposition of the Old, or as a code of rules to take the place of the code of Moses and his successors. What Jesus offers in his ethical teaching is not a set of rules of conduct, but a number of illustrations of the way in which a transformed character will express itself in conduct.[7]

The nonlegalistic approach of Jesus, even to the law itself, is clearly evident in the conversation he had with a lawyer, recorded in Luke 10:25-37. The lawyer asked Jesus, "What shall I do to inherit eternal life?" Jesus then asked him, "What is written in the law?" The lawyer gave the familiar summary of the law: supreme love for God and equal love for neighbor. The word of Jesus was, "Do this, and you will live." Then the lawyer, "desiring to justify himself, said to Jesus, 'And who is my neighbor?'" He asked Jesus to build a fence around neighbor and hence to place some limits on love.

Jesus replied with the familiar parable of the good Samaritan. Jesus did not answer the lawyer's question. "In place of a rule or covenant to obey he [the lawyer] is given a type of character to imitate. This is typical of the method of Jesus in dealing with moral questions. He refuses to legislate, because he is concerned with the springs of conduct rather than with the outward acts."[8] Jesus, at the close of this conversation, asked the lawyer a far more important question than the one the lawyer had asked. The question of Jesus was: Who "proved neighbor to the man who fell among the robbers?" In other words, how can one be a good neighbor rather than who is my neighbor? If you will think through the preceding, I believe you will see that it has considerable relevance for the matter of divorce and particularly the attitude of Christians and churches toward the divorced.

This should not be interpreted, however, as a soft, easygoing attitude toward divorce and/or remarriage. We should never forget that divorce falls short of God's purpose for the relation of husband and wife, and hence it is sin. And it may be that the sin was entering marriage without the proper care and prayer or may have resulted from too hurriedly seeking a divorce without a sincere effort to save the marriage and without a proper regard for the effects of the divorce on all who will be touched by it. It should be repeated, however, and possibly underscored for some church members that divorce is not an unforgivable sin.

As Christians we should all be grateful that we are not living under law but under grace. God's word to Paul, when he was struggling with his "thorn . . . in the flesh," was "my grace is sufficient for you" (2 Cor. 12:9). Our need may be drastically different from Paul's; but whatever the need, God's grace will be sufficient. If husband and wife will let his grace operate in their lives, it may help to preserve their marriage. For most of us outside and inside of marriage, there is no greater need than forgiveness for our sins. That may include a divorce too quickly secured, but it may also include the attitude of some toward the divorced.

We should never forget that God's forgiveness is available whatever the sin may be. That forgiveness, like most blessings that come from our Heavenly Father, is not unconditional. One condition, clearly stated by Jesus in the Model Prayer, is the forgiving spirit. The request for forgiveness in the prayer is the only petition commented on at the close of the prayer. The comment is, "For if you forgive men their trespasses, your heavenly Father also will forgive you; but if you do not forgive men their trespasses, neither will your Father forgive your trespasses" (Matt. 6:14-15). This clearly states one condition for forgiveness and restoration for the divorced as is true for any other sinner. The forgiving are forgiven, and the forgiven should be the forgiving. This includes all of us.

Possibly it should be said that the spirit of repentance and forgiveness, if genuine, can frequently prevent a divorce. When a divorce has occurred, there should be real repentance—all the responsibility for a divorce is seldom if ever entirely on one side.

Forgiveness should accompany the spirit of repentance. Furthermore, remarriage should not be considered unless and until there has been and is a genuine spirit of repentance accompanied by a willingness to forgive.

Those who advocate a nonlegalistic perspective concerning the biblical teachings regarding divorce often correctly suggest that divorce at times may be the "lesser-of-two-evils." Such a divorce, it is suggested, may represent a better solution than the continuance of a relationship that has lost all of its deeper meaning and is little better than legalized cohabitation. The inner unity has been destroyed; love is gone. True or real marriage cannot be produced by law or force. A marriage that has failed functionally cannot be restored simply by preserving it structurally.

This interpretation or attitude does not justify a hurried divorce and/or remarriage. An honest effort should be made to preserve the marriage by restoring or creating, as far as possible, the conditions for a fulfilling and meaningful union.

This discussion of law and grace, more or less naturally, leads to a consideration of the relation of the will of God to divorce and remarriage. The will of God is so deep, so broad, so meaningful that some distinctive terms are needed to describe it. Some make a distinction between the perfect and the permissive will of God. Weatherhead, in his little book on the will of God,[9] makes a distinction between the ultimate, the intentional, and the circumstantial will of God. More recently, in a compact but thorough study, Small distinguishes between what he terms the unconditional and the conditional will of God. His "unconditional" and "conditional" are practically the same as Weatherhead's "intentional" and "circumstantial" will of God.

Small applies over and over again his distinction to divorce and remarriage. He defines the conditional will of God as follows:

> By God's conditional will, we mean His grace-motivated accommodation to a fallen world in which His people must live and move and have their being. . . . The conditional will of God expresses his expectation that redeemed men and women cannot, under the conditions of this age, reach perfect righteousness.[10]

Small also says that, somewhat paradoxically,

we speak of God's absolute, unconditional will for man, while at the same time we speak of His conditional will which is administered in different modes. One time it is *law*, another *grace*. Under law, God acts graciously; under grace, God points to the law as the standard of His righteousness and as the goal of life in the Spirit.[11]

The ideal for the Christian is God's unconditional will or perfection (Matt. 5:48). This means, among other things, that the movement of the Christian's life should always be in the direction of the intentional or unconditional will of God. The result will be that the child of God will always live with some tension. There will be a constant tug to come up higher, to move toward the unconditional or intentional will of God. But there is no progress without such a tug or tension. This means, among other things, that divorce and remarriage should always be recognized as falling short of God's intentional will. The release for the tension that this creates is in the knowledge that the Heavenly Father understands, will forgive, and restore to full fellowship if his conditions for such restoration are met. Those conditions, as previously stated, are a recognition of responsibility for the sin that has been involved in the divorce, a request for forgiveness, the acceptance of that forgiveness, and a forgiving spirit toward those who have also been involved in the sin.

A rather serious problem for some conscientious Christians is whether remarriage involves one in a continuous adulterous relationship. In other words, does the couple commit adultery every time they have sexual intercourse, or is the adultery a one-time experience? We cannot speak dogmatically, but there is at least some possibility that it is a one-time experience. If this is correct, then it would be adultery for them to have relations with anyone other than the second mate.

There is at least one thing we can be sure about: our God is big enough to care for whatever sin or problem may be involved. Some way he can take care of it and evidently does in some cases. There are Christian couples who have been divorced and remarried who have matured in the Lord. And one does not and cannot grow and mature in the Lord without being right with or acceptable to the

Lord. There may not be many such couples, but there are some.

There are some additional insights into the life and ministry of Jesus that can be helpful as we consider the divorced and the church's attitude toward them. One is the fact that Jesus considered human need as more important than the law. He, on one occasion, said to the Pharisees, "The sabbath was made for man, not man for the sabbath" (Mark 2:27). The Pharisees had made the law of the sabbath a burden to the people. It had been provided, as was true of every other basic moral law, for the good of people. It is at least a possibility that some people tend to interpret what Jesus and Paul said concerning divorce so legalistically that it would negate at least the spirit of Jesus and the ultimate purpose of God in the divorce law.

Whether the preceding is correct, we do know that Jesus had a very generous, forgiving spirit in his relation to people who had sinned and fallen short of the purposes of God. Many illustrations could be given. There was the Samaritan woman at the well, who had practiced "progressive polygamy" but who was the first person, so far as we know, to whom Jesus clearly revealed that he was the promised Messiah (John 4:26). Other incidents, some of which have been previously mentioned, are: the woman of the street in the home of Simon, the Pharisee (Luke 7:36-50); the woman taken in the act of adultery (John 8:3-11).

Then there was Mary Magdalene "from whom seven demons had gone out" (Luke 8:2). There may be some question about the nature of the demons, but there is no doubt about her relation to our Lord. She was among the last at the cross and the first at the tomb. To her the resurrected Christ first spoke. To her he first entrusted the message of his resurrection (John 20:17-18).

There are numerous other illustrations that could be given that reveal the spirit and attitude of Jesus toward those who fell short of God's expectations. There was the thief or criminal on the cross, "Today you will be with me in Paradise" (Luke 23:43).

The divorced and all of us as sinners should not forget, however, that the criminal on his cross had cried out "Jesus, remember me when you come into your kingdom" (v. 42). It cannot be stressed too much that forgiveness of our Heavenly Father is never automatic and seldom unconditional.

This list of incidents in the life of Jesus that reveal his gracious forgiving spirit to those who had sinned would not be complete without a brief note about one of his closest followers—Peter. He was one of the inner circle of those who, on several occasions, were the only ones with Jesus. He was frequently the spokesman for the twelve. When Jesus predicted the desertion by his disciples at the time of his arrest, Peter bragged that he would never desert Jesus. He followed afar off as Jesus was led away to trial. In the judgment hall, he denied on three different occasions that he even knew Jesus. When he denied the third time, "the Lord turned and looked at Peter" (Luke 22:61—found only in Luke). Then Peter, remembering what Jesus had said about his denial, "went out and wept bitterly" (v. 62). What do you suppose was the expression on the face of Jesus as he looked at Peter? At least we know that it was a look that broke Peter's heart. This was the same Peter, forgiven and restored, who stood on the Day of Pentecost and preached that marvelous message about the crucified and risen Christ.

And let us remember again that great moral and religious teachers teach as much, if not more, by their spirits and attitudes than by anything they verbalize. This was definitely and to an unusual degree true of Jesus, the greatest Teacher who ever lived.

Although this is a book on the Bible and the family, it is considered wise to have at least a brief statement regarding the attitude toward and relation to the divorced by Christians and the church. From what has been said previously, there should be no question about the individual Christian's attitude. It should be the desire of every child of God to be helpful in relation to the divorced. Frequently, the divorced man or woman goes through a grief process comparable to the loss of a loved one through death. Entirely too often they are treated drastically different by Christian friends.

The church as an institution is somewhat different. At least the church has the problem of how the divorced can best be utilized in the structures of the church without compromising the church's message on divorce. Consideration also should be given to the possible influence on young people and others. There is no easy and universally acceptable answer to these and related problems. Small may slightly overstate the case when he says, "Strange, but one can be forgiven nearly any other failure known to life and be restored to a place of service within the church—confession and penitence does the trick. But to be divorced and remarried is to have committed the unpardonable sin for which there is no restoration to service for Christ in the church."[12]

"Confession" and "penitence" are the key words in the preceding statement. Without the right attitude toward the divorce, restoration to places of service is very doubtful. This may sound harsh, but divorce and remarriage should never be treated lightly. On the other hand, individual Christians and the church should exercise the same grace and generosity toward those whose marriages have failed as God had and continually has to exercise toward all of us in our failures and sins.

Ellisen says, "Spiritual leaders are not necessarily those who have made no mistakes, but those who have repented and learned from their mistakes, and, like penitent Peter, have more deeply appropriated the grace and strength of the Lord."[13] We should remember that "where sin increased, grace abounded all the more" (Rom. 5:20).

It may be wise for us to hear again and heed the warning: we should be careful not to permit the contemporary situation in our lives, in the lives of loved ones, in our world, or even in our churches to determine too largely our interpretation of the Scriptures concerning divorce and remarriage.

Notes

1. Stanley C. Brown, *God's Plan for Marriage* (Philadelphia: Westminster Press, 1977), p. 363.
2. E. Neufeld, *Ancient Hebrew Marriage Laws* (New York: Longman, Green and Co., 1944), p. 176.

3. Dwight Harvey Small, *The Right to Remarry* (Old Tappan, N.J.: Fleming H. Revell Co., 1977), p. 41.

4. There were other occasions when the Pharisees asked him, "Is it lawful"—to heal on the sabbath (Matt. 12:10) and to give tribute to Caesar (Matt. 22:17).

5. Some scholars attribute the unique elements in Matthew's conversation regarding and related to divorce to M, a source independent of Mark and also the supposed source of other material peculiar to Matthew.

6. Stanley A. Ellisen, *Divorce and Remarriage in the Church* (Grand Rapids: Zondervan, 1977), p. 99.

7. T. W. Manson, *The Teachings of Jesus*, 2nd ed. (Cambridge: Cambridge University Press, 1935), p. 301.

8. Ibid.

9. Leslie D. Weatherhead, *The Will of God* (New York: Abingdon-Cokesbury Press, 1944).

10. Small, p. 132.

11. Ibid.

12. Ibid., p. 10.

13. Ellisen.

10

Parents and Children

This chapter, to some degree and in some way, touches the lives of all of us. We may not be parents, but all of us are children of varying ages. We may be married but without children, voluntarily or unvoluntarily. Unfortunately, there are many children who live in one-parent homes—parents separated, divorced, or one dead.

Also, there is an increasing number of children who come into the world outside of an established family of a father and a mother who will welcome them into the home. According to the *New York Times* (10/26/81), in 1979 an estimated 957,800 babies were born in the United States to unwed mothers, which was about 17 percent of all births. This represented a 50 percent increase in the last decade and means that about 1 of every 6 American babies is born to an unwed mother. How unfortunate for both the father and the mother of such a child, but it is doubly tragic for the child.

In this chapter, an effort will be made to point out and to interpret the more significant teachings of the Bible regarding the relations and responsibilities of parents and children. There will be only two major divisions: "Parents to Children" and "Children to Parents."

Parents to Children

Some things will have to be assumed and not discussed. Among these is the fact that a married couple should have children. It is recognized, of course, that there are some wonderful couples who cannot have children. Also, there may be some who should not have children.

Another thing that we will assume is that every child has the inherent right to be wanted and welcomed by his or her parents.

This will involve careful planning and preparation for the coming of the child into the world. The preparation should involve not only the mother-to-be but also the father and other children, if any, in the home. The child who is planned for will usually be welcomed while on the way and when he or she arrives.

As we approach this discussion of the relationship of parents to their children, it should be recognized that being a good parent is one of life's major and sometimes most difficult achievements. Many men and an increasing number of women who may be considered successful from the world's perspective are, to varying degrees, failures as parents. Their children frequently pay a terrific price for that failure. Fathers and mothers may become conscious of their failure when the children reach the teen years. They may attempt to compensate for previous neglect; but in the vast majority of cases, they discover that it is too late. Some children are almost total strangers to their parents.

Love them. In the main, it is assumed in the Scriptures that parents will love their children. There are numerous references in the Old Testament where it does not say that parents loved or should love their children but such is clearly implied. Some examples are Moses and his mother; Rebekah and her favorite son, Jacob; Jacob and Joseph; Hannah and Samuel. Then think of the cry of David when he learned of the death of Absalom: "O my son Absalom, my son, my son Absalom! Would I had died instead of you, O Absalom, my son, my son!" (2 Sam. 18:33). Also there were the parents who pleaded with Jesus to heal a son or a daughter (for example, Mark 9:24; John 4:49).

Jesus, on some occasions, took for granted that parents loved their children. On one occasion he said, "He who loves ["cares for," NEB] son or daughter more than me is not worthy of me" (Matt. 10:37). In another statement, which does not contain the word *love* but where it is clearly implied, Jesus reminded his disciples, "If you then, who are evil, know how to give good gifts to your children, how much more will your Father who is in heaven give good things to those who ask him!" (Matt. 7:11). Good gifts are an expression of love.

The parable of the prodigal son (Luke 15) could just as

appropriately be called the parable of the compassionate father. When the son was on his way back to his father, "while he was yet at a distance, his father saw him and had compassion, and ran and embraced him and kissed him" (Luke 15:20). When the son started his confession, "Father, I have sinned against heaven and before you; I am no longer worthy to be called your son" (v. 21), he was interrupted by his father's command to his servants, "Bring quickly the best robe, and put it on him . . . and let us eat and make merry" (vv. 22-23). This is another illustration of love expressed.

Paul suggested to Titus that the older women "train ["encourage," NASB] the young women to love their husbands and children, to be sensible, chaste, domestic, kind, and submissive to their husbands, that the word of God may not be discredited ["dishonored," NASB]" (2:4-5).

One of the basic needs of all children is to have parents who genuinely love them and wisely express that love to them. Many of the problems and frustrations prevalent among contemporary young people could have been alleviated, if not eliminated, if they had matured in an atmosphere of genuine and wise parental love and concern.

Discipline them. Moses, speaking for God to the children of Israel, said, "As a man disciplines his son, the Lord your God disciplines you" (Deut. 8:5). God who is *agape* and who loves us disciplines us. There is no necessary conflict between love and discipline. Really, discipline of the right kind and in the right spirit is a product and proof of love. In contrast, a failure to discipline may be an evidence of a lack of love, at least of the right kind of love. It possibly should be added that only discipline that is motivated by love will be most effective.

There is a rather long reference to the relation of love and discipline in the great twelfth chapter of Hebrews. The writer first, quoting from Proverbs 3:11-12, said:

> "My son, do not regard lightly the discipline of the Lord,
> nor lose courage when you are punished by him.
> For the Lord disciplines him whom he loves,
> and chastises every son whom he receives" (vv. 5-6).

In other words, when discipline comes from the Lord, it can be assumed that he is treating us as sons and daughters. In contrast, the writer said, "If you are left without discipline, . . . then you are illegitimate children and not sons" (v. 8).

There follows a contrast between the discipline of earthly fathers and the discipline of the Heavenly Father, "They disciplined us for a short time at their pleasure, but he disciplines us for our good ["true welfare," NEB], that we may share his holiness" (v. 10). This rather lengthy passage on discipline is concluded with the statement, "For the moment all discipline seems painful," but "later it yields the peaceful fruit ["harvest," NEB] of righteousness to those who have been trained by it" (v. 11). The fruit of discipline, whether a child or an adult child of God, will be determined by whether he or she has been "trained by it." In other words, has some lesson or lessons been learned? And it might be added that, in human relations, the learning process is a two-way street: parents as well as children can learn from the necessary discipline.

This emphasis on the relation of love to discipline would not be complete without a reference to a statement made by the resurrected Christ to and through John on the island of Patmos. His word was, "Those whom I love, I reprove and chasten ["discipline," NEB]" (Rev. 3:19). This again underscores the fact that there is no conflict between love and the proper kind of discipline. In an excellent book, written some years ago, Gibson Winter makes the following statement: "In family life love and discipline seem to be alternating attitudes of parents to children, whereas the two are really inseparable. Undisciplined love spoils and unloving discipline burdens."[1] Unfortunately, some parents say they love their child "too much," particularly when small, to discipline him or her. Later they frequently discover that the child has matured into an undisciplined individual. Sometimes parents attempt to correct the mistake they have made and discover that it is too late.

Now, let us look at a few Scriptures that speak directly regarding parental discipline. There are several references in the Book of Proverbs. Before referring specifically to the verses, it may be wise to remember the general nature of Proverbs. The wise men had a distinct approach in their search for truth. They did not claim a unique revelation from God like the prophet. The latter's authoritative word was, "The Lord has said" or "The Lord has spoken." The wise men observed life and from their observation said, "This is the way things work." Generally speaking, they were right. Any exceptions to their observations do not nullify their general observations. Also, it should be remembered that some things said concerning discipline should be interpreted and evaluated in the light of the day in which the wise men lived.

Now, some special references. There is a verse that is not applied specifically to discipline by parents, but it is a good general statement:

> Whoever loves discipline loves knowledge,
> but he who hates reproof is stupid (12:1).

This is applicable to children, adults, to those of all ages.

Then there is the often-quoted verse:

> He who spares the rod hates his son,
> but he who loves him is diligent to discipline him
> (13:24).

Notice again the relating of love and discipline. We may disagree with the implied method of discipline; after all, discipline is more inclusive than physical punishment. But surely we will agree with the general tone and emphasis of the statement.

A couple more references from Proverbs will suffice:

> Discipline your son while there is hope;
> do not set your heart on his destruction (19:18).

There are two very meaningful verses in chapter 29:

> The rod and reproof give wisdom,
> but a child left to himself brings shame to his
> mother.
> . . . .
> Discipline your son, and he will give you rest;
> he will give delight to your heart (29:15,17).

Notice two or three specific aspects of these verses. "Left to himself" implies turned loose like a horse out in the pasture to roam where he will. Such a son or a daughter, so the wise man said, will bring shame to mother and/or father. Do you know of cases where this has been literally fulfilled? Many fathers and mothers can rejoice in maturing sons and daughters who are well-disciplined adults because they were properly disciplined as children.

There is at least one verse, and a very important one, in the New Testament which stresses the proper discipline of children. After Paul had stated the general principle of mutual subjection "to one another out of reverence for Christ" (Eph. 5:21) and after he had first applied this concept of mutual subjection to the relation of husbands and wives (5:22-33), he then applied it to the relationship of parents and children. He first addressed children (6:1), followed by the exhortation, "Fathers, do not provoke your children to anger ["wrath," KJV; "resentment," NEB]," or "you parents, too, must stop exasperating your children" (6:4, Williams). Colossians 3:21 adds, "lest they become discouraged." Fathers were specifically addressed because authority in the home at that time was primarily lodged in the father. But mothers were evidently included. At least, mothers as well as fathers were included in the exhortation to children.

How can a father and/or mother provoke or exasperate or discourage children? Phillips, which is a more interpretative translation than possibly any other except *The Living Bible*—a paraphrased version—says, "Fathers, don't over-correct your children or make it difficult for them to obey the commandment"—the commandment to honor father and mother. Parents may provoke or exasperate children by unjust, incorrect, unwise, or inconsistent discipline. This is particularly true if the discipline is not mixed properly with loving approval. "Be sure to have some honey mixed with the vinegar." Also, right relations between parents and children "may be destroyed as readily by parental harshness as by unfilial disobedience" (Int.B.)

Paul added that parents should bring up their children "in the discipline and instruction of the Lord" (Eph. 6:4) or "the training that is of Christ proceeding from Him and prescribed by Him" (Exp.G.). Christian fathers and mothers should remember that the discipline and instruction should be "of the Lord" or "with the sort of education and counsel the Lord approves" (Williams). Here Paul moved from the negative to the positive. Notice the combining of discipline and instruction. The former is one method of instruction. The latter—instruction—refers to instruction in general. Notice here, as elsewhere in his exhortations of mutual subjection or subservience (Eph. 5:21; 6:1), that the point of reference is always "in the Lord" or "of the Lord." The discipline, as well as the instruction in general, should be the kind that would be approved by the Lord and would mark that home as a Christian home, one centered around the devotion of its members not only to one another but to their common Lord.

The distinction between "discipline" and "instruction" "is not that between the general and the special, but rather between the training by act [discipline] and training by word" (Exp.G.). Whatever may be the correct definition, discipline is an integral and important aspect of the training of children in any home and particularly in a Christian home.

Teach and train them. Individuals are free to make most decisions they face. There are some decisions, however, where they do not have that freedom. Those decisions are made for them. For example, parents cannot decide whether they will be teachers of their children. In reality, parents are children's most important and influential teachers. There may be some exceptions, but this is generally true. Parents have a tremendous advantage over school teachers and Sunday School teachers. They have the advantage of time; the children spend far more time at home than at public school. The time advantage is far more pronounced when the home is compared to the church and Sunday School.

Also, parents have the child in the home during the first and most formative years of their lives. Frequently, the whole direction of the child's life, for good or bad, is well established before he ever goes to school. Furthermore, parents can be opportunistic teachers, relating the teaching to immediate situations that arise in the daily life in the home. Other teachers, school and particularly Sunday School teachers, have to imagine or erect more or less artificial situations. They can hope or trust that the child will succeed in carrying over into real life the truths they have sought to teach.

What help can parents find in the Scriptures for their teaching ministry? Since the Bible is not a textbook on family life or on any other subject, as stated before, a systematic discussion of the teaching and training of children should not be expected. Sometimes, however, teachings that are more or less isolated and incidental may be just as important as those in a more systematic treatment.

An example of the preceding is Deuteronomy 6, particularly verses 4 to 9. This is one of the richest passages in Old or New Testament on parental instruction of children, particularly the content and method of teaching. The first three verses of the chapter are introductory. Moses said, "Now this is the commandment, . . . which the Lord your God commanded me to teach you." Then notice the words that follow: "that you may do them." The purpose of the teaching was not only that they might know the commandments of God but that they should be obedient to them. This is just as true of parental teaching as it was and is of the teaching of Moses. And in verse 2 we see that the commandment was also for their sons and their sons' sons or grandsons. This was to be a continuing experience—"all the days of your life." Then notice in verse 3, "Hear therefore, O Israel, and be careful to do them." Parents or other teachers of children have not taught the child until he not only knows theoretically the commandment or truth of God but has also responded to or been obedient to that truth. In other words, it is doubtful if we ever fully hear or understand the truth until we seek to practice or express that truth in daily life.

Verse 4 begins with, "Hear, O Israel." This is the beginning of what the Jews called the Shema, which they used in their worship. *Shema* is Hebrew for "hear." These verses, along with Deuteronomy 11:13-21 and Numbers 15:37-41, "have been for many ages the first bit of the Bible which Jewish children have learned to say and to read" (Cam.B.). Verse 5 of Deuteronomy 6 was quoted by Jesus when he was asked about the great or most important commandment (Matt. 22:37). This commandment—supreme love for God—and the second like it in nature and importance (Matt. 22:39)—love of neighbor as oneself (Lev. 19:18)—are of major importance in the teaching ministry of parents.

What about the commandments of God in general? The contemporary world may be and is drastically different from the world in which Moses lived, but the basic needs of men and women, boys and girls are the same. This means, among other things, that the commandments of God and the basic teachings of the Scriptures, Old Testament as well as New Testament, are abidingly relevant. This is clearly true of the Ten Commandments.

Parents should help their children to understand that the basic commandments of God are applicable to our day. They also need to recognize that these commandments are for our and their good. What Jesus said regarding the sabbath is true of every fundamental law or requirement of God. He said, "The sabbath was made for man, not man for the sabbath" (Mark 2:27). There are few truths more important for maturing children than for them to understand that all of God's requirements or expectations are best for them. Just to cite one example, God knew what was best for young people, as well as husbands and wives and for society in general, when he said, "You shall not commit adultery" (Ex. 20:14). Parents should know and should help their children to know that God's laws are not the arbitrary requirements of some Oriental despot. They are provisions that are made for our good by our loving Heavenly Father.

There is at least one other emphasis in Deuteronomy 6 that should be a challenge to parents today. It suggests or implies that they should pass on to children their religious heritage. Beginning with verse 20, Moses said,

> When your son asks you . . . "What is the meaning of the testimonies and the statutes and the ordinances which the Lord our God has commanded you?" then you shall say to your son, "We were Pharaoh's slaves in Egypt; and the Lord brought us out of Egypt with a mighty

hand; . . . And the Lord commanded us to do all these statutes, to fear the Lord our God, for our good always, that he might preserve us alive, as at this day" (Deut. 6:20-24).

Notice "for our good always."

The children of Israel had a great heritage to pass on. Christian parents have an even greater heritage that they should pass on to their children. Through the grace and goodness of God, they have become children of God, born into the family of God. Through that experience, God has become their Heavenly Father. And it is hoped that, through the years since that initial experience when by means of their union with Christ they became new creations in Christ Jesus, they have matured in that faith and have a rich heritage that should be passed on to their children and ultimately to grand-children. And a wonderful, or it could be a fearful, truth is the fact that the communication of that heritage will be passed on not only by word of mouth but even more by the lives the parents live in the home, in the church, and in the world.

The preceding verses from Deuteronomy suggest that the primary responsibility for the teaching and training of children rested on the parents. This continued to be true in the Jewish home, at least until the beginning of the synagogue about 500 BC. The synagogue, however, did not displace the parents as the chief teachers of their children. The same is true in the Sunday School of our day. The synagogue simply supplemented and sought to strengthen the teaching in the home. And after all, some children, even in Jewish homes, grew up in communities where no synagogue was available or in homes where one parent was not Jewish. The latter was true of Timothy, who was evidently instructed by his mother and grandmother (2 Tim. 1:5). At least Paul reminded him that "from childhood you have been acquainted with the sacred writings" (2 Tim. 3:15). There were a few prominent and/or wealthy families in biblical days which may have provided tutors or special teachers for their children (1 Chron. 27:32), which may be the background for Paul's statement that "the heir, as long as he is a child, . . . is under guardians ["tutors," KJV] and trustees ["governors," KJV] until the date set by the father" (Gal. 4:1-2).

There are several helpful suggestions in the Scriptures concerning the method or means parents can and should use in teaching and training their children. Some of these are found in the verses from Deuteronomy 6. The first method suggested or implied was by example, "And these words which I command you this day shall be upon your heart; and you shall teach them diligently to your children" (Deut. 6:6-7). The order is not accidental. Parents cannot teach their children effectively unless the truths they would teach them have become vital parts of their own lives. There may be many exceptions, but generally speaking, children will walk in the steps of their parents. At least in most cases, the parents will determine more than anyone else the direction of the lives of their children. It would be well not only for parents but also for all of us as children of God to take seriously the words of Paul, "You then who teach others, will you not teach yourself?" (Rom. 2:21).

Joshua, at a critical stage in the history of Israel, demonstrated the impact that a father could and can have on his own family and his ultimate influence on an entire nation. After reminding the people that they had an option to serve the gods of their fathers or of the Amorites, his word to all of them was, "But as for me and my house, we will serve the Lord" (Josh. 24:15). The response of the people was, "We will serve the Lord. . . . The Lord our God we will serve, and his voice we will obey" (Josh. 24:21-24). What an impact a courageous father and/or mother can make on a family and in some cases on a whole nation!

Going back to the passage from Deuteronomy, it will be discovered that the teaching is to be diligent, "You shall teach them diligently to your children, and shall talk of them when you sit in your house, and when you walk by the way, and when you lie down, and when you rise" (Deut. 6:7). The main thrust of these words for contemporary parents seems to be that the word and work of God should be a natural, normal, inevitable part of the conversation in the home. This may and should include more formal teaching than is generally done in most Christian homes. More important, however, is the informal teaching through casual conversation and by the spirit revealed in the relations in the home. The Christian spirit should so permeate life in the home that it would be natural and more or less inevitable that the word and work of the Lord would be a topic of conversation at the table or while sitting together as a family in the den. Most parents have never realized the potential influence of the casual conversation in the home on the lives of growing and even mature children.

Deuteronomy 6 also says: "You shall bind them [the words of the Shema] as a sign upon your hand, and they shall be as frontlets between your eyes. And you shall write them on the doorposts of your house and on your gates" (vv. 8-9). Many Jews literally fulfilled these instructions. It will be unfortunate, however, if contemporary Christian parents push these instructions aside as not applicable to the training of children today. There is a suggestion here that is relevant for parents today. It is the fact that religious symbols can be used effectively as methods or instruments of teaching and training. The Bible on the table, the plaque or picture on the wall, the prominence of the Sunday School quarterly, denominational and religious magazines and publications can all make an impact on the lives of children in the home, as well as on parents and visitors in the home.

Worship is another phase of the parental teaching and training of children. There is nothing in the Scriptures about worship in the home except by implications. It can be assumed, however, that it was more or less prevalent in many homes.

There is abundant scriptural evidence of public worship and that children were included in those periods of worship (see Joel 2:15-16). In the days of Jehoshaphat, when Judah was threatened by her enemies, "all the men of Judah stood before the Lord, with their little ones, their wives, and their children" (2 Chron. 20:13). "And all Judah and the inhabitants of Jerusalem fell down before the Lord, worshiping the Lord" (v. 18). At the time of the dedication of the rebuilt wall of Jerusalem, Nehemiah and the leaders of Israel led the people in a great celebration of worship. Among other things: "they offered great sacrifices that day and rejoiced, for God had made them rejoice with great joy; the women and the children also rejoiced.

And the joy of Jerusalem was heard afar off" (Neh. 12:43). In the light of the customs of that day, it is rather surprising that the women and children were mentioned.

In one of the great praise Psalms, the psalmist said:

> Kings of the earth and all peoples,
> princes and all rulers of the earth!
> Young men and maidens together,
> old men and children!
> Let them praise the name of the Lord
> (148:11-13).

Children should be encouraged and trained to participate in family worship, which ought to be a regular feature of every Christian home. They should also participate with the parents in the worship services of their church.

There are some promises in the Scriptures which will encourage Christian parents as they seek to teach and train their children. One of the most frequently quoted promises is:

> Train up a child in the way he should go,
> and when he is old he will not depart from it
> (Prov. 22:6).

This is a wonderfully encouraging promise. It is somewhat greater, however, than many people realize. There are some rather common misinterpretations that tend to limit or restrict the promise. Some of the recent translations will enable one to interpret more accurately and see more clearly the real significance of the promise. For example, *The New English Bible* translates the verse as follows:

> Start a boy on the right road,
> and even in old age he will not leave it.

Let us note two or three things about this reassuring promise. Starting a boy or a girl on the right road involves much more than simply telling him or her the way in which he or she should walk. It also involves walking before the children in that way. They will learn much more by the example set by parents than by anything they say.

Also, what is "the way" children should go or "the right road" for them? Whatever the content of the teaching, it needs to be tailor-made for each child. The same training does not turn out the same for every child. Every child, even full brothers and sisters, are distinct individuals with unique abilities and needs. It is also possible that Proverbs 22:6 refers to the way a child ought to go. That way would be in harmony with the purpose and will of God.

Some have interpreted the promise in this verse to mean that children may depart from the way they have been taught, but when they are old they will come back to it. There may be, however, a greater truth suggested by the word *even* in *The New English Bible*—"Even in old age he will not leave it." If properly taught, the way in which a child ought to go or the road to be traveled will become so much an integral part of life that the child will never depart from it.

There may be exceptions to this promise. Exceptions, however, do not nullify the promise. It should be remembered that some exceptions, if properly examined, might not be exceptions at all. The conditions of the promise are much more demanding than most people realize. Furthermore, there are influences other than the home that touch and influence the lives of growing children. As they mature, they are increasingly responsible for their own lives; and sometimes they drift away from the instructions by and the impact of their parents. But in spite of all the preceding limitations, Proverbs 22:6 is a great promise.

Dedicate them. This section on the relation of parents and their responsibilities for their children would not be complete without a brief word regarding their dedication, which was previously discussed in chapter 4. The major illustration given in that chapter was Hannah's dedication of Samuel to the service of God. He was a gift from God. Hannah promised before his conception that, if God heard her plea and gave her a son, he would be given back to the Lord for service to him.

The prevailing perspective in the Bible is that every child is a gift or heritage from God. Parents have a stewardship responsibility for that gift. This is particularly true of Christian parents. Lockyer says, "In a Christian home all children born into it are received on trust, as belonging, first of all, to God. Thus they were dedicated to Him to use as he deems best."[2] There are occasions when Christian parents may feel a distinctive urge or have a conviction to dedicate a particular child in a unique way to the work of the Lord. This may be at conception, at birth, or some time after birth.

The preceding does not mean that every such child should be dedicated to full-time ministry or missionary service. This should not be done unless the parents are convinced that this is the purpose of God for that child. The most important thing is for parents to ask God to accept the child and to use him or her to promote the cause or kingdom of God in the world. And we can know and we should help them to understand that they will find the maximum fulfillment of every potential and every worthy motive as they seek to do the will of the Father. In other words, our gift and their gift of themselves will be abundantly rewarded. In this area of life, as is true everywhere else, we find life in its fullness by losing it.

There are occasions when the Lord himself seems clearly to be the initiator of the dedication. This was true in the case of Samson. This was also true of John the Baptist and Jesus. They are both dedicated from before their births to the unique purposes God had for them. John was to be "a man sent for God" (John 1:6) to be the forerunner of the Messiah. It was revealed to Joseph that Mary was to give birth to a son, "and you shall call his name Jesus, for he will save his people from their sins" (Matt. 1:21).

Some of God's great servants of the present, as well as the past, cannot be explained apart from the fact that God had special purposes for their lives. The lives they have lived, the services they have rendered, cannot be explained by their heritage or by the environment in which they grew up. They cannot be explained apart from God's grace and goodness. This seems to be true of many if not most of God's great men and women.

Children to Parents

The wise man gave the following appropriate admonition to children:

Hear, O sons, a father's instruction,
    and be attentive, that you may gain insight;
    for I give you good precepts:
    do not forsake my teaching (Prov. 4:1-2).

Again he said,

My son, keep your father's commandment,
    and forsake not your mother's teaching (Prov. 6:20).

Now, what are some of the teachings not only in Proverbs but elsewhere in the Bible concerning the relation of children to their parents? Every child owes a debt of gratitude for his or her parents. Without parents they would not be here. Children should be doubly grateful if they have had the privilege of coming into the world in and through a stable, loving Christian home with both father and mother in that home. God knew what he was doing not only when he decreed that children come into a home but also that a relatively long period be required for their maturing under the protective guidance of parents who love them. And although there are some excellent foster homes and institutions for homeless or neglected children, these are poor substitutes, with some exceptions, for the natural family.

Honor them. One emphasis that is found in the Scriptures is that children should honor their parents. The Fifth Commandment is, "Honor your father and your mother, that your days may be long in the land which the Lord your God gives you" (Ex. 20:12; see Deut. 5:16).

Honor means to reverence or respect (see Lev. 19:3). From the Old Testament perspective, duty to parents stood next in importance to duty to God. The penalty for cursing parents was the same as the penalty for blaspheming God (Lev. 20:9; 24:15-16). Notice that in the Fifth Commandment the mother was included along with the father. This would not have been true in most cultures of that time.

The command to honor parents "has a definitely Godward connotation and has been frequently grouped with the first four. From the Hebrew viewpoint, for example, parents stood in relation to their children as God's representatives."[3]

The command to honor parents, as is true of many of God's commands, has a promise attached to it, "That your days may be long in the land which the Lord your God gives you" (Ex. 20:12). The promise may be applicable to an individual or to the nation. If the former, it was a promise that children who honor their parents, generally speaking, will live longer than those who do not. If the promise was primarily to the nation, then it was a guarantee of national permanence or at least a long continuance of the nation. One Old Testament scholar, S. R. Driver, concludes that "a spirit of filial respect implies a well-ordered life in general, and so tends to secure prosperity both to the individual and to the nation" (Cam.B.).

Notice the closing words of the promise, "which the Lord your God gives you." It is not "has given you." It is a land that he will give you or "is giving you" (NEB). It was the Promised Land. His people were at its borders. But it would require a great deal of effort and struggle on their part. They had to take what was being given to them. This is just as true of many of God's good gifts to his contemporary children.

The command to honor parents was quoted by Jesus on at least two occasions. He quoted it when he dealt with the matter of corban, discussed later in this chapter. He also quoted it, along with some of the other Ten Commandments, when the rich young ruler asked him, "What shall I do to inherit eternal life?" (Luke 18:20). It could be that the reply of Jesus included more than Luke recorded. After all, as John said, the writers of the Gospels had to be selective (John 21:25). But if Luke fully recorded the reply of Jesus, it would be interesting to know why Jesus quoted the particular commandments: Do not commit adultery, kill, steal, and bear false witness and then closed with "honor your father and mother" (Luke 18:18-20), which in their original form preceded the others.

Paul, in his instructions to children, quoted: "Honor your father and mother" and then added "(this is the first commandment with a promise), 'that it may be well with you and that you may live long on the earth'" (Eph. 6:2). This suggests that Paul considered the promise a promise to children or individuals. Paul's exhortation was primarily, if not exclusively, to younger children who were still living in the home. Honoring parents, however, was applied in the Scriptures to mature sons and daughters, as well as younger children. Furthermore, it was a commandment or admonition that had and still has national implication and significance.

Some parents may not be very honorable, but sons and daughters should honor parenthood. An army private may not have much respect for a particular officer, but he is trained to salute not the officer but the insignia on the uniform. Parenthood is the "uniform."

Obey them. The honor enjoined by Paul is not that "of mere sentiment but of obedience" (Cam.B.) The two are distinct but closely related. "Obedience is the *duty; honor* is the disposition of which the obedience is born" (Exp.Gr.). In these two words—honor and obedience—"the whole distinctive duty of the child is summed up, in the Old Testament as well as in the New" (Exp.Gr.). Obedience of children is implied throughout the Scriptures.

The most specific word on children obeying parents is in the great passage by Paul on mutual submission (Eph. 5:21 to 6:9). His word to children was, "Children, obey your parents in the Lord, for this is right" (Eph. 6:1). The phrase "in the Lord"[4] creates some difficulty. These words are not in some of the ancient manuscripts and are not included in one or two translations (NEB, Williams). If "in the Lord" should be retained, then Colossians (which closely parallels Ephesians) may help to interpret its meaning. Paul, in Colossians, said, "Children, obey your parents in everything, for this pleases the Lord" (Col. 3:20). Paul was evidently counseling obedience in general. He was not saying, "Obey your parents if they are Christians" or are "in the Lord." Obedience as such was "in the Lord," approved by the Lord, an aspect of the will and purpose of the Lord. He further added the words, "for this is right."

Although obedience is the command of God and is right, there were and are some limits to that obedience. Supreme allegiance for the child of God should be given to God and to his will and purpose. In Ephesians, Paul did not consider occasions when there might be a conflict between the will of parents and the will of God. What about situations where ungodly parents would command a Christian son or daughter to do something that was obviously contrary to God's will or purpose for that son or daughter?

Jesus, as is true in many areas of life, demonstrated in his own life the obedience that should characterize a son or a daughter and the limitations of that obedience. At twelve years of age when Joseph and Mary found him in the Temple, the Record says, "He went down with them and came to Nazareth, and was obedient to them" (Luke 2:51). But there came a time, some years later, when he had to break away from his family to fulfill the will and purpose of the Father. So it may be at times in the lives of maturing sons and daughters. Too frequently, even in Christian homes, if mature sons and daughters continued to do just what their parents wanted them to do, they would not do the will of God and find the fulfillment and usefulness that comes through response to that will.

The preceding does not nullify Paul's word, "Children, obey your parents in the Lord, for this is right." There are exceptions to that rule or law, if it be a law, but exceptions do not nullify or abrogate a basic law of God. There may come a time, however, when a child will need to respond to a higher law or call of God.

Provide for them. Parents should seek to remain independent as long as possible. And children should help them maintain that independence. After all, the natural order of responsibility is parents for children rather than the reverse. Paul, in writing to the Corinthians, stated this concept. He said, "I am ready to come to you. And I will not be a burden, for I seek not what is yours but you; for children ought not to lay up for their parents, but parents for their children" (2 Cor. 12:14). This is God's order, and parents should remember it.

However, when a real need arises, it is just as clearly the responsibility of children to provide for their parents. This emphasis is very relevant for the contemporary world, with an increasing number and percentage of the population older people. Many of these are physically, mentally, and emotionally dependent on others to care for them. Entirely too many are neglected, if not forgotten.

Conditions today are drastically different from biblical days, but the basic principles set forth in the Scriptures are abidingly relevant. The Bible does not dictate how sons and daughters should provide for needy parents but it does plainly say that children should have a sense of responsibility for parents in need. Christian sons and daughters should be particularly alert and responsive to any real need of parents.

What do we find in the Bible? In the Old Testament, with its extended family, the older members of the family were not only cared for within the family circle, they were also frequently honored.

There was an incident in the life of Jesus when he related directly the Fifth Commandment—honor father and mother—to the provision for needy parents by mature children (Mark 7:5-13; Matt. 15:1-9). The scribes and Pharisees asked Jesus, "Why do your disciples not live according to the tradition of the elders, but eat with hands defiled?" (Mark 7:5). After quoting some words from Isaiah, Jesus said to them, "You leave ["neglect," NEB] the commandment of God, and hold fast the tradition of men" (v. 8). They considered "the traditions of the elders" just as authoritative and even possibly more authoritative than the written law. These traditions were the oral interpretations and applications of the law to the details of daily living. Jesus pointed out that those traditions, which were supposed to help them interpret properly and obey the law of God, were actually being used to violate one of God's clear commandments.

Jesus pointedly said to them, "You have a fine way of rejecting ["set aside," NASB] the commandment of God" (Mark 7:9). What was the commandment they were setting aside? It was the Fifth Commandment, "For Moses said, 'Honor your father and your mother.'" He then added, "But you say [these words stand in marked contrast to "for Moses said"], 'If a man tells his father or his mother, What you would have gained from me is Corban' (that is, given to God)⁵ then you no longer permit him to do anything for his father or mother, thus making void the word of God through your tradition which you hand on. And many such things you do" (Mark 7:10-13). Mark evidently thought it necessary to define the word *corban*—"given to God" or "set apart for God" (NEB).

The word *corban*, which had an honorable and legitimate use in the Old Testament, was being abused in the days of Jesus. A person could say, "It is corban" or "dedicated to God" and thereby evade responsibility for the material well-being of his parents. The most vicious part of the practice was the fact that the one making the vow could retain his possessions and use them as he pleased. "Then you no longer permit him to do anything for his father or mother" (Mark 7:12).

As suggested earlier, the natural order of responsibility is parents for children, but it is very clear in the Scriptures that children are responsible for parents who are in need. Paul, in 1 Timothy 5:5, refers to "real widows" or widows "in the full sense" (NEB). Who is the real widow? Paul said, "If a widow has children or grandchildren, let them first learn their religious duty to their own family and make some return ["repay what they owe," NEB] to their parents" (v. 4). He also said in the same chapter, "If any believing woman has relatives who are widows, let her assist them; let the church not be burdened, so that it may assist those who are real widows" (v. 16).

All of us are in debt to our parents, some much more than others. We can and should pay back a part of that debt by providing or caring for them when they are in need. Paul went so far as to say, "If any one does not provide for his relatives, and especially for his own family, he has disowned ["denied," NIV] the faith and is worse than an unbeliever" (v. 8).

It seems that the God-ordained natural responsibility for the needy elderly is as follows: (1) the natural family—children, grandchildren, and so forth, (2) the spiritual family—a church should care for its own needy, (3) the human family—community and state should provide for those who are not cared for by the natural or spiritual family.

Jesus, on one occasion, as he did in so many areas, revealed something of his love, concern, and provision for his mother. Jesus, hanging on the cross, "saw his mother, and the disciple whom he loved standing near, he said to his mother, 'Woman, behold, your son!'" And we should be grateful for the concluding words, "And from that hour the disciple took her to his own home" (John 19:26-27).

Conclusion

This chapter has been largely restricted to specific teachings of the Scriptures concerning the relation to and responsibility of parents to children—love, discipline, teach, dedicate—and children for parents—honor, obey, and provide for them. There are some rather important areas of the relation of parents and children that are either assumed or not mentioned at all in the Scriptures. The following is partially, but not entirely, based on the Scriptures.

Responsible relations of parents and children involve the following:

(1) Children should be planned for and welcomed into the home.

(2) Each child should be recognized as a gift from God.

(3) Since the above is true, parents should understand that they are responsible to God for the child. He or she should be given back to God for him to use as he will in his work and kingdom.

(4) Parents should also recognize that one of their major responsibilities is the proper teaching and training of the child.

(5) Proper training will involve, among other things, the provision in the home of a stimulating intellectual atmosphere and a healthy emotional and spiritual climate for growing children.

(6) An important phase of the training of a child is proper and loving discipline.

(7) One important phase of the training of children is for them to understand that they should honor and obey their parents. This means that parents should seek to be worthy of that honor.

(8) Both parents and children should properly utilize the resources of the community and their church in the various phases of their relations and responsibilities.

(9) In every area of their relations to and responsibilities for one another, the final point of reference for both parents and children should be God and his will and purpose.

Notes

1. Gibson Winter, *Love and Conflict: New Patterns in Family Life* (Garden City, N.Y.: Doubleday & Co., 1958), p. 66.
2. Herbert Lockyer, *All the Children of the Bible* (Grand Rapids: Zondervan, 1970), p. 43.
3. T. B. Maston, *Biblical Ethics* (Waco, Texas: Word Books, 1967), p. 19.
4. Ellicott, in his commentary, says that "in the Lord" is particularly prevalent in the epistles of the captivity, appearing twenty-one times.
5. This is the only place the word *corban* is found in the New Testament. The Hebrew word, usually translated "offering," is found approximately seventy times in the Old Testament, almost exclusively in Leviticus (see 1:2-3,10,14) and Numbers (see Num. 7 where it is found several times).

Supplementary Books from Broadman Press

Allen, Clifton J. *Life Is Worth Your Best*. Large type edition. (Senior adults)

Blackwell, William and Muriel. *Working Partners/Working Parents*.

Buchanan, Neal C. and Eugene Chamberlain. *Helping Children of Divorce*.

Chandler, Linda S. *David Asks, "Why?"* A book to use to help children, grades 1-6, with questions about divorce.

Couey, R. *Lifelong Fitness and Fulfillment*. Large type edition. (Senior adults).

Craig, Floyd. *How to Communicate with Single Adults*.

Crook, Roger. *An Open Letter to the Christian Divorcee*.

Davis, Cos, H., Jr. *Children and the Christian Faith*. A book for parents to use with older children who have expressed an interest in salvation.

Drakeford, John W. *A Christian View of Homosexuality*.

Dye, Harold E. *No Rocking Chair for Me*. (Retirement)

Favorite Hymns for Senior Adults. Large type edition.

Freeman, Carroll B. *The Senior Adult Years*.

Harbour, Brian. *Famous Singles of the Bible*.

Hendricks, William L. *A Theology for Children*. A book for adults which explains how to help children understand the Christian faith.

Hensley, J. Clark. *Coping with Being Single Again*.

Herring, Reuben. *Your Family Worship Guidebook*. A book to be used with older children and youth.

Howell, John C. *Senior Adult Life*. Large type edition.

Ingle, Clifford, editor. *Children and Conversion*.

Kerr, Horace L. *How to Minister to Senior Adults in Your Church.*
Mace, David and Vera. *Marriage Enrichment in the Church.*
Miller, Sarah Walton. *Drama for Senior Adults.*
Pearce, J. Winston. *I Believe.* Large type edition. (Senior adults)
_____ . *Ten Good Things I Know About Retirement.*
Pinson, William M. *Families with Purpose.*
Potts, Nancy D. *Counseling with Single Adults.*
Pylant, Agnes D. *Threescore and Ten—Wow!*
Self, Carolyn Shealy and William L. Self. *A Survival Kit for Marriage.*
Sessoms, Bob. *150 Ideas for Activities with Senior Adults.*
Steen, John Warren. *Enlarge Your World.* (Senior adults)
Stevens, Shirley. *A New Testament View of Women.*

Whitehouse, Donald S. and Nancy. *Pray and Play: A Guide for Family Worship.* Particularly good for families with preschoolers and younger children.

Wood, Britton. *Single Adults Want to Be the Church, Too.*

Index of Authors, Names, and Subjects

Abortion, 181
Abraham, 35, 46, 47, 49, 51, 87, 91, 93, 99, 132, 135, 140, 178
Absalom, 150
Achtemeir, Elizabeth, 180n
Adam and Eve, 46, 89, 150
Adultery, 54, 119, 191-192, 196, 198, 200, 206, 208, 211, 220
Age and Aging, 178 *ff.*; aged, 59; and the young, 135; attitudes toward, 142 *ff.*, 148; Genesis, 132; Jesus and, 134; New Testament and, 134; Old Testament and, 132-133; Paul and, 134-135; Prophets and, 133-134; Writings and, 133
Ahijah, 155n
Albrecht, R., 34n
Allen, Clifton J., 33n, 248
Amos, 21
Amnon, 150
Anders, Sarah Frances, 129n
Andrew, 70
Anna, 70, 111, 134
Apphia, 75
Appolos, 84n
Aquinas, Thomas, 84n, 179n
Artificial insemination, 181
Atkinson, D. J., 202n
Augustine, 28, 84n
Authority in the home, 78

Bailey, D. Sherwin, 202n
Barak, 64
Barclay, William, 33, 210
Barnabas, 136
Barnhouse, Ruth Tiffany, 202n
Barreness, 87, 88, 102
Barth, Karl, 84n, 179n
Black, M., 31
Blackwell, William and Muriel, 248
Betrothal, 51
Bible, as a rule book, 25; center in Christ, 19-20; divine/human nature, 17-18; her-meneutics (see also biblical interpreta-tion), 27, 81; interpretation (see also bibli-cal interpretation), 26 *ff.*, 157; message, 20 *ff.*; nature of, 35; promises of, 25; relevance of, 24 *ff.*; revelation, 17; two-dimensional (see horizontal/vertical rela-tions), 20-24; twofold message, 20; unity and diversity, 18-19
Biblical interpretation, attitudes toward, 28; books on hermeneutics, 34; commen-taries, 31-32; concordances, 30-31; har-monies of the Gospels, 32-33; hermeneu-tics (see Bible, hermeneutics), 27, 81; need for interpreting, 27; New Testament interpreting Old, 17, 20; principles for, 27-30; resources for, 30-33
Biblical translations, viii, 30
Bilnah, 88
Bowman, Henry, 57n
Bratcher, Robert, 33n
Bride, 54
Briffault, Robert, 57n
Brothers, 41, 55, 70
Brown, Stanley C., 223n
Buchanan, Neal C., 248
Buttrick, George, 32, 209

Cain and Abel, 46, 89, 122, 150
Caleb, 140, 147, 149
Calvin, John, 179n
Castration, 121
Celibacy, 40, 120 *ff.*, 182, 186, 188; (see also singleness); as a gift of grace, 125, 127; attitude of Jesus toward, 123; celibate marriage, 126; Paul and, 124; vocational, 126
Chamberlain, Eugene, 248
Chandler, Linda S., 248
Clark, Elizabeth, 84n
Chastity, 186
Chauvinism, 73
Child abuse, 86

Childlikeness, 107
Children, 39, 56-57, 59; and worship, 107-108; as gifts, 92-93, 238; attitude toward, 86; care of, 93, 226; children of promise, 91-93; creation of, 89; customs related to, 98 *ff.*; dedication to God, 100, 102-103, 238-239; desire for, 87 *ff.*; disciplining of, 227-231; gratitude to parents, 240; honor of parents, 240-242; illegitimate, 39; obey parents, 242-243; providing for parents, 243-246; provoking to anger, 230; purification, 100; teach and train, 231-238; weaning of, 102; will of God as obedience, 242-243
Christian immaturity, 139
Chronological age, 130
Chuza, 72, 123
Circumcision, covenant, 99; new covenant, 99
Clemens, Lois, 65, 84n, 201n
Clement of Alexandrea, 84n
Cobb, John B. Jr., 34n
Cobble, William B., 106, 108n
Companionship, 40, 188
Complementarity, 65
Concubinage, 46, 55
Conjugal rights, 174
Conjugal union, 43, 45
Contraception, 181
Cook, James I., 58n
Corban, 245
Courtship, 49
Covenant, husband/wife in the New Testament, 178; husband/wife in the Old Testament, 176-178
Couey, R., 248
Craig, Floyd, 248
Creation of sexes, 65, 66, 165
Crook, Roger, 249
Cross, Earl Bennett, 58n
Cross, the, 24

Dana, H. E., 28, 34n
Daniel, 123, 141
David, 18, 35, 46, 110, 132, 150, 175
Davis, Cos H., Jr., 248
Deaconness, 76

Deborah, 64
Decision making, 26
Deen, Edith, 83n
de Vaux, Roland, 57n, 58n, 84n
Discipline, 39, 53, 230-231
Divided homes, 161-162
Divorce, adjustment to the ideal, 211; adultery, 206, 208, 211; attitudes toward the divorced, 216-223; biblical teachings concerning, 119 *ff.*; Christians and, 213, 215; certificate of, 210; confession and penitence, 223; Deuteronomy 24:1-4, 205 *ff.*; exception clause, 208, 211-213; forgiveness, 218; increase in, 203; Jesus and, 119, 207-212; Malachi 2:16, 207; Old Testament and, 119, 205 *ff.*; Paul and, 119-120, 174, 212-216; Shammai and Hillel, 209; summary statements, 204-205; uncleanness, 206; will of God and, 205, 210; 1 Cor. 7:10-16, 212
Dorcas, 117
Dowry, 51
Doyle, Patricia M., 83n
Drakeford, John W., 248
Dummelow, John R., 31
Dutile, Gordon, 173, 180n
Dye, Harold E., 248

Eleazar, 110
Elder, 135 *ff.*; as a role, 136; development of the term, 135; in the early church, 136-137; Old Testament and, 135
Eli, 103, 132, 150, 155n
Elihu, 138, 144
Elijah, 84n, 110
Elisha, 108n
Elizabeth, 92, 93, 134
Elkanah, 88, 92, 93, 102, 103, 175
Ellisen, Stanley A., 215, 223, 224n
Endogamy, 50
Enoch, 132
Ephraim, 145
Epstein, Louis M., 58n
Esau, 90, 93, 145
Esther, 64
Ethiopian eunuch, 27, 121
Eunuchs, 120-121, 186

Euodia, 75
Exogamy, 50
Ezekiel, 97, 111, 115, 123
Ezra, 50, 63

Family, biblical symbology, 159; choice of companion, 159-162; churches as, 55; creation of, 35, 37; divisions in, 41; extended 47, 142; failures, 42; first, 35; Genesis, 35; hierarchical view of, 79; history, 57; ideals, 42, 56; kingdom of God, 125; natural order, 42; nature, 42-45; need for redefinition, 128; nuclear, 142; purpose, 39-42; sociology, 57; source, 35 *ff.*; symbolic use, 53-55
Family life and birth and death, 143
Father, 53
Fatherless, 21, 53, 96, 115
Female inferiority, 66
Feucht, Oscar E., 47, 58n, 170, 179n, 180n
Fischer, Fred, 33
Forgiveness, 23
Freedom of the child of God, 169
Freeman, Carroll B., 249
Friedrich, G., 33
Froment, E., 34n

Genesis 2, interpretation, 37-38
Genetic engineering, 181
Glaze, R. E., Jr., 28, 34n
God as Father, 54, 55; as husband, 53; as person, 24; "I AM" 24
Good wife, 63
Gray, Robert M., 130, 154n, 155n
Grelot, Pierre, 180n
Gundry, Stanley L., 33

Hagar, 49, 87
Hannah, 88, 92, 93, 102, 103, 175
Harbour, Brian, 248
Hardesty, Nancy, 84n
Harris, Charles S., 155n
Heflin, Boo., 84n
Heflin, J. N., 64, 65
Heim, Ralph D., 32
Hendricks, William L., 248

Hensley, J. Clark, 248
Hermeneutics, 27 *ff.*
Herod, 104
Herring, Reuben, 248
Hiltner, Seward, 155
Hiram, 110
Holmes, Urban T., III, 202n
Home, 39
Homosexuality, 192-195; contrary to the purpose of God, 194-195; ministry to, 195; Paul and, 193-194; sodomy, 193
Honeycutt, Roy, 102, 108n
Horizontal/vertical relations, (see Bible, two dimensional); 20-24
Hosea, 18
Howell, John C., 168, 179n, 180n, 248
Hulcah, 64
Husband, 53
Husband/wife relations, 55, 56; Christ and the church, 172-173; contemporary perspectives, 164; husbands, responsibilities, 172; Jesus and, 163; nature and roles, 165-168; New Testament perspectives, 163; Old Testament perspectives, 162; Paul and, 163-164; sex relations, 186-189; union of, 209-210; wives' responsibilities, 175

Image of God, 36-37, 38, 64, 65, 109, 165, 197
Incest, 50, 77
Indecency, 206
Ingle, Clifford, 108n, 248
Intermarriage, 161
Isaac, 44, 52, 91, 93, 99, 132, 135, 140, 155n, 160, 175, 178
Isaiah, 17, 21, 84n, 97, 101, 114, 122, 135, 144
Ishmael, 49

Jacob, 35, 46, 51, 87, 90, 91, 93, 98, 132, 135, 138, 140, 145, 155n, 175, 178
Jairus, 95
James, 70, 107
Jeremiah, 54, 90, 97, 115, 122, 135
Jerome, 84n
Jesus and children, 105; blessing of children,

105; Jesus and childhood, 103; Jesus' birth, 103-104; teaching from observing children, 106
Jesus and ethical principles, 217
Jesus and women, 68 ff.; attitude toward, 68-69, 81; balanced treatment of sexes, 70; Luke's account of, 70; parables, 70; women's response to Jesus, 71-72; women who ministered to Jesus, 72-73; women who traveled with Jesus, 72
Jewett, Paul K., 57n, 65, 83n, 84n, 85n, 164, 171, 179n, 180n
Joanna, 72, 123
Job, 89, 116, 138, 144
Joel, 18, 133, 141
John, 70, 107
John the Baptist, 18, 70, 92, 93, 108n, 123, 140
Joseph and Mary, 52, 98, 100, 101
Joseph of Arimathea, 70
Joseph (O.T.), 91, 93, 132, 135, 141, 145, 146
Joshua, 99, 132, 140, 147-149, 235
Justice, 22

Kahana, K., 58n
Kerr, Horace L., 248
Kingdom of God, 40, 56
Kirk, Jerry, 192, 194, 202n
Kittel, G., 33
Kübler-Ross, Elizabeth, 152, 155n

Laban, 87
Laetsch, Theodore, 122, 129n
Lamech, 46
Landis, Judson and Mary, 57n
Lazarus, 56, 71
Leah, 52, 87
Levi, 56
Levirate marriage, 48, 113
"little ones," 105
Lockyer, Herbert, 83n, 84n, 91, 92, 108n, 238, 247n
"loose woman," 62
Lot, 47
Love, 22, 43
Love drama, 177-178

Luther, Martin, 84n, 179n
Lydia, 75

Mace, David, 48, 57n, 58n, 182, 201n
Mace, David and Vera, 58n, 249
MacGorman, J. W., 125
Malachi, 97
Male/female roles, 35, 37-39, 62, 67, 83, 124; contemporary perspectives, 166, 170; cultural influences, 165-166; equality/submission, 168 ff.; roles in Scripture, hermeneutics for, 231 ff.
Male superiority, 66
Manasseh, 145
Manoah, 102
Manson, T. W., 217, 224n
Mark, 72
Marle, Rene, 34n
Marmor, Judd, 202n
Martha, 56, 70, 71, 152
Marriage, 39; age for, 49; and culture, 127; arrangements, 62; biblical concept of, 44-45; by capture, 48; ceremony (see also wedding), 52; creation of, 55; customs and laws, 48-52, 67; exclusiveness, 44; failure, 44; forms, 45-48; history of, 57; impediments to, 51; nature of (see also "one flesh"), 42, 43; Talmud, 49; will of God concerning, 127
Mary Magdalene, 71-73, 123, 221
Mary of Bethany, 56, 69-71
Mary, the wife of Clopas, 73
Maston, T. B., 33n, 58n, 129n, 247n
Matthew, 56, 72
Maxwell, Robert J., 155n
Mbiti, John S., 58n
Methuselah, 132
Micah, 22
Michel, 175
Mickelsen, A. Berkley, 34n
Midwives, 98
Miles, Herbert J. and Fern Klarrington, 179n
Miller, Sarah Walton, 249
Miriam, 64, 122
Mixed marriage, 212, 213
Moberg, David O., 130, 154n, 155n

Moffatt, James, 43
Monogamy, 44, 47, 119, 124
Morrison, Clinton, 31
Moses, 17, 24, 46, 53, 84n, 93, 110, 132, 135
Mother, 41
Motherhood, 94, 101, 122
Muehl, William, 202n
Mutuality, 78-79, 173-175, 213-214
Mutual subjection/submission, 173, 230, 242

Nahor, 58n
Naomi, 111
Nazirite, 102, 108
Neglected children, 40
Nehemiah, 50, 51, 63
Neufeld, E., 57n, 58n, 201n, 205, 223n
Never married, 59, 109, 124-125
Newport, John, 33n
Nicodemus, 70
Nicoll, W. R., 32
Nympha, 75

Old age, 130
Old folks revolution, 131
Older adults, 130, 245; adjusting to aging, 147-148; and example, 147-149; biblical promises, 154; care for, 142, 145-146; changing attitudes, 143; church's ministry for, 148-149; crises of, 149 ff.; danger of stereotyping, 141; death, 151; declining health and vitality, 150; disappointment in children, 150; disrespect for, 144; maturity, 139; memory, 140; prevailing family type, 142; productive lives 140; qualities and character traits, 137 ff.; respect for, 143-144; understanding and wisdom, 137
"one-flesh," 43, 168, 183-185
Oneness, 43
Onesimus, 75
Ordination, 82-83
Orphah, 111
Orphans, 96 ff.; the Law and, 96; the Prophets and, 96-97; the Writings and, 96

Osborn, Segerberg, Jr., 155n

Parents, as teachers, 231; communicating heritage, 234; Deuteronomy 6:4-9, 232; family worship, 236; Jesus attitude toward, 93-95; parenting, 39-40, 94, 101, 122, 226; providing for children, 243-246; setting examples, 237; suggested methods, 235
Parent/child relations, 56, 69, 93, 94, 104; assumptions of, 225 ff.; responsible relations, 246
Patriarchy, 47
Paul and women, attitude toward, 74-75, 80-82, 126; freedom, 76-78; hermeneutical principles for women in church and society, 74; hermeneutics, 74-75, 77-78; instruction/advice about women, 74; Paul, women, and submission, 77-79
Pearce, J. Winston, 249
Peninnah, 88
Personhood, 36
Peter, 18, 41, 56, 70, 84n, 107, 141, 222
Philemon, 75
Philip, 27, 121
Phillips, J. B., 30
Phoebe, 76, 84n
Physical intimacy, 38, 40, 43
Pinson, William M., 249
Pittenger, Norman, 202n
Polygamy, 46, 55
Potts, Nancy D., 249
Prayer, 23
Price, Thomas, 58n
Priestesses, 64
Prisca/Priscilla, 76
Procreation, 188
Prodigal son, 54, 124
Propagation, 38-39
Prophetesses, 64
Prophets, 21
Prostitution, 189-191, 200
Pylant, Agnes D., 249

Rachel, 51-52, 91, 93, 98, 175
Rahab, 122
Ramm, Bernard, 27, 28, 34n

Real widows, 117-118, 245
Rebekah, 44, 51-52, 91, 93, 175
Redemption, 24-25
Rehoboam, 46
Relational, 40
Remarriage, 113-114, 127; innocent party, 208, 210, 213; Pauline privilege, 214; will of God concerning, 219-220
Reuther, Rosemary Radford, 83n
Richardson, A., 33
Richardson, Herbert, 84n
Robertson, A. T., 32, 33, 79, 84n, 136, 153, 210-211
Robinson, James M., 34n
Rowley, H. H., 31
Ruth, 48, 64, 111

Salome, 72
Samaritan woman at the well, 70, 71, 221
Samson, 92
Samuel, 88, 91, 93, 102-103, 108n, 132, 140, 150
Sarah, 52, 87, 91, 93, 99, 135
Saul, 138
Scanzoni, Letha, 84n
Selection of a wife, 49
Self, Carolyn Shealy and William L., 249
Sessoms, Bob, 249
Seth, 132
Sex organs, male, 121
Sex urge, 40
Sexual immorality, 195-196, 196-197, 199-201
Sexual intercourse, 52, 124, 188; abstinence from, 188-189; in a monogamous relationship, 193; outside marriage, 189-197; purposes, 184-185; a union, 183-184; within marriage, 186-189
Sexual morality, 125
Sexual passion, 125, 128
Sexual purity, 198-199
Sexual revolution, 181
Sexual temptation, 125
Sexuality, and Christian calling, 124-127; basic concepts, 181 ff.; body as temple of the Holy Spirit, 199; considered evil, 182; curse or blessing, 182-183; gift of God,

181-183; image of God, 183; misuse of the body, 185-186; sanctification of, 197-199
Shukri, Ahmed, 58n
Simeon, 134
Simon the leper, 56
Simon the Pharisee, 56, 72, 199-200, 221
Single adults, 59; Bible and, 109; church and, 127-129; ministry to, 109
Singleness (see also celibacy), and the will of God, 120; as never married, 122; as an opportunity to discover the will of God, 128; as a spiritual gift, 120; New Testament and, 123-124; Old Testament and, 122-123; Paul's advice on, 126
Sisera, 64
Sisters, 70
Small, Dwight H., 207, 219, 223, 224n
Smith, Ebbie C., 180n
Solomon, 35, 46, 50, 110, 138, 175
Son, 54-55
Stagg, Frank, 70, 77-80, 136, 137, 141, 155n
Stagg, Frank and Evelyn, 83n, 84n, 85n
Steen, John Warren, 249
Stephanas, 84n
Sterilization, 181
Strong, James, 31, 129n
Submission (see also mutual subjection/submission), conclusions from the New Testament, 173; Paul, 170 ff.; subordination/submission, 170 ff.; 1 Peter, 171, 174
Surrogate mothers, 181
Susanna, 72, 123
Swaddling clothes, 98
Syntyche, 75

Tabitha, 117
Tamar, 48, 113
Taylor, Gordon R., 57n
Ten Commandments, 62
Thomas, Robert L., 33
Timothy, 55, 84n, 117-118, 146, 234
Tournier, Paul, 152, 155n
Trible, Phyllis, 58n

Unmarried, 40
Unwed mothers, 59

Vaughan, Curtis, 119, 129n
Vine, W. E., 33
Virgin/virginity, 63, 186, 198, 206
Von Allmen, J. J., 33

Watson, Wilbur H., 155n
Weatherhead, Leslie D., 219, 224n
Wedding, 52
Wegner, Walter, 48, 58n, 177-178
Westermarck, Edward, 50, 57n, 58n
Whitehouse, Donald S. and Nancy, 249
Widow at Zarephath, 110
Widow of Nain, 112
Widower, 111
Widows, 21, 40, 59, 109; attitude of God
  toward, 116; early church and, 116-117;
  etymology of in the Old Testament and
  New Testament, 112-113; Hebrews and,
  113; high priests and, 113; James and,
  118-119; Jesus and, 112, 116; justice for,
  114; law regarding, 114; life-style, 114,
  118; named in the Old Testament, 111;
  nameless, 110; named in the New Testament, 111; Paul and, 112, 117-118; Prophets and, 114-116; remarriage of, 113-114;
  Writings and, 116; younger widows, 118
Wilkinson, John, 27, 34n
Williams, Charles B., 30, 84n
Winter, Gibson, 228, 247n
Wisdom, 63
Women, 61-62; and subordination, 68, 79;
  contemporary attitudes, 82-83; dress of,
  79; Jesus' attitude toward, 68-69 (see also
  Jesus and women); Old Testament attitude, 81; ordination of, 62; prominent,
  63-64; protection of, 63; respect for, 63;
  speaking/silence in public worship, 79-80;
  temptation and fall, 67; traditional role
  of, 83, 168; who prophesied, 78
Women's revolution, 59, 166
Wood, Britton, 249
Wright, G. Ernest, 55

Young, Robert, 31

Zaccheus, 56
Zechariah, (N.T.) 70, 92-93, 108n, 140
Zechariah, (O.T.) 97, 115

Index of Passages Cited

OLD TESTAMENT

Genesis

1 .... 37, 43, 55,
         64, 81, 84
1:1 to 2:3 37
1:26 .... 65, 109
1:26-27 36
1:26-31 65
1:27 .... 64, 65
1:27-28 40
1:28 39,
         89, 184
1:31 .... 66, 182
2 .... 37, 40, 43,
         55, 81, 84
2:4 37
2:5-25 37
2:7 66
2:18 .... 37, 38,
         40, 66, 166
2:18-24 66
2:18-25 37
2:21 66
2:22 66
2:23 .... 66, 67
2:24 .... 39, 40,
         43, 44, 67,
         178, 183,
         184, 185,
         207, 209
2:25 45
3 .... 46, 67, 84
3:16 .... 55, 67
4:1 .... 184, 193
4:14 46
4:17 184
4:19 46
4:25 .... 89, 184
5 .... 122, 132
5:1-2 65
5:3 39
5:24 132

9:1 122
14:14 47
16:1 87
16:2 87
16:4 87
17:2 99
17:4 99
17:7 99
17:10-13 99
17:16 91
18:1 91
18:11 .... 91, 135
18:12 62
18:19 47
19:5 .... 193, 202
21:4 99
21:8 102
21:21 49
24 .... 45, 160
24:1 .... 132, 135
24:2 132
24:3-8 49
24:14 160
24:19 160
24:22 52
24:58 45,
         49, 160
24:60-61 52
24:65 52
24:67 .... 52, 175
25:8 .... 132, 135
25:21 91
26:16 160
27 105
27:1 .... 145, 155
28:8-9 49
29:17-18 87
29:20 .... 87, 175
29:21 51
29:23 52
29:24 52
29:27 87
29:29 52

29:30 175
29:31 87
39:1 88
30:3 88
30:22-23 91
33:5 90
34:12 51
34:31 190
35:17 98
35:29 135
38:11 113
38:11-24 190
38:14 113
38:19 113
38:25-27 190
38:28 98
41:16 141
41:25 141
41:46 141
42:38 132
43:27 132,
         135, 145
43—50 145
44:20 .... 132, 135
44:29 132
45:3 145
45:13 145
45:23-28 145
46:4 145
47:12 47
48:2 145
48:10 .... 145, 155
48:21 145
49 105
49:28 145
49:33 146
50:7 135
50:7-9 146

Exodus

1:12 98
1:15-17 98
1:20-21 98

2:1-10 93
3:1-12 84
3:14-15 24
4:22 53
10:9 135
12:21 136
13:1-2 102
13:2 100
13:12 100
13:13 100
13:14-15 102
15:20-21 64,
                     122
20:12 146,
               240, 241
20:14 191,
               199, 233
20:17 62
21:1-11 62
21:5 175
21—23 191
22:14-17 191
22:16 51
22:22 114
22:29b-30 102
22:23-24 114
23:23-33 50
34:19-20 102
34:28 191

Leviticus

1:2-3 247
1:10 247
1:14 247
9:1 136
12:8 100
18:6-18 50
18:19-28 206
18:20 206
18:22 193
19:2 197
19:3 240
19:18 .... 22, 233
19:29 190
19:32 .... 143, 155
20:9 240
20:10 .... 191, 206

20:13 193
20:17-21 50
20:26 198
21:7 119,
               190, 207
21:9 190
21:13-14 113
21:14 119,
               190, 207
22:13 113
22:19 121
22:24 121
24:15-16 240
27:1-8 63,
                    144
27:2-8 145

Numbers

3:47 102
5:13-14 206
5:20 206
6:2-21 108
6:5 103
7 247
11:16 136
11:24-25 136
11:30 136
12:1-16 122
14:22-24 147
15:37-41 232
16:25 136
18:15-18 102
27:8 62
30:1-15 63
31:7-9 110
31:13-17 110

Deuteronomy

1:31 53
4:13 191
5:16 240
5:18 191
5:21 62
6:2 232
6:3 232
6:4 232
6:4-9 232

6:5 .... 22, 233
6:6-7 235
6:7 235
6:8-9 236
6:20 233
6:20-24 234
7:1-8 50
7:3-4 50
8:5 .... 53, 227
10:16 108
10:18 114
11:13-21 232
14:28-29 96
14:29 114
15:19-20 102
16:11-14 114
17:17 47
20:7 51
21:10-14 48,
                    63
22:13-21 63,
                    206
22:19 205
22:22 191
22:23-24 51,
                    191
22:23-27 51
22:25-27 191
22:28-29 191,
                    206
22:29 205
23:1 121
23:17-18 190
24 210
24:1 .... 208, 209
24:1-4 81,
              119, 163,
              174, 205,
              206, 207
24:4 206
24:5 51
24:17 114
24:19-21 114
25:5-10 .... 48, 113
26:12-13 96,
                    114
27:19 114

258

27:20-33 50
28:50 155
30:6 108
33:27 .... 25, 154

Joshua

2:1-21 121
2:1-24 190
5:4-5 99
6:22-25 121
8:10*b* 136
13:1 132
14:6-12 147
14:10-11 148
14:12 148
15:16-17 49
20:1-9 136
24:15 235
24:21-24 235
24:31 136

Judges

1:12-13 49
2:7-10 136
2:17 190
4:5 64
5:7 64
8:27 190
8:33 190
11:1-3 190
13:2-7 92
13:3-5 102
13:8 108
14:1-3 49
14:1-20 49
14:12 52
16:1 190
19:16 155
19:17 155
19:20 155
19:22 155,
        193, 202
19:25 184
19:26 62

Ruth

1:9-13 114

1:16-17 111
1:20-21 113
4:2-11 136

1 Samuel

1:2 88
1:4-7 88
1:5 175
1:8 88
1:11 103
1:19-20 92
1:19 184
1:20 88
1:22 103
1:28 103
2:12 150
2:20 103
2:21 103
2:22 132
2:25 150
2:26 108
2:31-32 155
3:2 155
8:1 132
8:3 150
8:4-5 136
8:5 150
18:17-20 49
18:20 175
18:25 51
25:39-42 114
29:28 133

2 Samuel

13:1-14 150
13:23-29 150
15:18 150
15:16 46
16:11 150
16:20-23 110
18:5 150
18:33 .... 150, 226
20:3 .... 46, 110

1 Kings

7:14 110
11:1 175

11:1-3 .... 46, 51
14:24 190
15:12 190
17:8-24 110
19:9-16 84
22:46 190

2 Kings

4:1-7 110
4:8-37 108
22:14-20 64

1 Chronicles

27:32 234

2 Chronicles

11:21 46
20:13 236
20:18 236

Ezra

5:5 136
5:9 136
6:7-14 136
9:1 50
10:3 177
10:8-14 136

Nehemiah

8:2 63
10:28-31 63
12:43 237
13:23-26 51
13:24 .... 50, 177

Job

1:21 89
1:29 96
12:12 .... 137, 138
12:13 138
12:16 138
12:20 138
29 96
29:12 96
29:13 96
29:15-16 96
31 96

31:15 90
31:16 116
31:17 96
32:4 144
32:9 138
42:17 155

Psalms

10:14 96
10:18 96
14:1-3 25
23 154
23:4 152
33:6 36
37:7 154
45 175
55:22 154
68:5 116
68:5-6 53
68:11 64
71:9 151
74:16-17 154
90:10 133
90:12 133
103:13 53
113:9 90
119 84
119:73 36
119:98 139
119:104 139
127:3 90
128:3 90
131:2 101
139:13 90
146:9 .... 96, 116
148:11-13 237

Proverbs

1:20 63
2:16 62
3:11-12 227
4:1-2 240
5:3-6 190
5:15-16 187
5:15-21 187
5:16 187
5:18 187

5:18-20 187
5:21 187
6:20 240
6:23-26 190
7:4 63
7:4-27 190
7:5 62
9:11 63
12:4 63
13:24 229
15:25 116
16:1 144
17:6 155
18:22 163
19:13 163
19:14 163
19:18 229
20:29 135
21:9 .... 62, 163
21:19 .... 62, 163
22:6 .... 237, 238
22:15 229
23:22 143
25:24 62
27:15-16 .... 63, 163
29:17 229
30:18-19 49
31 .... 63, 163
31:10 163
31:10-31 84

Ecclesiastes

5:18 133
6:12 133
7:1 133
9:9 175

Isaiah

1:4-15 97
1:10-20 21
1:11 115
1:13 .... 21, 115
1:16-17 .... 21, 97, 115
1:23 115
3:5 144

3:9 193
6:1-8 84
7:6-7 115
8:3 64
10:1-2 115
20:4 135
22:3 115
25:8 152
41:10 154
43:7 90
44:2 90
46:4 144
49:14-15 101
50:1 .... 47, 205
54:4 113
54:5 177
54:5-8 53
54:6-7 47
56:3-5 122
60:13 36
61:10 52
62:1-5 53
62:4-5 47
62:5 .... 52, 176
63:16 53
64:8 53

Jeremiah

1:5 90
1:5-19 122
1:6 90
2:1-12 104
2:2 54
2:13 104
2:20 104
3:1-2 190
3:6 190
3:8-9 54
3:19 53
3:19-20 54
5:7 191
5:28 97
6:11 135
7:9 191
7:34 52
9:1-2 192
9:25-26 108

260

16:1-9 122
16:9 52
20—21 23
23:14 191
25:10 52
29:23 191
31:31 155
31:31-33 196
33:11 52

Lamentations

2:21 155
4:6 193

Ezekiel

7:26 136
8:11-13 136
9:6 155
14:1-5 136
16:8 .... 176, 191
16:15 191
16:16-17 191
16:26 191
16:28 191
16:32 54
16:59-60 191
20:1-4 136
22:7 .... 97, 115
23:37 191
23:37-38 54
23:41 191
24:16-17 111
24:18-27 111
44:22 .... 114, 207

Daniel

2:25-30 141
2:45 141

Hosea

2:16-19 176
11:1 53
11:3-4 53

Joel

1:2 133
2:15-16 236
2:28 .... 141, 155

Amos

2:6-8 22
3:11 23
4:1 62
5:10-12 22
5:10-13 23
5:21-24 22

Micah

6:8 22
7:8 .... 25, 154

Zechariah

7:9-10 .... 97, 116
7:12 116
8:4 133
8:5 134

Malachi

2:14 .... 177, 207
2:16 119,
                205, 207
3:5 .... 97, 116

NEW TESTAMENT

Matthew

1:18-19 52
1:21 239
1:23 34
1:25 184
2:1-12 104
2:13 104
2:20 104
3:1-17 123
4:4 18
4:6 18
4:10 18
5 197
5:17 196
5:21-48 208
5:27-28 196
5:28 .... 196, 197
5:29-30 29
5:31-32 208
5:32 .... 119, 208,
                211, 217

5:48 220
6:9 54
6:12 23
6:14-15 23,
                218
7:9-11 54
7:11 226
8:14-15 56
9:18 95
10:34-36 41
10:37 .... 41, 226
10:42 108
11:10 18
11:16-17 106
11:19*b* 63
11:28 25
11:23-30 154
11:30 .... 68, 104
12:10 224
12:17 18
12:46 94
12:46-50 41
13:17 196
13:33 70
13:55 104
14:1-12 123
15:1-9 244
15:7 18
15:17-20 197
16:16 71
16:18 56
16:25 179
18:1-5 107
18:5-6 106
18:10 106
18:12-13 106
18:14 106
19 .... 208, 209
19:3-12 207,
                208
19:5 .... 40, 44,
                184
19:6 .... 44, 119,
                209, 210
19:8 .... 81, 205,
                210
19:8-9 19

261

19:9 .... 119, 208,
210, 211,
217
19:10 .... 120, 212
19:10-12 209
19:11 120
19:11-12 212
19:12 120,
121, 186
19:13-15 105
20:20-28 107
20:25-28 171
21:13 18
21:14-17 108
22:2-14 52
22:17 224
22:23-33 58
22:37 233
22:37-38 22
22:39 .... 22, 233
22:40 23
25:1 124
25:1-13 52,
70, 159
25:40 108
25:45 108
26:6-13 56
26:24 18
26:31 18
27:22 160
27:55 72
27:56 124
27:61 124
28:1 124

Mark

1:2 18
1:4-9 123
2:19-20 52,
159
2:27 .... 221, 233
5:23 95
5:41 .... 34, 95
6:14-29 123
7:5 244
7:5-13 244
7:6-7 18

7:8 244
7:9 244
7:9-13 146
7:10 17
7:10-13 244
7:12 245
7:20-23 197
7:24-30 96
9:24 226
9:36-37 107
9:42 106
10:2-12 208
10:7 .... 40, 44
10:7-8 184
10:10 211
10:11 211
10:13-16 105
10:35-45 107
12:36 18
12:40 116
12:41-44 112
15:22 34
15:34 34
15:40 124
15:41 72
15:47 124
16:1-9 124

Luke

1:5-25 123
1:7 134
1:8 140
1:15 .... 92, 108
1:18 134
1:30-31 92
1:39-80 123
1:46-56 70
1:67-79 70
2:7 98
2:12 98
2:15 104
2:19 104
2:21 98
2:21-39 111
2:22 100
2:22-23 100
2:22-32 70

2:25-35 101
2:36-38 70,
134
2:38 101
2:40 .... 93, 104
2:48-50 94
2:51 94,
104, 243
2:52 .... 93, 104
3:1-22 123
3:4 18
4:38-39 41
5:29-32 56
7:11-17 112
7:14 112
7:31-32 106
7:34 199
7:35 63
7:36-50 56,
199, 221
7:37-38 71
7:38 200
7:39 200
7:47 200
7:48 200
8:2 .... 124, 221
8:2-3 72
8:3 123
8:26 95
8:40 95
8:42 95
8:43-44 95
8:54 95
9:7-9 123
9:46-48 107
9:48 107
10:25-37 217
10:38-42 56
10:39 69
15:2 199
15:8-10 70
15:11-32 54,
70, 124
15:13 199
15:20 227
15:21 227
15:22-23 227

262

15:30 199
16:18 208
18.1-5 112
18:1-8 70
18:15-17 105
18:18-20 241
18:20 241
18:28-30 42
19:1-10 56
19:5 .... 40, 44
19:6 44
19:40 108
20:47 116
21:1-4 112
21:4 112
22:24-27 107
22:61 222
22:62 222
23:27-31 73
23:42 221
23:43 221
23:55-56 73
24:10 124
24:27 27

John

1:6 .... 123, 239
1:15-37 123
1:23 18
1:29 195
1:42 34
2:2 47
2:1-11 .... 52, 94
3 70
3:16 172
3:29 159
4:9 69
4:14 71
4:24 71
4:26 .... 71, 221
4:27 69
4:49 226
7:53 to 8:11 202
8:1-11 200
8:3-11 .... 84, 221
8:10-11 200
8:32 169

8:34 169
8:36 169
9:7 34
10:30 19
11:1-44 56
11:25 71
11:26 152
11:27 71
11:32 69
12:1-8 56
12:3 .... 69, 71
12:3 ff 200
12:38-41 18
14:2 54
14:9 19
14:27 154
15:13 172
17:22 19
19:25 124
19:25-27 70,
                    73
19:26-27 95,
                    246
20:1 124
20:11-18 124
20:11 ff 71
20:16 73
20:17 .... 71, 73
20:17-18 221
21:25 .... 93, 241

Acts

1:16 18
2:14-21 18
2:17 141
2:25-26 18
4:25 18
4:36 34
6:1 116
8:26-40 27,
                    121
8:31 27
9:36-42 117
9:1-6 84
10:1-33 84
11:30 .... 136, 137
13:8 34

14:23 .... 136, 137
15:4 137
15:6 137
15:22-23 137
16:11-15 75
16:16-18 75
17:4 75
17:12 75
18:2, 18, 26 76
20:17 137
21:8-9 123
21:18 137

Romans

1:1 23
1:24 194
1:26 194
1:26-27 194,
                    196
1:28-32 196
2:21 235
2:28-29 100
3:10 .... 25, 201
3:23 25
5:20 223
6:16 201
6:20-22 169
7:14 to 8:4 182
8:14-17 54
8:15-16 55
8:28 .... 25, 154
8:35 154
9:25-26 18
9:27-29 18
10:5 17
11:2 201
12:1 151,
                186, 199
13:1 56
13:8-10 22
14 .... 26, 74
14:10 55
14:13 55
16 112
16:1-2 76
16:3 76
16:3-5 76

1 Corinthians

1:11 78
3:1-2 139
3:1-3 77
3:16 201
5:1-2 77
5:6 201
5:11 195
6:2 201
6:3 201
6:9 ....195, 201
6:9-10 193
6:11 193
6:12 77
6:13 *ff* 185
6:15 185,
                199, 201
6:16 ....40, 44,
                184, 201
6:19 ....151, 201
6:20 186
7 ....78, 161,
                204, 214
7:1 ....78, 124
7:1-4 174
7:2 ....124, 188
7:2-7 213
7:3 188
7:3-4 174
7:5 188
7:6 124
7:7 ....125, 186
7:8 125
7:8-9 40
7:9 125
7:10 213
7:10-11 174,
                207
7:10-16 212
7:12 216
7:12-16 174,
                213
7:13 216
7:15 215
7:15-16 208
7:16 ....215, 216

7:17 126
7:17-24 125
7:20 126
7:22 78
7:24 126
7:26 126
7:27-28 126
7:32-35 126
7:35 126
7:36-38 126
7:39 117,
                161, 162
7:40 117
8 ....26, 74
8—10 77
8:1 ....26, 78
8:11-13 55
8:13 74
9 ....26, 74
9:13 201
9:24 201
10 ....26, 74
10:24 74
10:31 74
10:32 74
11 ....78, 79, 80
11:14 77
11:2-16 78,
                170
11:3 ....78, 164
11:3-10 79,
                164
11:4 79
11:5-6 213
11:6-15 29
11:8-9 66
11:11-12 38,
                66, 79,
                164
12:1 78
12:12 *ff* 74
12:13 171
14 ....79, 80
14:28 34
14:33-36 170
14:33-40 78
14:34 213

14:34-35 80
14:34-36 79,
                80
15:26 152
15:55-56 152
16:1 78
16:19 76

2 Corinthians

3:17 76
6:14 ....161, 162
6:14*b* 213
6:14-16 161
6:16-18 54
11:2 159
12:9 ....25, 218
12:14 243
12:19 154

Galatians

1:15 92
3:26 54
3:28 ....36, 74,
                77, 79, 163,
                165, 171
4:1-2 235
4:6-7 55
5:1 ....76, 169
5:2 169
5:6 98
5:13 ....76, 163
5:14 22
5:16-17 182
5:16-21 182
5:17-23 195
5:19-21 182
5:22-23 182
6:15 98

Ephesians

2:8-10 23
2:21 173
4:1 199
4:11 23
4:22-32 195
4:25 199
5 171

5:1 199
5:3 195
5:21 171,
230, 231
5:21-33 55,
170, 214
5:21 to 6:4 56
5:21 to 6:9 242
5:22 171
5:22-23 171,
230
5:23-24 163
5:25 172
5:28 172
5:31 .... 40, 184
5:33 175
6:1 .... 171, 230,
231, 242
6:1-4 171
6:2 241
6:4 230
6:5 .... 163, 171
6:5-9 171
6:21 55

Philippians

1:1 84
1:20-21 153
2:6-7 171
3:12-15 139
3:14 139
4:2-3 75
4:12 149
4:19 .... 149, 154

Colossians

1:19 19
2:9 19
2:11 100
3:5-17 195
3:11 171
3:18-19 170
3:18-21 56
3:20 242
3:21 230
4:15 75

1 Thessalonians

4:3 .... 197, 198
4:3-8 .... 198, 199
4:4 198
4:5 198
4:6 198
4:7 199
4:8 199

1 Timothy

1:18 55
2:8-12 80
2:8-13 170
2:8-15 164
2:15 157
3:8-13 84
4:3-4 186
4:14 137
5:1-2 .... 135, 146
5:3-4 146
5:3-16 117
5:4 .... 146, 245
5:5 .... 118, 245
5:6 118
5:8 .... 117, 128,
146, 245
5:9 146
5:10 118
5:14 118
5:17 137
5:19 137

2 Timothy

1:5 234
2:1 55
3:15 234
4:19 76

Titus

2:2-6 135
2:4 175
2:4-5 .... 170, 227

Philemon

2 25

Hebrews

1:1-3 68
1:3 19
5:12-14 140
6:1 140
11:31 .... 122, 190
12:5-6 227
12:8 228
12:10 228
12:11 228
13:4 197
13:22 197

James

1:27 .... 97, 118
2:14-26 23
2:17 118
2:21-26 190
2:25 122
5:14 137

1 Peter

1:15-16 198
2:13 .... 171, 174
2:16 169
3:1-7 174
3:7 .... 171, 175
3:8 175
4:7-10 23
5:1 137
5:1-5 137

2 Peter

1:21 17
2:6-10 193

1 John

4:8 .... 172, 195
4:16 .... 172, 195

2 John

1 137

3 John

1 137

Jude

7 193

Revelation

1:8 24
3:19 228
4:4 137

4:10 137
5:5-6 137
5:8 137
5:11 137
5:14 137
7:11 137
7:13 137
7:17 152

11:16 137
14:3 137
19:6-9 55
19:7 159
19:9 52
21:2 .... 55, 159
21:9 .... 55, 159
22:17 55

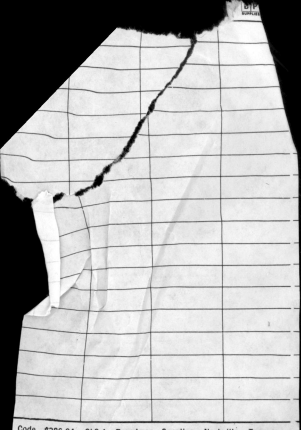

Code 4386-04, CLS-4, Broadman Supplies, Nashville, Tenn.,
Printed in U.S.A.